Business Reports
for
Busy People

Timesaving, Ready-to-Use Reports
for Any Occasion

BUSINESS REPORTS
FOR BUSY PEOPLE

Greg Holden

3 1336 08540 9861

CAREER
PRESS
Pompton Plains, NJ

BUSINESS REPORTS FOR BUSY PEOPLE
EDITED BY KATE HENCHES
TYPESET BY EILEEN MUNSON
Cover design by Rob Johnson/Toprotype
Printed in the U.S.A.

To order this title, please call toll-free 1-800-CAREER-1 (NJ and Canada: 201-848-0310) to order using VISA or MasterCard, or for further information on books from Career Press.

The Career Press
220 West Parkway, Unit 12
Pompton Plains, NJ 07444
www.careerpress.com

Library of Congress Cataloging-in-Publication Data
Holden, Greg.
  Business reports for busy people : timesaving, ready-to-use reports for any occasion / by Greg Holden.
    p. cm.
  Includes bibliographical references and index.
  ISBN 978-1-60163-042-1 -- ISBN 978-1-60163-740-6 (ebook) 1. Business report writing. I. Title.
  HF5719.H65 2011
  651.7--dc22
                                                2010034228

To Peggy

Acknowledgments

Many people take part in the creation of a book, and it's impossible to acknowledge everyone who brings the work to print. However, I do want to acknowledge the help of those I was involved with personally. These include my longtime assistant and collaborator, Ann Lindner, and my agent, Neil Salkind, of Studio B Productions. I also wish to thank Michael Pye of Career Press, who got the project started, and Kirsten Dalley, who saw it to fruition.

CONTENTS

Part V: Human Resources

Part VI: Other Reports

Business Reports for Busy People, as its name implies, is designed to be a practical source of information that's easy to find when you're trying to get through a hurried business day. When you're tasked with writing a business report and find yourself staring at an empty page, you need a jump-start to get you going. Each chapter contains a variety of jump-start material: an introduction that helps you focus on the goal and purpose of the report; step-by-step instructions for assembling the report, checklists, and ready-to-use reports and excerpts tailored to different types of businesses. The intent is to help you do your work better and more effectively—right now.

Business Reports for Busy People is broken into nearly 30 chapters for a reason. I wanted to include as many different kinds of business reports as possible, to increase the chances that you'll find one that fits the task at hand. At the same time, each chapter is packed with concrete information, useful techniques, and practical tips. That way, you can jump to the general type of report you want and still find the specific bits of advice you need.

I invite you to leaf through the book to find the data that applies to your own situation. Also keep in mind that each chapter is tabbed on the outside margins so you can quickly find the chapter you need first. Read the chapters that apply to your own business needs, because each chapter stands alone. Then flip through the book to find resources that apply to all business reports and that are likely to help you as well.

In the corporate world, business reports are regarded by many executives as an important benchmark in managerial success. Your ability to prepare a good report will not only help your organization, but it is likely to play a role in your ability to move up in the company or find a job if the need arises. You'll find this book helpful in learning to write an effective business report; read it, use it, and you'll have a key to business success.

Getting Started

PART

I

Chapter 1

Essentials of Successful Business Reports

Business reports are challenging and frequently used tools for virtually any organization. Whether you work in the corporate world, in a nonprofit environment, or in education, you need to organize information and present it in a format that your colleagues or others find easy to understand and interpret. Your job is to focus and shape the information; you don't necessarily need to worry about tone, structure, or including standard elements; that's where this book will help you.

Business reports are far more challenging than business letters. Reports are by nature more complex and detailed, and often need to make a case—that the company is on budget, that a building project needs to be awarded to a certain contractor, or dozens of other reasons. Often, reports require supporting documentation, and the process of gathering and deciding how best to present the data can take a long time. But the basic elements and structure are similar, and ones with which you are probably familiar.

Considerations of a Business Report

Whenever you are faced with a business task of considerable size—and many business reports can be lengthy—it helps to break the task into separate components. As you'll see in the chapters later in this book that are devoted to specific types of business reports, the contents themselves can be broken into separate sections such as an introduction, charts, and a conclusion.

The success of your report depends on whether or not you present well-focused and comprehensive content in a way that your audience can understand. Simply copying a previous report and inserting new figures or information won't work. Before you even start writing, a few preliminary steps will help you get started. The preliminaries can be broken into separate components. These include the audience, the general organizational plan for your report, and the writing style you are going to employ.

Identify Your Audience

The individuals who are going to read, analyze, and possibly make decisions based on your report will help you determine the length and detail of the contents. Take care in identifying exactly who is going to receive your report, and to analyze their communication needs as well. Ask yourself a few questions, and jot down the answers:

1. Who requested this report? (List the person's name and job title.)

2. What is this person/these persons expecting from your report? A recommendation? A detailed analysis? A comprehensive set of data?

3. How would you like the recipient(s) to respond after reading your report? With a specific decision? With conclusions will they communicate to the rest of the company?

4. What is the single most important piece of information you want to communicate in your report?

Managers are busy, and many only have the time to absorb a limited amount of information at once. Don't try to cover more ground than your readers want. The most important of these points of consideration is the last one: the most important piece of information you have to communicate. You may have many points to discuss, but be sure to get this one across first. Focusing your information and keeping your report as brief as possible—telling your readers only what they most need to know—is essential for effective business reporting.

Communicating With Higher-Ups

If your report is intended for your supervisors, or others who are higher in the organizational chain of command than you are, make sure you tactfully take into account the differences in your level of experience and background knowledge. Don't try to impress. Chances are your readers are able to draw their own conclusions about what you present. Simply being decisive and comprehensive, and summarizing the points you present will be enough. Then present your supporting information.

Communicating With Peers and Others

Just as you should avoid trying to impress your higher management, avoid talking down to those you supervise. Simply being clear and complete is enough. If you draw conclusions in your report, simply state them without issuing arbitrary orders.

If you are communicating with your peers, you can get into more technical detail than you would for other audiences, because you can be certain your readers will understand the subject at hand. If you are preparing a grant proposal or other report in which you are making a case for a project or for funding, however, you need to be a marketer as well as a reporter. After presenting your supporting information, you need to persuade your readers why they should fund your endeavor. Otherwise, when speaking to peers, it's best to present the facts and draw reasonable conclusions without trying to be overly persuasive.

Get Organized

Getting organized, when it comes to writing business reports, means focusing on your message; identifying the most important points you need to convey; and determining what kinds of presentations (for instance, charts or tables) you will use to communicate with your intended audience. Creating an outline is always a helpful idea. Beyond that, jotting down a few notes about your main message and how you will present your contents will keep you on track as you write your report.

Focus on Your Message

As stated before, busy managers don't like to read lengthy introductions or cover more information than they really need. Keep sight of your main point. State it at the beginning of your report, and restate it at the end, to keep your message on target and at the forefront of your reviewers' attention.

List Your Central Points

Before you begin your report, make a list of your most important points. Each of these points can then take the form of a heading that leads readers through the report and gives it structure and direction. For instance, if you are preparing an analysis of marketing methods, you might jot down the following list:

▶ Word-of-mouth marketing is increasingly valuable.

▶ Newspaper advertising is expensive and results are hard to quantify.

▶ Radio advertising is effective if placed during programs that attract our customers.

▶ Emphasis should be placed on our Website and the Internet.

When you are drawing up an outline of your report, you can then create a section called Advertising Approaches. The previous subjects can take the form of subheadings, like this:

> Advertising Approaches
>> [sublist] Importance of the Internet
>>> [sub-sublist]Website
>>> [sub-sublist] Word-of-Mouth Marketing
>> [sublist]Traditional Advertising
>>> [sub-sublist] Radio
>>> [sub-sublist] Newspapers

Headings point the way for readers. They indicate your most important topics. Use them to make your report more readable and help readers understand the most important points you want to communicate.

Decide How to Present Your Data

Tables, charts, and illustrations are essential parts of virtually all business reports.

Writing With Style

The saying "form follows function" should help you when deciding the tone and style you'll use to prepare your report. Generally, reports contain only a few types of information:

▶ Good news.

▶ Bad news.

▶ A persuasive case.

▶ An analysis.

The message you want to send determines your style. If you are conveying good news, you state it directly. Bad results or unsuccessful outcomes require a more indirect approach. A persuasive case calls for marketing; enthusiasm and a positive approach can help make the case you wish. An analysis that does not involve persuasion and does not reach positive or negative conclusions can be a straightforward, "just the facts" matter. In general, though, a report that impersonal is less engaging than one that is personal, interesting, and lively. Your goal, after all, is to get your intended audience to *read* your report. The following sections suggest ways to achieve an engaging style and to avoid a writing style that is stodgy and machine-like.

Tips for Good Report Writing Style

You aren't writing a personal letter, and you aren't writing a memo either: Your report needs to be personal as well as informational. In order to strike a good balance, try for the following:

▶ Use words that are in common use rather than stilted, literary terms (for example, *shallow* rather than *otiose*).

▶ Make your sentences and paragraphs short and direct. Try to break paragraphs after the third or fourth sentence, unless you are making an important point that requires more explanation.

▶ Use active voice. "Conglomerated Materials had a subpar year" is better than "It was a subpar year for Conglomerated Materials," for instance.

▶ Make people rather than objects the subject of your sentences.

▶ Keep figures, percentages, and ratios simple and easy to understand. Round numbers (use 2 instead of 1.987, for instance).

That last point requires further explanation. Chances are your audience is more interested in the comparative value of organizations or items than in their absolute value. Because you're probably not writing a scientific report, you don't have to present numbers exactly. For instance, instead of breaking down a series into percentages (15% nuts, 20% bolts, 42% nails, and 23% clamps, for instance) consider saying "nearly half consisted of nails. The next highest was clamps, followed closely by nuts, and lastly bolts."

Stylistic Pitfalls to Avoid

Many business reports are prepared in order to support a recommendation or suggest a particular course of action. It's important to make sure your facts, and not your style, support your conclusions. Let the facts and observations speak for themselves. At the same time, be sure you get your points across clearly. Your writing style should avoid problems such as:

▶ **Seeming prejudiced.** Spell out assumptions you are making, and provide sufficient evidence to support the conclusions you reach.

▶ **Vagueness.** By starting out each section with a clear topic sentence, you will help your readers track where they are in your report and what the significant points are that you want to make. Also sum up sections with a restatement of the main point and a transition to the next section.

▶ **Mixing past and present tense.** As a general rule, it's good practice to stick with present tense to discuss topics that are occurring now and that will occur in the near future, as well as trends and facts that occurred in the past and that still exist currently. (Of course, you have to use past tense to describe events that occurred and that are over or that have since changed.)

In addition to these good textual practices, you need to use supporting graphics and documentation wisely. Only use graphics that pertain directly to your text; keep your report short and to the point by omitting ones that aren't useful. Be sure to refer to graphics in your text and explain what their significance is. (For instance, "Figure 1.4 shows the relative success of radio advertising compared to newspaper ads.") If you use material created by others, be sure to give them credit and include the source of the material either as a footnote or in a bibliography.

Chapter 2

Components of a Business Report

The preparation work outlined in Chapter 1 should help you when you are assembling the components of your business report. You can take each of the bits of background information you gathered in your initial groundwork and translate them into specific parts of the report. The sections that follow describe the components that are common to most reports. After all, some reports (such as appraisals) have special contents that don't apply to other subjects. But this chapter will examine the components that will apply to most business reports you are likely to prepare. You'll also learn how to take the answers to the questions you asked yourself in Chapter 1 and plug them in to the appropriate parts of your report.

Beginning Your Report

In Chapter 1, you asked yourself some basic questions, such as: Who will read your report? What are your readers expecting? What is the single most important piece of information you have to convey? This information should help you get started with your report.

If your audience is primarily technical in orientation (such as a group of IT professionals), your report should have a technical, straightforward title: Securing the Company's Network Infrastructure, for instance. If you are making a recommendation about a vendor or contractor, the subject in question should be in the title—though not the answer, as you should save that for your introduction and summary. For example: Evaluation of Apartment Building Contractors would be better than Recommendation of Apex Construction Company for Building Project.

Suppose, for example, you are writing a business plan of the sort described in Chapter 13. Your audience is likely to be people who will provide you funding: bank officers, or venture capitalists. They probably don't understand the kind of business you are planning to run. You not only have to explain what you want to do, but you need to make a good business case for it. You

2. Components of a Business Report

need to gain the trust of highly skeptical funders. The sections that follow will convey general instructions for putting together the components of a typical report as well as specific suggestions for this kind of report.

Hooking Interest With a Title

Your title should describe the subject and purpose of your report in a brief format that is specific but does not give too much information. The specific length isn't the most critical thing. Though many editors would say titles of three to six words are best, the important thing is to be specific about the report's subject and primary goal and to hook the reader's interest.

A business plan report should not be flippant or humorous. It should immediately indicate what you plan to do. If you can convey a sense of enthusiasm and inspire confidence about your business, so much the better. There's nothing wrong with including the words *Business Plan* in your title, by the way. For example:

Business Plan Titles

Good	Better
Business Plan for North Side Bar	Creating a New Gathering Place: A Plan for Joe's Pub & Grill
Business Plan for Organic Farm	Plan for Latching on to the Organic Farm Trend
Koala Road Gifts Business Plan	A Business Plan for Kids' Specialty Store, Koala Road Gift

There's nothing wrong with the last title. By being more specific, you immediately gain the interest of readers who are probably flooded with such proposals. You distinguish yourself from other stores, and you hint at the approach that sets your store plan apart from the competition—the fact that your plan will sell kids' specialty items, which implies that your target audience is young, affluent parents looking for unusual, exclusive merchandise.

Author and Date

This component is straightforward. After your title, you need to provide your name and the date your report was prepared. The date is important for reports that need a timely decision: for instance, if an appraisal is being made for property that is up for purchase, or if a recommendation is being made for a contract that needs to be awarded soon.

Along with your name, you may want to include additional information, such as:

▸ Any certifications or degrees you can list along with your name, such as PhD, MD, and so on.

▸ Your job title, if it is relevant to your report.

▸ A university affiliation, if that would lend credibility to your report.

Using titles might seem like boasting, but if they are relevant to the subject of your report, it's well worth adding them. For instance, if you are writing a business plan for a medical practice, by all means include your MD or other title after your name. If you are a certified real estate appraiser and you are preparing an appraisal report, include the appropriate C.R.E.A. or other title after your name.

Introduction

The opening of your report is one of the most important sections within it. Here, as elsewhere, you need to take into account who your readers are and how much they need to know. It's also important to ask how much the readers know already. If they consist of higher management within your organization, you don't have to explain to them what your company is, what it does, and what its plan is for the future. They are already aware of such things.

Your introduction should accomplish two goals:

1. It should speak directly to your readers, taking into account their level of authority and the amount of knowledge they already have about the topic.

2. It should state the main topic, summarize what the report will accomplish, and "hook" readers by indicating why they should pay attention to the contents.

Despite all your hard work, you can't depend on busy managers to read your entire report in the detail you would like. You have to put your main points in the introduction. Following the traditional writing "pyramid" used by journalists to write news stories is often a good principle to follow.

Topic Sentence

As a former journalist, I was often called on to write news stories in which readers were immediately given the Who, What, When, Where, Why, and How of what was happening. That was all presented in the opening paragraph, which took the form of an "inverted pyramid." The concept is illustrated in Figure 2-1 on page 24.

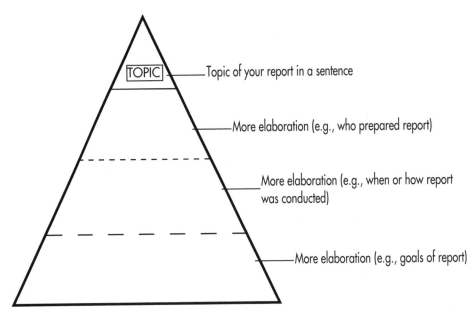

Topic of your report in a sentence

More elaboration (e.g., who prepared report)

More elaboration (e.g., when or how report was conducted)

More elaboration (e.g., goals of report)

Figure 2-1

Your report should start out the same way a news story does: with the "lead," or most important point, summarized in a single sentence. Here are some examples:

▶ The year 2010 saw record profits and a new headquarters for Consolidated Systems as well as unprecedented market growth. (Annual Report)

▶ Work on assembling a redesigned Website has passed the design phase, with editorial content and programming still remaining to be done. (Progress Report)

▶ Switching from the current natural-gas heating system to a more environmentally conscious solar heat system will cost $100,000 initially but pay for itself in savings over a 10-year period. (Evaluation Report)

▶ The current baby boom in the Atlanta area means affluent young parents need a retail outlet for high-end children's toys and furnishings such as the business described in this plan. (Business Plan)

The temptation, with any lead sentence, is to try to say too much in a limited number of words. It's preferable to create a lead that only says one thing, such as the What of the five Ws (Who, What, Where, When, and Why—as well as How). Other subjects, such as Who and Why, can be covered in subsequent sentences.

Elaborating on Your Topic

The introductory paragraph of a news story is likened to a pyramid because the most focused and succinct information—the "point" of the story—is presented first. Subsequent sentences elaborate on the first bit of information. The elaboration isn't essential, but provides important background information that helps the reader understand the topic better.

For instance, the last topic sentence in the preceding list introduces the need for a children's store in the Atlanta area. Subsequent sentences could elaborate on this in a number of ways:

▶ Who: "The store will be opened by two parents who have run clothing businesses in Miami and other cities."

▶ Where: "The store will be located in the Atlanta Underground, one of the best-traveled shopping areas in the United States."

▶ When: "An opening in September will provide plenty of time to build clientele and assemble inventory for the all-important holiday shopping season."

In addition, the elaboration can also summarize the reason the report was requested, or the goal(s) of the report:

"This report will analyze the growth and success of the store over the coming five years. It will analyze the existing competition, describe how this store's selection will be different from others, and how growing numbers of young parents will be attracted through innovative marketing campaigns."

As you can see, a report that is intended to make a case or solicit financial support, such as a business plan, needs to express enthusiasm and confidence. A statement of the goals leads the reader naturally into the main body of the report.

Main Contents

The main body of the report is where you make a supporting case for the conclusions or assertions stated in the opening. You present data that you have gathered, either through observation or calculation. You present the data using easy-to-interpret visual aids such as charts. You finish up with conclusions and recommendations that are all the stronger for the information that has preceded them.

Executive Summary

Some, but not all, reports contain a section called an Executive Summary. This is a high-level statement of the most important points in the report. It's similar to a topic sentence and elaborations. However, the summary also includes some data and descriptions of properties, companies, projects, or other subjects the report has covered.

Only include an Executive Summary if a) your managers have requested one, or b) the report is intended only for higher-level management in your company. An Executive Summary enables management to absorb the most important points of your report without having to read the whole body of work. Because you would rather have them read the contents in their entirety, you should offer an Executive Summary only on request, or only if you are specifically told to do so.

Body

In the body of your report, you move step by step through the assessment, recounting of details, description of the situation, or other contents. The exact contents depend on the report; the arrangements can vary widely, which is why each of the subsequent chapters presents you with step-by-step instructions to follow and suggestions of the kinds of topics you can cover.

Conclusions/Recommendations

Although you summed up your conclusions in the opening paragraph, and may have done the same in an Executive Summary, you should state your conclusions or recommendations one more time at the end of your report. Why the repetition? Because your views and statements are likely to be informed, and possibly colored, by the presentation of data that has come before it. Your opening paragraph or executive summary might only state your conclusion in a sentence or two. In the summary at the end, you can go into detail about your recommendations and explain why you are making a particular choice or recommending a specific course of action.

For instance, instead of simply saying:

"It is my recommendation that we award the job to Pinnacle Graphics."

You can take time to elaborate in the end-of-report summary, so that your case is made in a stronger and more reasoned way:

"Many of the design firms interviewed by the evaluation team were obviously competent and well experienced. And some of the team members came up with initial recommendations that are slightly different than those of the main group. But all members agreed that Pinnacle Graphics was worthy of consideration. The most important factor in our decision was the depth of technical support that the company can provide, especially on weekends. Our recommendation, then, is clearly to award the job to Pinnacle Graphics."

Secondary Information

Sometimes, words aren't enough. Some readers respond more readily to images and charts rather than textual information. In fact, don't be surprised if, when you hand out your report to a group in person, some recipients skip ahead immediately to the charts and figures, and examine those in detail before they even read a word.

Graphics and Charts

Because you're likely to be using the popular Microsoft Office package to prepare your report, it makes sense to explore the chart-making and graphing abilities of those programs. If you use Excel, for instance, consider converting your spreadsheets to charts, and taking advantage of that application's sophisticated chart-formatting capabilities.

Microsoft Office, however, does not have a sophisticated graphics program, one that will help you crop and edit photographic images. A program like Adobe Photoshop Elements (*www.adobe.com*) or Paint Shop Pro (*www.corel.com*) would be ideal. But if you only have a limited number of images and don't want to purchase a new program, you can insert images with Microsoft Word, but cropping them requires you to use the program's Picture toolbar.

To add an image:

1. Open Word, and position the cursor at the point in the report where you want the image to appear.
2. Click the Insert menu.
3. Click Picture, and then slide your mouse pointer to the right and choose From File from the submenu (or, if the image is still on your digital camera, choose From Scanner or Camera).
4. When the Insert Picture dialog box appears, single-click the image to highlight it.
5. Click Open.

After you insert a photo into a Word file, it appears with six rectangles at the corners and on the sides. These are selection handles. To make the image smaller, hold the Shift key down, click a handle, and drag inward. (Holding down the Shift key preserves the images existing proportions so that it doesn't become distorted as you change the overall size.)

To crop an image, single-click it to select it. Selecting it causes the selection handles to appear. When you select it, the Picture toolbar should appear automatically. If the Picture toolbar does not appear automatically, you can display it by following these steps:

1. Click the View menu.

2. Choose Toolbars.

3. Slide your mouse to the right and choose Picture from the submenu.

4. When the menu appears, pass your mouse over each of the images in turn to see what they do. The Crop tool is about seventh from the left; click it, and a set of cropping handles appears over your image.

Distribution List

The distribution list shows all the recipients of the report. It is important not as a tool to build your credibility, but as a managerial tool that ensures completeness. Be extra careful, when you assemble your list that you:

> Have not left out anyone who needs to receive your report.

> Have spelled everyone's name right and listed all job titles correctly, if necessary.

> Have not included people who should not have access to the report.

Tip: It's important to crop an image for two reasons. First, it allow the reader to focus in immediately on the most important contents without distracting backgrounds or other images. Second, it reduces file size. If you take a high-quality JPEG image with a digital camera, it can take up 1 megabyte (1MB) or more in file size. When you insert that into a Word document as part of a report, that makes the file size considerably larger. Add half a dozen or more images, and suddenly, your document is too large to send by e-mail. Cropping images makes them smaller and more portable.

Have someone double-check the distribution list so it is correct when you first send out your report, and so you don't have to correct it later on.

References

If you have applied for a job, or reviewed the resumes of those who are going through the application process, you know the importance of references. When it comes to reports, references provide documentation of facts and assertions you have taken from different publications.

References don't simply provide you with a safeguard against plagiarism. They demonstrate that your report is well supported by outside documentation. Choose your reference material with care: The more reliable your sources are, the more reliable your report will be. Instead of citing popular magazines such as Time or newspapers such as *USA Today*, turn to the library and turn up scholarly material that is related to the subject you are exploring.

Chapter 3

Formatting Your Business Report

Most books about business communications focus primarily on content, and that's appropriate because contents are the most important aspects of business letters, reports, memos, and other communications. But the fact is that your message can be seriously diluted by a report that is marred by typographical errors, that has missing sheets, or that is poorly presented. And by the same token, a report that is professional in appearance builds credibility, supports your message, and generally makes you look good in the workplace. In this chapter, you get some tips for how to format, edit, and present your work so it makes the impression you want.

Editing and Proofreading

After you create your report, you're probably eager to get it off your desktop and into the hands of those who are looking for it. You might be on deadline and in a hurry. The temptation is to get your work out the door as quickly as possible so you can move on to other tasks. If you have ever made a mistake in distributing business communications, you know the embarrassment of having errors pointed out and having to redo your work just to fix them. You know the value of taking your time and proofreading your work, and that applies even more to business reports because of their length and complexity.

Tip: *The Chicago Manual of Style*, produced by the University of Chicago, is an indispensable source for information about copyediting and rules of use.

Copyediting Your Report

Copyediting is the practice of reviewing and correcting text to free it of spelling an grammatical errors and to improve its readability. There are five good practices to follow when copyediting your report (or any other lengthy document, for that matter):

Rule 1: Get someone to help you.

After writing your report, you may be too close to the contents and know them too well to be able to find errors. It's almost always a good idea to find a colleague who is unfamiliar with the text to read it through and check it carefully for errors. Find someone in your office who is adept at finding textual mistakes and solicit that person's help.

Rule 2: Print out your report.

Not everyone is proficient at reading text on a computer screen. For many, it's easier to copyedit on paper. Print it out and ask him or her to mark corrections in print.

Rule 3: Wait before you edit.

Don't try copyediting or proofreading your text just after you have finished writing it. Above all, don't try to do editing when you're tired. Take a break and get some coffee before turning to this text, so you can concentrate better.

Rule 4: Find a quiet, well-lighted place.

The fewer distractions you have the better you'll be able to concentrate. It often helps to be somewhere other than your office or your usual work space.

> Tip: If your document is particularly lengthy and contains specialized terms (such as scientific words), consider making a style sheet. This is a sheet that tracks any spelling and grammatical usage that is specific to your document. It's a tool for you and any copyeditors/proofreaders with whom you work to make sure your spelling is correct and your usage fits company style.

Rule 5: Use a ruler or other tool.

While you're reading, keep track of your place in your report with a ruler or straight-edge as you go down the page. That way you will only be looking at one line at a time and can find your way back easily.

Looking for Possible Improvements

When you're copyediting, you aren't always looking for outright errors or typos. Those are good to find, but you should also look for ways to improve your text. Be sure the report:

▶ Says what you want it to say.

▶ Doesn't use redundant or unnecessary words or phrases, dangling modifiers, or split infinitives.

▶ Is consistent in tone, punctuation, and spelling from beginning to end.

▶ Has accurate URLs and other references.

If you list Web page addresses in your file, make sure that, at a later time, you open a Web browser and actually visit the sites referred to in the links to make sure they are accurate and the addresses are correct.

Formatting Your Text

It's important to divide your text into sections and organize the contents with headings to maximize the chances that your readers will pay attention to what you are saying and (hopefully) read the entire text. Chances are they will jump around only to the sections that interest them, which is normal. The most important sections are the Executive Summary or Introduction, the Conclusions, and any Recommendations, if you have them.

Title Page

This is a separate page that contains the title of your report, your name, and the date. It only takes a few seconds to insert a separate page before the beginning of your report text. Creating a title page makes any document look better no matter how it's presented (as separate sheets, in a binder, or as a PDF file).

Reference Sections

For a particularly long report, especially one that has multiple images, charts, or drawings, you might be well advised to include additional material that helps your readers organize the contents and interpret what you have to say. Typical reference sections that might go at the front of a lengthy report include:

▶ A list of figures or illustrations. This enables readers to jump to the data they are most interested in.

▶ A list of technical terms. If your report uses special jargon or technical terms that your readers might not understand, a brief list of terms and their definitions placed at the beginning of the document would help them.

▶ A Table of Contents. This is probably the most important bit of reference material you can have. A Table of Contents is useful for reports of, say, 10 pages or more (though this is hardly a firm rule). Be sure to include not only top-level chapter headings in your table, but the first level of subheadings beneath them. For example:

   ▸ White Paper on New Cell Phone Service

   ▸ Introduction

   ▸ Executive Summary

   ▸ List of illustrations

- Chapter 1: The Current State of Cell Phone Communications
  - Current Protocols
  - Variations in Coverage
- Chapter 2: Improvements in Our New Service
  - 4G Network
  - Wi-Fi Access

In a report such as a white paper that can reach to 30, 40, 50, or more pages, a table of contents can be a useful way to direct managers and other reviewers to the most important parts of information for them—the ones they need to act on.

Introduction

See Chapter 2 for more on a typical introduction, which might take the form of an "inverted pyramid."

Executive Summary

Every report should have an introduction. The Executive Summary can either take the role of the introduction or supplement it. If it serves as an introduction, the Executive Summary can use the same "inverted pyramid" structure. If it is added on, it can consist of a listing of the main points, your conclusions, and any recommendations you have.

> Tip: For some senior managers, the Executive Summary will be the only part of the report they read: try to make it a standalone document, and don't simply copy from the report itself.

Conclusions

Like the Executive Summary and Introduction, the Conclusions section is a "must-read" for every manager in your organization. This is where you make statements about what you observed, what the state of affairs is, and what course the company should take—but make it clear that your statements are based on data you observed and compiled, and not on your opinions.

Physical Presentation

The traditional method of distribution for a business report is in print: You print out multiple copies, one for each recipient, and distribute them in person or by interoffice mail. Major reports can be elaborate, however. You might have all the sections listed above, as well as others. The most elaborate reports will have:

- Cover.
- Title Page.
- Table of Contents.

3. Formatting Your Business Report

▶ Table of illustrations/figures.

▶ Executive Summary.

▶ Introduction.

▶ Main text.

▶ Conclusions.

▶ Recommendations.

▶ Appendices.

▶ Bibliography.

▶ Index.

Only the longest reports will have indexes; these can be prepared with Microsoft Word if needed. In addition to these sections, longer reports might also include a letter of authorization from the official in the organization who assigned the report. You might even be asked to include a letter of acceptance, officially acknowledging that you are responding to the request. This letter might include an Executive Summary for the benefit of the person who assigned the report. But such letters are uncommon, and usually, your report will consist of the sections listed earlier in this chapter. Options for printing or otherwise distributing the report follow.

Presenting as Separate Sheets

Even in the age of computers and the Internet, printing out reports has its advantages. Printed documents can be given a cover and placed in a binder or folder, which makes the entire work look more professional. If needed, you can cut down on the number of pages by placing the list of figures on the same page as the table of contents, for instance.

Creating a Booklet

The length of comprehensiveness of a report doesn't determine if it should be placed in a binder with a transparent cover or bound by the local duplication shop. It's the level of importance of the report that matters, and that's something only you can determine. If you do prepare a report that requires this level of formatting, consider a cover page that lists the title, your name, and the date, followed by a "title fly" page that presents only the title. After this, other preliminary contents such as the table of contents would appear.

Electronic Reports

Reports that are short and whose contents aren't terribly critical can be distributed electronically. In this case, you can format the document either in Microsoft Word or whatever word-processing program you used to prepare it, or you can convert it to PDF format as described in Creating a PDF (Page 34).

Distributing a File by E-mail

If you distribute by e-mail, make sure you accurately record the names and e-mail addresses of everyone on the distribution list. Leaving someone out will embarrass that person. You then attach the Word document to the outgoing e-mail message and write a cover message. This message might provide some background as to the reason for the report and when it was assigned. For instance:

> *Six months ago my department was asked to evaluate the need for a new headquarters for this company and, if a move is warranted, to suggest possible new locations. After a lengthy study, we have determined that the company would benefit greatly, both financially and in terms of employee morale, by locating the headquarters outside the city. The following report explains the reasons for this recommendation and suggests possible locations for a new building.*

Creating a PDF

PDF stands for Portable Document Format. It is a format created by Adobe Systems Incorporated in order to allow the transmittal and sharing of documents that have complex formatting that needs to be preserved. If a file uses non-standard typefaces and has lots of complex images and graphics included in an elaborate design, PDF is ideal. Converting a file to PDF not only embeds the typefaces, images, and graphics in the document, but it compresses the file as well so it can be easily transmitted by e-mail or other electronic means.

Some programs, like Adobe Photoshop, have the ability to convert a file to PDF automatically. If you don't use Photoshop, you can download an application such as CutePDF (*www.cutepdf.com*). Converting the document to PDF is then as easy as printing: Click the File menu, choose Print, and then choose CutePDF Writer from the options shown. Some other applications, such as QuickBooks, also provide a PDF conversion application from the Print dialog box.

Posting a Web Page

A business report can also be posted on the company Website, but if you attempt to publish online, you need to be aware that restricting access to the file requires special programming. The most common option for publishing online is to give all visitors to your Website the ability to see the file. If the file is meant to be confidential, don't publish it on the Web.

3. Formatting Your Business Report

Business Planning

PART II

Chapter 4

Recommendation Reports

Often, a recommendation report is commissioned by a business owner or manager. A consultant who has expertise in the area concerned (design, development, investment, and so on) examines the situation and recommends the best course of action. Whether the report is commissioned or assigned internally, it's important to maintain impartiality. The person paying the consultant may be biased toward a particular decision. But your report should always take an objective and realistic view and not be swayed by office politics or other issues.

Note: Investigation reports can amount to several volumes of writing. There are times, however, when a business is confronted with a more minor or local problem. In that case, a report that provides the information needed to make an important decision is necessary. See Chapter 24 for more on investigation reports.

If the report is commissioned and you are a contractor working from outside the company, you may want to include a letter of transmittal with the features that follow. An Executive Summary will provide the company with the facts at a glance. These and other features that apply to a recommendation report are presented here.

▶ The title of a recommendation report might present the recommendation itself in a flash: "Why investing in hedge funds is overly risky in the present climate," for instance.

▶ The Executive Summary briefly identifies the problem or situation. Rather than a single paragraph, however, some Executive Summaries elaborate by describing the type of investigation that was done to reach the conclusion and suggest the final conclusion of the best way to address it.

▶ The body of the report outlines factors that led to the decision: the economy, a location, personnel availability, the current need, and so on.

▶ The investigation outlines what was done to establish the cause and what was discovered about possible solutions.

▶ The outcome recommends what should be done and who should do it.

▶ The evidence provides documentation to support the recommendation, such as calculations and illustrations.

Your recommendation should be straightforward. If, however, your examination of the situation points to more positive outcomes that would result from different courses of action, list those as well.

Step-by-Step Guide

This chapter assumes that you have already conducted the research work needed to prepare the recommendation report. You should have already accumulated data and prepared supporting elements such as charts and tables that support your conclusion. If, however, you have any doubts about the nature or focus of your report, be sure to clarify them with the manager who assigned you this task. Be sure, before you write the report, that you have the following questions in your own mind:

▶ What is the purpose of the report?

▶ What is the scope of the report? Are you expected to cover a particular period of time?

▶ Are you expected to provide different alternatives, or a single best recommendation—or both?

Making these questions clear in your mind will help you as you assemble your material.

Step 1: Executive Summary/Introduction

In a lengthy report that has been commissioned on a contract basis, an Executive Summary is advisable. It provides those who requested the report with a quick "at a glance" view of what you discovered. Because the Executive Summary describes the entire contents of the report, at this initial stage you should just write a one-sentence version and fill in the rest after finishing the report:

Catalyst Enterprises will save in transportation and property tax costs and achieve benefits for a majority of its employees by relocating to a new facility in Marist County, New York. The move should be conducted in the next calendar year to take advantage of tax incentives being offered by the state of New York.

Step 2: Introduce the body of the report.

When beginning the body of your report, you might restate your recommendation:

Why Catalyst Enterprises Should Relocate to Marist County, New York

Beginning this subtitle with the word *why* signals that you are now going to explain your recommendation in detail.

Step 3: Explain the origins of the report.

Section I of the body should provide some background about how the report came to be: Explain what the need for the report is, and what specific situation the organization is facing.

Also explain something about how the report was conducted, to demonstrate that it is credible and comprehensive. For instance: Six members of our consulting group traveled to the location in New York.

* *Detailed inspections were done of three possible building locations.*
* *Phone interviews were conducted with three Marist County officials.*
* *Personnel records of Catalyst Corporation for the last 10 years were reviewed in detail.*
* *A sampling of six employees was interviewed to determine the impact of a relocation.*
* *The Business Services director for Catalyst was consulted to obtain tax records, utility bills, and other costs associated with the present location in Dayton, Ohio.*

Also, if alternates to the recommendation were explored as well, be sure to mention them. This lets reviewers know that you examined multiple options, not just the one you are recommending: "A smaller facility in the current down of Dayton was also examined," for instance.

Step 4: Examine the current situation.

No matter what recommendation you are planning to make, it's a good idea to examine the advantages and disadvantages of the current situation. This way, you illustrate the impact of the status quo, and illustrate the need for a change. This section heading might be:

"Positive Aspects of the Current Location."

Step 5: Describe current financial/political/business trends.

Your recommendation is likely to be influenced by outside factors, and in this early step it is appropriate to describe those factors. You might describe:

- Financial market trends
- The state of the real estate market
- Business property vacancy rates
- Consumer buying habits

The exact trends will vary depending on what you are recommending. But be sure to analyze any financial or geographic factors that affect the property or business you are examining.

Step 6: Costs and other analyses

Because it's likely your recommendation will depend on financial factors, you should include an analysis of any costs, such as purchases, rentals, reimbursements, or other figures, that will affect the company's bottom line if your recommendation is implemented.

Step 7: Negative implications

Every course of action has either a real or potential downside. It's necessary to take into account the effects of the action you are recommending. Doing so shows your clients or management that you have taken all factors into account.

Step 8: Projections

How will your course of action affect the company into the future? How will the organization be different one, two, or five years down the road after your recommendations become reality? Tell company management now, so they can be prepared. Hopefully, your projections will be positive ones, which will encourage them to adopt what you are proposing.

Step 9: Illustrations

If at all possible, prepare maps, drawings, charts, tables, or other illustrations to demonstrate visually what you are saying in your text.

Step 10: Recommendations

You have already stated your position, in the title and in the introduction or Executive Summary. But at the end of your report, restate your recommendations briefly. Include any alternate courses of action as well. Recommendations should follow naturally from the data presented. Try to be direct, and begin your statement with "We recommend" or "It is recommended."

Often, recommendations are made only after a disaster or other significant event has taken place. (An obvious recent example is the report issued by the special commission looking into the 9/11 terrorist attacks in the United States.) In such a case, you need to be sure you distinguish between conclusions and recommendations. Conclusions describe the cause of the event. Recommendations are actions that should take place to prevent such events from recurring.

A conclusion:

The accident at River Road and Northwest Highway on March 11, 2008 occurred because of a mixture of environmental factors as well as equipment failures. Heavy rains contributed to slick driving conditions. Poor lighting in the area made visibility low. The brakes on the bus were inadequate, and the steering mechanism was too loose. In addition, the driver heading south on River was traveling too fast for conditions.

A set of recommendations:

Reliable Bus Company should be cited for poor maintenance, and all vehicles on its line should have brakes and steering checked immediately. New street lights should be added to the intersection of River and Northwest Highway.

Checklist

❑ Include an introduction or Executive Summary.

❑ For contract reports, include a Letter of Transmittal.

❑ Make the body heading state the recommendation.

❑ Explain the Why and How of the report.

❑ Examine the current situation's pros and cons.

❑ Include relevant business or other trends.

❑ Analyze costs.

❑ Mention negative implications.

❑ Include charts or tables.

❑ Make direct recommendations that are supported by data.

4. Recommendation Reports

Recommendation Report Template

TITLE PAGE

Why Catalyst Enterprises Should Relocate to Marist County, New York

Prepared for: James Bardonet, President

Catalyst Enterprises

Maryanne Glastonbury, Manager

Property Research Division

MG Mortgage Services

1234 Colorado Blvd.

Pasadena, CA 10024

April 15, 2010

LETTER OF TRANSMITTAL

April 15, 2010

MG Mortgage Services
Commercial Division
1234 Colorado Blvd.
Pasadena, CA 10024

Mr. James Bardonet, President
Catalyst Enterprises
448 Wilshire Blvd.
Los Angeles, CA 17738

Dear Mr. Bardonet:

I am pleased to present you with the report you requested on March 1 of this year, determining the advisability of relocating Catalyst Enterprises headquarters to Marist County, New York.

The report shows that the proposed move will result in substantial savings in taxes, plus other financial incentives to be provided by Marist County. The savings combined with the sale of the current building will more than offset costs of relocation. Of course, many employees will be unable to move with the company, so compensation should be provided. But the long-term benefits to the company outweigh the short-term complications.

I am pleased to be able to share these recommendations with you and am available by phone for further consultation as needed.

Sincerely yours,

Maryanne Glastonbury
MG Mortgage

Executive Summary

Recommendation

Catalyst Enterprises will save in transportation and property tax costs and achieve benefits for a majority of its employees by relocating to a new facility in Marist County, New York. The move should be conducted in the next calendar year to take advantage of tax incentives being offered by the state of New York.

Investigation

Site Analysis. The Current Catalyst Enterprises headquarters is a 60-year-old building in need of repair for which the company pays $176,000 per year in taxes. The building can hold 450 employees, but the company only has 210, so much of the structure is unoccupied.

Market Trends. Taxes in California continue to increase, and a 3 percent hike is expected in 2010. In New York, taxes run 1/3 to 1/4 lower. The current recession means that real estate across the country is inexpensive.

Building Specification and Cost Analysis. MG Mortgage located a building in the desired state of New York, in Marist County. The three-story, 60,000-square-foot building, similar to the current headquarters, will hold 250 employees. Parking is available for 300. Total renovation will cost $380,000, but the considerable tax incentives being offered by Marist County mean that virtually no tax bills will be levied for three years. After that, a reduced rate of $100,000 will be levied. The construction should thus pay for itself in four years.

Financing Information. Financing can be arranged at 5.1 percent over a 30-year period on $300,000 of the total project cost.

Body of Report

Why Catalyst Enterprises Should
Relocate to Marist County, New York

Report Background

This report will consider the advisability of moving the Catalyst Enterprises headquarters from its present California location to a new building in New York. It evaluates the advantages and disadvantages of such a move, considers remaining in its current location, and calculates costs associated with the operation.

The MG Mortgage staff gathered information for this report from Catalyst's own business department and other sources:

- Six members of our consulting group traveled to the location in New York.
- Detailed inspections were done of three possible building locations.
- Phone interviews were conducted with three Marist County officials.
- Personnel records of Catalyst Corporation for the previous 10 years were reviewed in detail.

4. Recommendation Reports

- A sampling of six employees was interviewed to determine the impact of a relocation.
- The Business Services director for Catalyst was consulted to obtain tax records, utility bills, and other costs associated with the present location in Dayton, Ohio.

All of these sources gave us a solid foundation on which to make a recommendation. We also based our recommendation on consideration of the location, market trends, renovation costs, tax incentives, and personnel implications.

Current Location

The company's current location is too big and too expensive for the company's needs. Taxes and utilities amount to $228,000 per month. If part of the building was rented out to a company employing 50 to 100 individuals, perhaps $75,000 of this cost would be recouped, but this be reduced as taxes are expected to increase steadily over the coming decade.

Transportation

As residents know, the Los Angeles area lacks good public transportation. Nearly all of the Catalyst employees drive to the headquarters. Perhaps 8 percent take some form of public transportation. Many of those travel one to two hours to reach the location. To accommodate commuters, the company went to staggered work hours. The result is a disorganized work schedule, as shown in Table 1:

Table 1: Work Hours in Current Headquarters

	Start 7 a.m.	Start 8 a.m.	Start 9 a.m.	Start 10 a.m.
End 3 p.m.	18	4	-	-
End 4 p.m.	2	73	4	-
End 5 p.m.	1	2	116	2
End 6 p.m.	-	-	5	45

Moving to a new location with good public transportation would allow virtually all employees to work on the same schedule.

Cost Analysis

Moving to New York would cost the company considerably initially, but pay for itself in only four years. Costs are broken down in the sections that follow:

Building Costs. We strongly recommend purchasing an existing structure rather than building new, as many good buildings lie vacant and can be purchased cheaply in the New York countryside. We estimate total building costs to be $745,000 for the entire development project. As shown in Table 2, this includes renovation costs of $112,000 and resurfacing of the parking lot for $10,000.

4. Recommendation Reports

The purchase cost is $350,000. For a 60,000-square-foot structure, this works do approximately $58 per square foot. This compares favorably with commercial office costs in Los Angeles, which run about $85 per square foot.

Table 2: Renovation and Relocation Cost Summary

Item	Cost
Hard Costs	
Purchase of new HQ	$610,000
Renovation	$112,000
Extra improvements	$40,000
Landscaping	$22,000
Parking lot resurfacing	$10,000
Moving costs	$22,000
Relocation compensation	$150,000
Subtotal	$922,000

Item	Income/Savings
Sale of Current HQ	$785,000
Tax incentives	$110,000 per year
Subtotal	$885,000 (year one)
	$997,000 (year two)

4. Recommendation Reports

Negative Financial Implications

Loan Package. If financing is required to cover the purchase price plus expenses the company will incur long-term debts. Hopefully those can be paid off in five to 10 years. A loan of $500,000 can be obtained for 5.3% interest over a five-year period.

Operating Costs. Heating and other costs associated with moving to a cold climate will be incurred; however, many of the costs are currently being absorbed by the company in its current building.

Table 3: Operating Costs

Item	Per square foot per month
Property taxes	$11.6
Insurance	.99
Maintenance	4.4
Janitorial services and supplies	3.4
Utilities	8.3
Property management	2.8
Contingency	0.2
Total	$31.69

We estimate that current costs for the California location are $29.95, so the difference is not substantial but worthy of note.

Recommendation

The high cost of operating the current building in California, coupled with high taxes and other costs, mean that moving the headquarters to New York will pay for itself in only two years. In addition, the fact that many higher managers already live in New York will save the company substantially in travel costs and result in greater staff cohesiveness.

The considerable pain and inconvenience of relocation for rank-and-file employees is offset by the lower cost of living in New York and better public transportation. On the whole, we enthusiastically recommend this move, and urge the company to make the switch in the coming calendar year to take advantage of considerable tax incentives being offered them.

Templates for Types of Recommendations

Template 1: Post-Accident Recommendations

After an accident or natural disaster, a report that provides analysis and conclusions is nearly as important as one containing recommendations. Include both in separate sections:

Conclusions

The fire in the power plant occurred because of inadequate cleaning of combustible materials that were piled in various locations. At the same time, the introduction of cleaning solvents into the space very likely induced combustion.

Recommendations

The power plant should be rebuilt with new sprinkler systems. In addition, better disposal of cleaning materials should be undertaken, with regular laundering to be conducted at least once a week. In addition, solvents used in cleaning and manufacturing should be stored in an airtight container.

Template 2: Recommendations for New Procedures

Often, recommendations are made in order to determine new ways of teaching, selling, or conducting business. In this case, you aren't telling management to make a specific purchase but to rethink how things are done currently and adopt new methods. Often, this is a "hard sell," so you have to make a particularly persuasive case. Include sections like the following:

Problems With Current Teaching Methods

Why Other School Districts Are Performing Better

Why Immediate Action Is Required

Consequences of Failure to Act

Template 3: A Recommendation That Goes Against "Conventional Wisdom"

Sometimes, you need to make a recommendation that runs counter to conventional wisdom or even purchasing rules. This can occur if you do not want to choose the lowest bidder for a project. If that is the case, you need to provide several credible reasons for doing so:

Best Choice: Lake County Press

Bids were solicited from four printers to produce the annual report. The lowest bid was received by the University's in-house printing department. However, I recommend going with the second-lowest printer, Lake County Press, for the following reasons:

- The University Printing Department has proven unreliable on previous occasions.

- The University Printing Department's bid came in three days later than requested.

- Lake County Press has printed similar jobs before for this office with good results.

- The difference between the two companies' bids, $1,344, is less than 10 percent of the total printing cost.

Chapter 5

White Papers

If you are tasked with preparing an in-depth investigation of a new technology or business process about a complex topic, you'll need to create a white paper for your major donors, high-level executives, or board of trustees. A white paper is a lengthy report with multiple sections that examines a topic in detail and that often (though not always) puts forth a position or suggests a decision to make. A white paper differs from a simple recommendation in its depth and in the complexity of a topic: Its purpose is to educate and make business managers understand how things work or how processes flow as much as to promote a position. By educating managers, you help *them* make important decisions.

It's not necessary to publish a white paper-like book, but often, binding it in a professional way is recommended. Part of the reason for compartmentalizing the text is to make it user-friendly for busy readers. But by carefully spacing your material you will also be instilling confidence that you've done thorough research on your feasibility study, project report, or product analysis. Here are the components:

▶ Writing a cover letter is a way of conveying a report from one organization or person to another. One type of cover letter is called an executive summary because it gives a company's leaders political or financial information that would be unsuitable for all readers or out of place as part of the report itself.

▶ The title page is visually attractive but yet packed with vital details. The title of the report should strike a balance between being informative and short. The name of the person or organization for whom the report was prepared is listed, as well as who prepared the report. The date should be centered at the bottom.

▶ The main message is boiled down in the executive summary. Although it is brief, it should include the purpose, main findings, and outcome.

▸ The table of contents page is helpful to the reader by providing page numbers. But it may be even more important to give an overview of what is contained in the report and how it is organized.

▸ An introduction sets the stage for the report by describing important background and looking ahead to the purpose and scope of the report.

▸ The discussion is the main part of the report. Details are presented clearly and concisely from the initial approach to the analysis of findings to the presentation of results.

▸ Conclusions sum up the parts of the report with a focus on the main findings and the results.

▸ If it would be helpful to list references, a bibliography would go here.

▸ The appendices are evidence. This is where you put detailed data that supports the discussion. It's okay to be technical here.

Step-by-Step Guide

The following is a short white paper that you can rewrite and expand for your own uses. What you see here is a miniature white paper; your own will probably be longer. At the side of the page, you'll find brief explanation of the most important parts of the report given the products and services you want to provide. They are described briefly in the sections that follow.

Step 1: Write a cover letter.

April 3, 2008

To: Ted Jones, Vice President of Golden Chariots Unlimited

From: Michael Boyer, Director of Market Research

Re: Report on Prospective Car Buyers

Enclosed is George Murphy's white paper on market research. This is a second draft to fulfill the contract we awarded to his firm to determine why customers who had leased one of our vehicles did not make the decision to buy when their lease was up. After receiving the first draft, I asked Mr. Murphy to address some issues more specifically.

Two points about this report:

(1) He means it when he says the estimates are not a bid for the work he recommends. I asked him to add them. They are ballpark estimates only, and the simplest way for him to make them was to guess what he would charge.

(2) Mr. Murphy's first draft did not discuss a customer survey. He told me that, while he thought customer surveys would provide valuable data, he did not recommend them originally because of the cost. I asked him to discuss their merits and to provide an estimate.

I will schedule a meeting so that we can discuss the report. Please respond by end of business April 10.

Step 2: Prepare introductory material.

It's usually a good idea to provide an Executive Summary or even a single sentence summarizing your findings and providing readers with the most important points. A Table of Contents, however brief, is common as well.

A Brief Research Agenda for
Golden Chariots Unlimited

Step 3: Create a table of contents.

For example:

I.   *Executive Summary*
II. *How Do Our Customers Feel?*
III. *Leasing vs. Purchasing*
IV. *Conclusion*
V.   *Recommendation*

Step 4: Discussion

This section of the report will analyze the pros and cons of the various quantitative research studies.

Step 5: Conclusion

The conclusion summarizes your findings as a result of your examination. The research and investigative work you have already done should support your conclusions. You aren't necessarily giving your opinions; rather, your conclusion should be a natural extension of the contents that have come in the Discussion section.

> Recommendations are not necessary but include one if asked to do so. White papers can also be purely informational, providing explanations about technical subjects or business processes.

5. White Papers

Checklist

☐ Do you have background to present or topics to explain that warrant a white paper?

☐ Does your cover letter explain who prepared the report?

☐ Did you provide an Executive Summary?

☐ Do you have a Table of Contents?

☐ Did you illustrate with graphics or charts?

☐ Does your report contain subheadings?

☐ Does your report contain a conclusion?

Note: Before you start, make sure a white paper is the appropriate report. White papers are heavily informational. They explain technologies, options, or business processes. They frequently provide historical background about a topic. If you are asked to explain options and provide recommendations, a recommendation report is more appropriate; see Chapter 4 for more information.

White Paper Template

The following is a short white paper that you can rewrite and expand for your own uses. What you see here is a miniature white paper; your own will probably be longer. At the side of the page, you'll find brief explanation of the most important parts of the report given the products and services you want to provide. They are described briefly in the sections that follow.

COVER LETTER

April 3, 2008

To: Ted Jones, Vice President of Golden Chariots Unlimited

From: Michael Boyer, Director of Market Research

Re: Report on Prospective Car Buyers

Enclosed is George Murphy's white paper on market research. This is a second draft to fulfill the contract we awarded to his firm to determine why customers who had leased one of our vehicles did not make the decision to buy when their leases were up. After receiving the first draft, I asked Mr. Murphy to address some issues more specifically.

Two points about this report:

(1) He means it when he says the estimates are not a bid for the work he recommends. I asked him to add them. They are ball park estimates only, and the simplest way for him to make them was to guess what he would charge.

(2) Mr. Murphy's first draft did not discuss a customer survey. He told me that, while he thought customer surveys would provide valuable data, he did not recommend them originally because of the cost. I asked him to discuss their merits and to provide an estimate.

I will schedule a meeting so that we can discuss the report. Please respond by end of business April 10.

Introductory Material

It's usually a good idea to provide an Executive Summary or even a single sentence summarizing your findings and providing readers with the most important points. A table of contents, however brief, is common as well.

A Brief Research Agenda for
Golden Chariots Unlimited

Table of Contents

Executive Summary

Golden Chariots Unlimited (GCU) is a distinctive car dealership with a unique position in the community of vehicle providers. Yet, compared to its competitors, the company knows very little about its current customers, its prospective customers, and its past customers.

We recommend the following five quantitative research studies:

(1) To learn how GCU customers compare and differ from customers choosing other dealerships, we recommend the Cooperative Dealership Research Project. These baseline data provide insights into what new customers expect of GCU and serve as building blocks for further research.

> You can also include a one- or two-sentence "Bottom Line" statement along with your executive summary.

(2) The Car Purchasing Experience Questionnaire provides insight on how current customers view GCU's sales and service. It also allows GCU to compare its success in these areas with similar dealerships. From this research, GCU learns what its customers expect from their dealership experience and identifies needed improvements.

(3) A custom-designed Climate Study allows GCU to explore issues specific to its clientele, develop a more complete profile of the satisfied GCU customer, and test the attractiveness of everything from a new service facility to improving the free coffee.

(4) A study of those who lease but do not buy is the most effective way to learn how to increase GCU's customer base. The earlier studies will provide a profile of the satisfied GCU customer. The inquiry survey will allow GCU to identify the most likely GCU customer among the prospects and find marketing techniques that will be most effective in attracting them to GCU.

(5) GCU should continue using the Satisfied GCU Customer Questionnaire to gain insight into why those who lease do not choose to buy. Additionally a follow-up telephone survey can take an in-depth look at the more generic findings of the Satisfied GCU Customer Questionnaire.

Discussion

This section of the report will analyze the pros and cons of the various quantitative research studies.

Below we describe a research agenda designed to help Golden Chariots Unlimited compete more effectively for viable prospective customers, improve retention of those who lease to encourage their ongoing business and their decision to purchase a car, and create a better sales environment. Each survey builds on what is learned from the previous effort with the goal of generating a clear and concise picture of the distinctive Golden Chariots Unlimited experience and to present that experience most effectively to customers. The surveys needed, in sequence, are illustrated in Figure 5-5.

(Insert your sample surveys, figure 5-5, here.)

How Do Our Customers Feel?

The first and least expensive step would be to administer the Cooperative Dealership Research Project to all new customers. This is the study that will allow GCU to compare the attitudes and opinions of its new customers with those who have chosen to do business with other dealerships. These baseline data will also provide insights into what new customers expect of GCU and help anticipate the services that they will seek.

The Car Purchasing Experience Questionnaire is a straightforward profile of GCU's current customers. It gives demographics of each individual as well as a snapshot of the types of communities they represent. This data will be most useful in encouraging current customers to "spread the word" about GCU to friends, family members, and neighbors. Our goal is to build a satisfied customer base that will generate new prospective customers by word of mouth.

While it is useful to know about the car-buying public in general, the custom-designed Climate Study allows GCU to explore issues specific to its own clientele. It identifies qualities that are unique to GCU customers. Data will be collected on, for example, the products and services that each customer purchased in the past year. Their satisfaction will be measured not only in the result of their purchase but in the "bells and whistles" of conducting their transaction. Questions will be asked about the staff in regard to competency and congeniality. Data will be collected on how long the person had to wait for an appointment, to be seen when they arrived on the premises, and for the transaction to be completed. In addition to multiple choice responses, comments will be encouraged. In short, a Climate Study can improve the effectiveness of the marketing effort by defining the "idea" GCU customer. It also can make the decision making process concerning internal changes far more effective.

Leasing Versus Purchasing

Customers who lease but do not buy are the key to increase GCU's customer base. Why would a person be initially attracted to GCU products and services but

5. White Papers

then not pursue their initial interest? Knowing how this group views GCU and the kinds of things that might have converted them to becoming customers can provide volumes of valuable information. The earlier studies will provide a profile of the satisfied GCU customer. The inquiry survey will allow GCU to identify the most likely GCU customer among the prospects and find marketing techniques that will be most effective in attracting them to GCU.

> This white paper is a miniature version of a real one. White papers can be 6-20 pages or more in length.

A follow-up telephone survey can take an in-depth look, which can be combined with the more generic findings of the Satisfied GCU Customer Questionnaire. The goal would be to determine the attributes and interests of the customers who choose GCU, those who should have chosen GCU but did not, and those who never really considered GCU.

Conclusion

We realize that we have outlined an ambitious research program for GCU. But we do so to ensure that GCU can continue to compete for highly motivated customers who will bring return business to GCU. This program will create a mosaic that should provide more effective ways to identify and attract prospective GCU customers while generating actionable ways to increase satisfaction among current customers.

Recommendation

My opinion, based on comparative figures assembled by my staff, is that a typology of the GCU customer would be very useful. We would be able to determine the characteristics of the "near misses" who never took GCU seriously and avoid wasting valuable staff time in pursuing them. Using this data will help GCU better serve its current customers, encourage more customers to explore our products and services, and persuade those who currently lease to purchase a vehicle from us. As we all know, good research raises additional questions. An essentially new questionnaire could be administered every year to learn more about the prospective customer. Realistically, we recommend that GCU repeat crucial questions and delve further into some new areas every three or four years. An annual survey could be justified if mailed paper and pencil questionnaires were effective. We have found, however, that the response to mailed surveys is unsatisfactory. Telephone surveys, therefore, are the more effective but much more costly alternative.

> Recommendations are not necessary but include one if asked to do so. White Papers can also be purely informational, providing explanations about technical subjects or business processes.

Chapter 6

Primary Research Reports

A primary research report is a report that presents findings based on research you or your colleagues conducted. The audience for a primary research report has two basic questions: (1) What are the facts? and (2) How do you know? A primary research report gives equal importance to the second of these questions as well as the first. Your job is to convince your reader that your report is reliable. You do this by stating your purpose, methods, and scope.

> A secondary research report would be a summary of research that others have conducted.

Nothing can be judged unless you know the goals, so it is essential that you give a clear and explicit statement of the purpose. The history or background of the problem need not be lengthy. But it must include one sentence that is a pointed and concise statement of the problem that you set out to solve. Then you can follow up with background for clarification. If the extent of the description would be distracting, the reader may be referred to the appendix.

A primary research report addresses two overarching topics: methods and scope. The two topics may be presented separately or combined. *Scope* covers what you intended to cover; *methods* answers the "how do you know" question. Sometimes your reputation as a researcher speaks for itself and you don't need to explain your methods in great detail. But if your findings are new or surprising, you must take care to convince your readers that your research methods were sound. Your goal in the primary research report is to show that your facts have a solid basis in valid research. Examples of primary research reports include:

▶ Scientific tests of new products—medicines, chemicals, or physical substances like steel or plastic.

▶ Investigations of events in the recent past. If your company had a downtown, for example, you might be called on to discover the reasons for it.

▶ Personnel issues. These can include labor disputes, hiring of contractors, replacing staff with automated process, or outsourcing.

▶ Networking or computer-related systems. Explaining how database and application servers work or analyzing why a system crashed and how it can be improved is a good use of a research report.

▶ Sales trends. If sales have been going down steadily for a period of six or seven years, you need more than a simple investigation. You need to do market research to see if your products are still in demand, and a research report will address this need.

Note: A primary research report differs from an investigative report of the sort described in Chapter 24. Whereas an investigative report looks into the reasons behind a single event or topic, a primary research report presents results based on testing, tracking, surveys, reviews of data, or some other form of research.

Step-by-Step Guide

A primary research report can only be prepared after a considerable amount of work has been done—in other words, the very research on which you are going to report. The contents of a research report differ depending on the topic being researched, but general contents are presented in the sections that follow.

Step 1: Provide an introduction.

Don't delve into the problem you were investigating or the results you found just yet. Your introduction should provide no more than a paragraph or two of background information such who requested the report, your qualifications, and when the report was done:

The executive committee asked my office to investigate the impact on sales of a proposed smoking ban in restaurants and bars in the neighboring towns of Quihonsett and Banks. I have a background in demographics and sociology so I was able to contribute considerably methodology to the investigation.

Step 2: State the problem.

In a brief paragraph, summarize the subject of your research report:

Smoky Joes is a chain of tobacco stores in the northeastern U.S. Two of the towns in which stores are located are preparing to vote on a smoking ban in bars and restaurants. My department was assigned to research the potential impact on the company. A similar ban in Chicago, Illinois and its impact on another chain of tobacco stores was studied over a three-month period.

Note: You don't have to be researching a problem as such. You might also title this section "The Situation," or simply "Background."

Step 3: Describe the scope of your work.

Discuss your objectives in conducting the research, and explain how much you expected to cover. Be sure to mention topics you specifically did *not* attempt to cover.

Step 4: Explain your method.

It's possible the readers of your research report will try to duplicate your work and results in their own local area. To do this, you need to discuss the methods you used. The description can take the form of steps: Step 1, step 2, and so on. Or you can simply say "To begin, I did this. Next, I followed another approach."

Step 5: List the materials used.

Describe the facilities you used and any special equipment you employed, so others can replicate your results if needed.

Note: This section can either be part of the Method section or stand on its own.

Step 6: Review existing literature.

In some cases, you won't be the first person to conduct primary research in your chosen area. Here, describe any books, articles, or encyclopedia listings that are relevant to your own study. What do the other authors have to say about their topic, and how does it compare to your own?

Step 7: Report your results.

The most important part of a primary research report is the information you collect through your research. This should be presented in charts, graphs, or tables placed in the body of the work.

Graphics that illustrate your findings can also be placed in an appendix. This is a good idea if they are especially long and will interrupt the flow of your report.

Step 8: Draw your conclusions.

Once you present your data, you need to draw conclusions from it. The numbers don't speak for themselves; busy managers need to know what they mean. Tell them if the results were predictable or if there were surprising elements. Make recommendations or projections as to how the results might affect the future of your business:

The success of tobacco shops in Chicago indicates that the impact of a smoking ban on our own operation is minimal. A surprising result was the popularity of Hookah stores, which indicates that the market for smoking paraphernalia is strong in the 18 to 30-year-old demographic. Smoky Joes would do well to branch into this area.

Step 9: Add a bibliography.

Research reports typically draw on authoritative sources for their methods and conclusions. It's important to include references citing the work done by others on the same topic. A bibliography appended to your report will make it more credible and give future researchers information to draw on if and when they attempt to replicate your results. For example:

Bibliography

> *Mandel, Howard.* Tobacco Through the Ages. *New York: Houghton Mifflin Co., 2001.*
>
> *"Starting Your Own Hookah Store,"* Smoker's World, *May 2006.*
>
> *Ziv, John Cabot.* Meditation and Smoke Rings. *Kabbalah Publishers, 1987.*

> Refer to the *Chicago Manual of Style,* published by the University of Chicago Press, for instructions on how to format a bibliography.

Checklist

- ❑ Have your clearly defined the goal of your research?
- ❑ Have you limited the scope and described it clearly in your report?
- ❑ Have you clearly stated the problem?
- ❑ Do you have charts or graphs to illustrate your data?
- ❑ Have you explained the methods and materials you used?
- ❑ Have you mentioned other reports related to your own?
- ❑ Have you included a bibliography?

Primary Research Report Template

Introduction

Information Please Inc. has ten years of experience investigating retail stores and researching shoppers' needs and tastes. We were asked to investigate the most popular stores in a two zip codes by the Newton County Chamber of Commerce. Our work was conducted over a two-month period in 2010. We used a mixture of phone calls and in-person surveys done at 20 stores in the designated area that are targeted specifically at young women.

The Bottom Line

Women between the ages of 25 and 35 from the zip codes of 52030 and 52050 are more likely to shop at Slam Glam Boutique than any of the alternative clothing establishments, and this success brings increased business to surrounding commercial establishments, according to this market survey prepared for the stockholders of Slam Glam Boutique by Information Please, Inc.

The Situation

The Chamber of Commerce seeks to attract more shoppers in the high-spending ages 25 to 40 range, especially females. They want to know what sorts of stores currently in their immediate area are attracting the most young females so they can encourage more such stores to open in different locations, thus increasing options for shoppers in that age range. The malls located in the two aforementioned zip codes are losing customers, especially younger shoppers, and there is a need to attract them back to the local shops.

Scope of Research

Information Please was only asked to investigate the 52030 and 52050 area codes. Only major stores in those areas were researched. Primary research was done only with female shoppers in the ages 25 to 40 range.

Methods Used

The following methods were used in conducting the primary research:

- Phone interviews (25)
- In-person surveys (22)
- Review of sales receipts (1)
- Newspaper reports (2)
- Magazine articles (1)
- Radio stories (1)

Materials used were simple: a tape recorder, a phone, and a clipboard and paper.

Population and Buying Units

Although Slam Glam Boutique is located in a shopping mall with a zip code of 50402, which is surrounded by middle-class, single-family homes and assisted care facilities, women from the surrounding region are willing to drive to the facility. The population of women of all ages in zip code 50402 is 35,000, but only 500 of those who indicated on a survey that they had shopped at Slam Glam Boutique were from that zip code. All those women were between 20 and 40.

In contrast, 85 percent of those customers who had made a purchase at Slam Glam Boutique within the last year were between 25 and 35 years of age and were from the zip codes of 52030 and 52050. We did a survey of shoppers visiting the shopping mall. Representative comments are presented in Table 6.1.

Table 6.1: Survey of mall shoppers

Topic	Comment	Age
Location	"It's difficult to get here. I would rather walk."	23
Parking	"You have to park so far away, it's an ordeal in winter. Why no indoor parking?"	38
Stores	"Some of these places have been here 30 years. Who shops here?"	35
Prices	"Good range of prices, but not enough bargain stores."	39
Merchandise	"Where are the new designers?"	27
Dining Opportunities	"Aside from Rainforest Cafe, there's no restaurant I would ever visit."	23

Buying Income

Although the women who shopped at Slam Glam Boutique had incomes ranging from $20,000 to $85,000, 75 percent made between $30,000 and $40,000. However, 50 percent of the respondents indicated that they spent more than 50 percent of their disposable income on clothing. Many did not own their own car, but 90 percent had access to a car belong to a friend or family member. Only 7 percent owned a home or condo; most rented or lived with their family of origin. Only 35 percent were married to a working spouse. The differences found in the research are illustrated in Table 6.2:

Table 6.2

Venue	Annual Income	Percent Spent on Clothing
Mall	$40–$60,000	20%
Neighborhood Stores	$25,000–$30,000	15%
Slam Glam	$20,000–$85,000	52%

Retail Sales

The high percent of income spent on clothing by this demographic group and the large amount of young women who are willing to travel to shop at Slam Glam Boutique explain why the profit margin of the Coolness Mall ($1.2 million in the last fiscal year) is so high. In contrast, nearby discount stores and resale shops are either breaking even or operating at a loss.

Overall Business Factors and Stability

Although surrounding retail establishments are going out of business as a result of the economic downturn, Slam Glam Boutique profits improved during the recent recession. Thirty percent of the respondents on the survey had been laid off and were buying suits they could wear to job interviews. Another 40 percent indicated that they would sacrifice in other areas, even spending a large portion of their unemployment check, for an outfit that made them feel good about themselves. Twenty percent were splurging on a party dress for a special occasion. The remainder were buying clothes for every day, but still wanted them to be high quality fabric and to make them look attractive. All of Slam Glam's customer's were more interested in purchasing clothes that were stylish and trendy that they would wear for only one season as opposed to classic clothes that would be a long-term addition to their wardrobe.

Business Activity

Coolness Mall estimates that 80 percent of its business is now related to the success of Slam Glam Boutique. Examples include stores that specialize in music, custom make-up, and cell phones. Construction has averaged $5 million more than in the surrounding area, and rents have increased 20 percent. There is a waiting list of businesses that are eager to relocate to Coolness Mall. Five new restaurants and two new gourmet health food stores have opened.

6. Primary Research Reports

Results

It's clear that Slam Glam Boutique has been highly successful in attracting young women in the 25 to 40-year-old range to its facility. What's more, the success of the store has had a ripple effect, boosting business in Coolness Mall and other nearby retail outlets. The store's success is due to the fact that it offers trendy clothing at affordable prices.

Conclusions

More stores like Slam Glam are needed in the 52050 zip code particularly, where the Staid Mall is losing business and in danger of closing. Tax incentives should be provided for young entrepreneurs who want to open such stores in the neighborhood.

Bibliography

Mandel, Howard. *Retail Sales to Young Females.* New York: Houghton Mifflin Co., 2001.

"Starting Your Own Clothing Store," *Wearer's World,* May 2006.

Ziv, John Cabot. *Meditation and Clothing.* Kabbalah Publishers, 1987.

PROJECT MANAGEMENT

PART III

Chapter 7

Progress Reports

Many business projects span long periods of time, from a few weeks to a number of years. Progress reports tell company managers what is happening with the project at any given time. Progress reports tend to be informal, consisting of only a few pages. However, they contain important information such as lists of materials, analysis of costs incurred, diagrams, and schedules projecting the project's completion. Progress reports also describe any problems or complications that have arisen while the project is ongoing. For short-term projects, only a single progress report may be needed. For long-term projects, a progress report may be called for every month or every quarter. These periodic progress reports have a more rigid and well-developed structure is that needed for less complex short-term projects.

The general types of progress reports you might need to create are:

▶ Status reports that describe the progess of a job to a particular point.

▶ Completion reports that present highlights and suggestions of what to do if the projects is repeated in the future.

▶ Investigative reports that describe problems encountered during a project.

The types of projects discussed in progress reports are virtually limitless, but here are a few general examples:

▶ Reports that inform clients of the projects of short-term manufacturing contract jobs.

▶ Construction of large-scale construction projects, such as power plants or transportation systems.

▶ Major publications jobs, such as annual reports, that can take several months to produce.

▶ Scientific studies of health issues or developments of new medicines.

Step-by-Step Guide

The following is a set of steps that describe the preparation of a typical progress report. The specific contents vary depending on the types of projects being discussed. But, in general, sections such as Summary, Background, and Progress are included in most reports. Progress reports tend to be less formal than formal investigative reports or primary research reports. You can present your report as a memorandum, as shown in the template corresponding to this chapter.

Step 1: Introduce your report.

Don't assume that everyone who reads your report has intimate knowledge of the project you are writing about. Restate it briefly, even if it seems well known to you and the person who commissioned the report; others in your organization may read your work as well. Describe the project you are examining, state the reason for your report, and give a brief (one-paragraph) summary of the report's contents.

> *It's hard to believe that only a few short years ago we were isolated individuals who were alone with our love of thimbles. The purpose of this report of the Thimble Lovers is, first of all, to congratulate ourselves over having found each other, and to assess the progress we have made. The next is to determne how to carry our love of thimbles to a wider audience. This report summarizes the growth of Thimble Lovers, summarizes where we are now, and looks ahead to a bright future.*

Step 2: Summarize your progress to date.

This first section summarizes where the project stands currently. Look at this section as a sort of Executive Summary: a two- or three-sentence statement of your findings: Is the project in trouble? Is it thriving? How much of the project is complete? Are the organizers close to reaching their goals? Give readers a quick overview of what they will find when they read your report in detail. For example:

> *Thimble Lovers was formed in 2010 and started with just three members. As its 10-year anniversary approaches, the group has grown to 300 members nationwide, and holds a successful annual meeting. Its initial goals have been fully met, but new challenges await as members head into their second decade.*

Step 3: Provide background.

This looks back to the past and summarizes events leading up to the current state of the project. It is a summary of the situation. Not only that, but the Background section should summarize the group, topic, organization, or situation whose progress you are examining. This is a chance to point out the importance of the subject you are examining, and to summarize the purpose of the group or subject. For example:

Thimbles have been instrumental throughout history, and the earliest examples are found in ancient Greece. Thimbles have been used everywhere from the household to the nursery to the battlefield. Surprisingly few clubs exist to celebrate the nearly limitless variety of thimbles found around the world and throughout the ages. Thimble Lovers was the first thimble-related group created in the United States. The group has a charter from the Association of American Associations. The occasion for this report is the group's first decade.

Step 4: Give progress details.

This gives a brief sense of the work that was planned to be done, describes the work that was actually done, mentions the problems encountered, and gives an account of whether the schedule was affected. Challenges should be described in detail, action should be explained, and an explanation should be given as to the success of the efforts. When talking about the schedule, the difference should be quoted in hours, days, or weeks. Here is an example:

> Note: It's a good idea to remind your readers of the purpose and background of the situation in order to fully understand the issues at stake and to evaluate progress that has been made.

The construction of the bridge over the Patuxet River was planed for nearly a decade before ground was finally broken in April 2002. At the time, the general contractor, Hammer Company, projected that the work would be done by April 2003. The Patuxet City Council asked Construction Advisors Inc. to evaluate the progress that has been made so far and project the actual completion date. The report was commissioned as a result of slowdowns and accidents that have set the project back considerably.

This report was conducted in November and December 2002. Meaurements were taken of the amount of bridge work done to date, and the amount remaining to be completed. Extensive interviews were conducted with Hammer Company in November. However, discussions broke off after a section of the bridge fell into the river, injuring three workers. Hammer Company has since been unresponsive and Construction Advisors has been working on its own. We found the following:

- *The job is currently six weeks behind schedule.*
- *Only 40 percent of the work has been completed.*
- *We project that construction will not be completed until September 2003 unless changes are made (see Conclusions, below).*

> ◆ *Faulty workmanship and a too-small, non-union workforce resulted in weak bracing of the bridge that led to the section collapsing just as our investigation was underway.*
>
> ◆ *We recommend either replacing Hammer Company or hiring another company to oversee their efforts.*
>
> ◆ *We recommend increasing the number of workers by 10 to 20 percent.*

Step 5: Describe supporting data.

It's a good idea to include a Supporting Data section if your evaluation of progress stands a chance of being controversial in some way. If you discover that the progress that has been made to date falls short of original goals, for instance, you can expect that the people whose job it was to achieve those goals will take issue with your conclusions. Having supporting data on hand is essential to counter their arguments and to provide your readers with real, unbiased information to back up your conclusions rather than your opinions. For example:

▶ The original budget for the bridge construction project was $10 million. To date, 80 percent or $8 million has been spent. Yet, the project is only 40 percent complete.

▶ The distance to be spanned is 3,000 feet. To date, only 1,245 feet has been spanned, and 1,755 feet remain.

▶ The contractor has requested additional funds of $5 million, which would put the project 50 percent over budget.

▶ Our scientific lab discovered that structural steel being used for the project has not been approved by the National Highway Association, which is tasked with approving bridge construction projects in the United States.

▶ Complaints have been filed by the Patuxet City Council and the Franklin County Board of Directors.

▶ Two fired workers have reported to the media that the company is using unsafe materials.

In addition, special devices used to measure the strength of bridges have been installed on two of the supporting columns on the west side of the river and found that strength is 10 percent below federally approved standards.

Note: This is an optional section, but it could include forms, statistical data, and other documentation that relates to the project.

Step 6: Draw up a plan of action.

Moving forward, this section looks to the future. It elaborates on plans for upcoming work and incorporates any adjustments to the schedule that will need to be made. This section is different than the Conclusions section: Conclusions summarizes the main point of the report—the progress that has been made—whereas the Plan of Action section looks to improvements or changes that need to be made. Those conclusions and recommendations do not necessarily need to address shortcomings; you can make recommendations that are designed to maintain the current level of progress or simply to maintain the success or "health" of the organization or project being examined.

Step 7: Present your conclusions.

Note: Only include this section if asked to to do. You aren't being asked to prepare a recommendation (see Chapter 4); your primary goal is to describe progress so far. However, if asked to recommend action, be sure to base your views on the progress that has been made.

After presenting your data, summarize what it all means for your readers. Let the facts speak for themselves rather than being an advocate for a particular position. Being overly critical of substandard progress leaves you open to the charge that you are biased against the group being examined. On the other hand, being too enthusiastic makes you look too biased and not credible.

Note: Chances are you will have a chance to advocate for a position in discussions of your report. Keep the report itself objective so it is credible to your readers.

Checklist

❑ Do you have a clear picture of the purpose of your report?

❑ Are you expected to focus solely on progress to date, or do you need to recommend actions as well?

❑ Have you presented an introduction?

❑ Did you include a Background section that prvides historical information about the project or group you are examining?

❑ Did you provide details about the current progress?

❑ Did you list data that supports your assessment of the progress?

❑ Did you include a plan of action, if that is required by the group that commissioned your progress report?

❑ Have you drawn conclusions from your research and data?

Progress Report Template

Introduction

It's hard to believe that only a few short years ago we were isolated individuals who were alone with our love of thimbles. The purpose of this report of the Thimble Lovers is, first of all, to congratulate ourselves over having found each other, and to assess the progress we have made. The next is to determine how to carry our love of thimbles to a wider audience. The group is doing well now, but we feel we can do better and widen our membership base beyond the Midwest. This report summarizes the growth of Thimble Lovers, summarizes where we are now, and looks ahead to a bright future.

Background

Thimble Lovers was formed in 2010 and started with just three members. The founder, Don Jacobs, died in 2008. Marlene Bobodich has been our president ever since. As its 10-year anniversary approaches, the group has grown to 300 members nationwide, and holds a successful annual meeting. Its initial goals have been fully met, but new challenges await as members head into their second decade.

Summary: Progress to Date

Our members mainly come from the Midwest; 100 live within a 500-mile radius of Chicago. The largest number of members in any state (52) is in Wisconsin. We have a newsletter and a Website. Our income from membership dues just covers our costs, with only a $1,200-per-year profit. We need to increase revenue and membership without making the group too expensive to afford.

Progress Details

Today, we have a schedule of events, a newsletter, and a Website that "say it loud and say it proud: we love thimbles." Yet we also need to be realistic about our goals for the future. How wonderful it would be to have space to call our own. Here we could display portions of our impressive collections. We could have our meetings whenever we choose without having to pay rent and reword our meetings for the convenience of others. We could get together a library of materials to increase our own storehouse of knowledge as well as spread the word about the glory of thimbles.

Supporting Data

To consolidate our goals, we held a focus group last month. Our objectives were to find out how folks currently felt about thimbles and to determine what would motivate them to officially join our ranks. We began by identifying our target audience and making attempts to reach them. Notices were posted in grocery stores, coffee shops, sewing establishments, and the scrapbook club. To make sure we would not be biased by our surroundings, we held the event in the recreation center of the Village Inn. Participants were given name tags, asked to introduce themselves, and to give a one-sentence statement about what thimbles meant to them. Rewatching the video tape dozens of times and reviewing the transcripts revealed some important points. For example, although participants were specifically asked not to bring thimbles with them, the competition among owners is more fierce that we expected. Several can clearly be seen fondling their thimbles in their pockets and others brought them out to openly display. At times the lust was palpable.

Admission to this event was $10, $5 for members. The event mentioned previously attracted 75 attendees Yearly membership dues are $300.

Plan of Action

One aspect of our proposed meeting space is that there will be the opportunity to cross boundaries. Quilters, for example, are avid users of thimbles. We need a venue to bring them in under our umbrella. There may also be the occasional user of thimbles who need to be educated about the delights that await when that first thimble is put on their finger. For example, an expectant mother or grandmother may be sewing for the first time to present the next generation with a handmade heirloom. They need to know that thimbles can be an important part of the process.

We propose a modest increase in yearly dues to $325, and event admissions to $20/$10. This, we project, will increase annual revenues to $2,000.

Conclusions

In conclusion, we realize that Thimble Lovers need to find ways to be collaborative as a group while still respecting the rights of others to hoard their treasures if that is their choice. We believe that putting thimbles on display on a rotating basis will solve the problem. We will certainly allow donors to remain anonymous if they fear that their security would be risked by revealing the extent of their thimble collection. Another challenge is to improve the diversity of our demographics to include more persons of color, more youth, and more men. A subcommittee for each of these groups has been formed to brainstorm about how to make it okay to identify oneself as a thimble lover and still remain secure in important parts of one's identity. In fact, we have reevaluated our goals of forming a permanent home. We can use the basement of the fabric shop for our library and display location. We believe more members of underrepresented groups would attend meetings if they would not be identified by the passerby with their cars being seen in our parking lot. Instead we intend to use our funds for education and to donate thimbles to the needy.

Chapter 8

Time Accounting Reports

No place is the saying "time is money" more accurate than in the workplace.

If you take a business trip and have to account for time spent on meetings, or if you work in an organization that requires you to record time spent at work as well as time spent on holidays and other days off, a time accounting report is ideal. An employer needs to know that when staff are paid an honest day's wages that they have put in an honest day's work. In some cases, that simply means punching a time clock. But as staff work from remote locations and become craftier about ways to misuse the system, logistical complications increase. Other reasons for preparing a time accounting report include:

▶ Tracking attendance (for example, in a school).

▶ Billing (for example, the work done by lawyers is usually calculated in "billable hours").

▶ Scheduling vacations.

▶ Tracking sick time.

▶ Reporting required furlough days taken.

▶ Compensating for overtime.

> The general types of functions you might accomplish when creating a time accounting report are listed here:
>
> ▷ Collecting time.
>
> ▷ Managing time.
>
> ▷ Processing time.

The other component of tracking time has to do with billable hours. Everyone is watching costs these days. A client is more likely than ever to scrutinize every penny on a bill. Instead of doing a cost estimate based on an overall project, companies are more likely to demand detailed accounting. Often different hourly fees are imposed for different kinds of work. Whether travel is involved or other forms of telecomputing, the costs need to be factored into the equation.

If you work in an organization that reports to a federal or state government, chances are you will have to account for your time in some way.

There does not need to be an emotional component to time. Simply setting up a system and recording it accurately should be second nature to employees at all levels, managers, and clients. As always, the key is good reporting to explain, implement, and maintain the process. But even more important is the report that processes and analyzes the results.

Step-by-Step Guide

Step 1: State the purpose of the report.

In a sentence or two, describe the reason for your time accounting. Those who process your information will want to know what job you were working on, what your own position is, and possibly your ID number if you have one:

Greg Holden

Director of Communications

Jane Addams College of Social Work

ID 6638277766

This is a record of work done January 1–May 30, 2010

Step 2: Give the project or position involved.

In some cases, billable hours may need to be charged to a client for work on a single project—a series of related activities designed to achieve a well-defined purpose. You may be required to organize the work you performed on the project into specific tasks. The client may want to know how much time was spent on planning, how much spent on transcribing, how much taking depositions, and so on:

The project being reported on is the legal case involving a lawsuit against Rebel Trophies by a customer who slipped in front of the store, Mabel Normand. Time spent on the case is broken into:

- *Depositions*
- *Meetings with client*
- *Photography of store*
- *Review of city code*

Step 3: Company policy regarding time accounting

In case the people who read your report are not familiar with your time accounting methods, it's a good idea to state them. That way everyone will be on the "same page" as far as the citations and regulations you are using for your report. For example:

Note: It's also useful to state the policies and procedures for time accounting in case you are creating a time accounting report template to use for your office. Such a template is included with this book's CD-ROM.

Employees of the Jackson and Jackson and Smithfield Ltd. law firm shall account for the following: The beginning and ending times worked each day, and the times spent on any absences during the work day, such as illness, doctor's appointments, and vacations (except for the standard one-half hour lunch break). These must be recorded for each day. This information will be used for client billing as well as pay calculations.

Step 4: List the period covered.

This might seem obvious, but it's essential to mention the time period covered, whether it is a pay period (a week or a month) or a billing cycle. In addition, you might go into detail on time spent or attendance by listing such items as:

- ▶ The times you started or ended work each day.
- ▶ The times you were absent (not including lunch breaks).
- ▶ Any credit hours you used during your attendance (if in school).
- ▶ Any compensatory hours you compiled that you will be able to make up at a later day by taking time off.
- ▶ Any overtime hours you worked, for which you will be paid (or the client will be charged) extra.
- ▶ Any time you worked on a specific project or task, along with the names of those projects or tasks.
- ▶ Any time you spent on leave during the period you are reporting on.

Step 5: State the methods used to track your time.

This section is optional, but if your employer requires it (or if you want to require it for your own employees) state the methods to account for your time or attendance. These days, chances are you will use some sort of online time accounting system. But some organizations still require forms to be printed out, filled in, and submitted. In cases where two or more time accounting methods are available, it's important to note which one you used:

- ▶ Automated or Web-based systems used in many organizations.
- ▶ Paper copies of sign in/out times.
- ▶ Employee Attendance Records or other applicable forms.

> Be sure to include any job codes you'll need to bill your client, or any course numbers, if you are recording school attendance.

Step 6: Summary of time remaining

This section, too, is optional, but you can keep track of time remaining, whether it is the number of vacation hours you have left in the year, or the number of hours you expect to spend on the project before completion. For example:

Total Hours/Year	Spent This Month	Year to Date	Time Remaining
75.0	10.0	25.0	50.0

Checklist

☐ Did you identify yourself, your ID number, and your position?

☐ Did you describe the project or class for which you are counting time?

☐ Did you state company policies on time accounting, if needed?

☐ Did you list the time period covered?

☐ Did you break out individual tasks, if the client or your supervisors want you to do so?

☐ Did you record the method used to track your time?

☐ Did you calculate the time remaining, if needed?

Time Accounting Report Template
Cover Memo

April 11, 2010

To: John B. Murphy, President
Illinois State Dept. of Transportaton
111 Wacker Drive
Springfield, IL 60533

Dear Mr. Murphy:

When I founded this company thirty years ago, the process of time accounting was more straightforward than it is today. You explained your needs, we produced text, you signed off on the results, we counted up the hours and multiplied them by one standard rate, you paid us, and we were all happy. All was done on good old-fashioned paper with either a typewriter or a number-two pencil.

What we are seeing today is technology that is changing on an ongoing basis. Your needs are more diverse and complex, and we want to work with you to make sure that our product gives you a leg up on your competition. That requires both print and electronic media. We work hard at Copy Corral to stay one step ahead of the latest trend. We want to give you cutting-edge technology not only in our creative copy but also in the way we prepare our bills. It has been said that if you can't beat them you should join them. So I hope that you will take a few minutes to review your next invoice to assure yourself that it is our way of using the latest technology to assure that you get the most bang for your buck. Our new system will allow us to be much more fair in giving you true value for each component of your project. You will find attached our time spent on various tasks rates for services such as research, brainstorming, fact checking, writing, editing, and proofing, as well as costs for project management and administrative tasks. We are eager to receive your feedback and look forward to working with you during this transition.

Sincerely,

John Bademus
Principal, Archer & Lane, Attorneys at Law

8. Time Accounting Reports

Purpose of Report

The purpose of this report is to explain to clients of Copy Corral the changes you will see on your next invoice. Time is now being accounted for in 15-minute increments to maximize accuracy and efficiency. We are tracking time spent to date and providing you with an estimate of time remaining.

Project or Position Involved

Case #101, Lawsuit filed by customer against Rebel Trophies for slipping on sidewalk in front of building.

Archer & Lane: Policies Regarding Time Accounting

1. When compiling billing hours at the end of a reporting period, normally a calendar month, staff are to record figures for the projects or tasks worked on during the reporting period and the amount of time worked on each project or task during the same period.

2. When an attorney or other staff person is traveling or doing training, begins or completes work at a location other than the client's office, or is absent for the entire day, the staff person is to record the time and task information when he or she has an opportunity to access the computerized time-management system. Otherwise, the supervisor or a designated staff member is to record the time data on behalf of the employee.

3. Attorneys and paralegels must be aware of the work time and absence of employees for whom they are responsible to ensure the accuracy of billable time information.

4. Employees shall abide by Archer and Hill polices regarding overtime and work schedules.

5. Every Archer and Hill staff person shall establish procedures for time and attendance accounting in conformance with the policy spelled out in this document.

Time Accounting Responsibilities of Archer and Hill Employees:

a. Accurately record the precise start and end times of hours worked, to the quarter of an hour, the amount of overtime worked, and absences that should be charged to leave, charging the appropriate account numbers with the time actually spent.

b. Verify that the correct project(s) or task(s) have been charged with the amount of hours worked, in quarter-hour increments.

c. Verify the correct recording of time and attendance information each pay period and make sure the data is correct.

d. Receive approval to work overtime in advance.

e. Request and receive approval for leave in advance.

f. Protect their passwords for automated time and attendance systems to maintain security within the system. Handing out of user IDs and passwords is not allowed.

g. Timekeepers shall, if a paper time and attendance process is used to prepare timesheets:

- Be thoroughly familiar with the time accounting procedures and adhere to the time and attendance reporting procedures described therein.

- Verify the correct data entry of time and attendance information on the Staff Attendance Record each pay period and validate by signature that this information is correct.

- Require each subordinate staff person to verify, by signature, hours worked and any leave taken on the Staff Time and Attendance Report each pay period.

- Use the Staff Attendance paper records to enter timesheet entries into the automated Time and Attendance system for electronic certification by the supervisor.

- Keep an accurate record of subordinate employees' time and attendance information. Leave is chargeable in accordance with the provisions of SM 370.630.

Supervisors shall:

h. Be ultimately responsible for the proper recording and reporting of all time and attendance data, including the time worked on projects or tasks during the reporting period, for employees under their authority. Supervisors shall certify the accuracy of time and attendance data either manually on the Employee Attendance Record or electronically in an automated system. Supervisors shall also, whenever feasible, certify the Time and Attendance Reports themselves or have the timesheets certified by an approved alternate.

i. Determine whether any excess time indicated on the time accounting document constitutes authorized overtime (for example, resolve possible errors in recording of hours worked). If payment should be authorized for the reported excess time, the supervisor shall ensure that the necessary documentation has been completed to justify compensation. Errors related to the recording of hours worked shall be corrected in the time and attendance system or on the time accounting document and brought to the employee's attention.

j. Archer and Hill managers must record all work performed in their organizations into projects or tasks and assign at least one account number to each project or task.

Data Recording Requirements

If paper timesheets are used, the timekeeper shall maintain the file of time and attendance system records, including sign-in/out sheets or any other documentation used to prepare the Time and Attendance Reports. These records may be disposed of after six years or after an audit by the General Accounting Office, whichever comes first.

Period Covered

Feb. 15–April 15, 2010

Method Used

Instead of agreeing on a price per project, we will be charging you an hourly rate that will be determined on fifteen-minute increments. To back up a minute to the beginning of a project, we will be more accurate and clear in making estimates when we present you with a bid. We will be able to e-mail you a weekly accounting of where we stand in regard to that estimate. When we are in danger of going over our agreed upon amount, we can work with you to adjust our assignment accordingly. Our talented staff is looking forward to this new process. No longer will they experience the dread of not knowing what to do next. They will have a much better sense of how much time they have available.

The Archer and Hill Time Accounting System was used to record this data

Time Spent

Time Accounting Report

Page: 1 of 1

Report Time: 4:52PM

Report Date: 04/10/2010

Archer and Hill, Attorneys at Law Requested By:
System Administrator

1 of 2

Dates Included: 03-15-2010 to 04-15-2010

Timekeeper Selected: All

Client Selected: All

Matter Selected: All

Billing Type Selected: All

Task Code Selected: All

Client	Number	Staff Person	Number Date	Ticket	No. of Hours	Task	Code	Activity
Johnson vs. Rebel	111	John Smith	Mar. 20, 2010	A111	5.0	deposition	03-1098	recording
Johnson vs. Rebel	111	Amanda Bynum	Mar. 29, 2010	A118	2.5	deposition	03-1098	transcription
Johnson vs. Rebel	111	John Smith	Mar. 30, 2010	A122	1.25	prep	03-1098	phone call w/client
Johnson vs. Rebel	111	John Smith	Apr. 3, 2010	A151	0.25	travel	03-1099	go to court
Johnson vs. Rebel	111	Tom Pagnum	Apr. 3, 2010	A152	1.0	photo-graphy	03-1999	photograph Rebel Trophies facility
Johnson vs. Rebel	111	Amanda Bynum	Apr. 4, 2010	A155	1.75	photo-graphy	03-1999	process and edit photos

Summary of Time Remaining

For your convenience, we are tracking the time remaining on this lawsuit, based on original estimates:

Total Hours/Project	Spent This Month	Year to Date	Time Remaining
75.0	10.0	25.0	50.0

8. Time Accounting Reports

Chapter 9

Incident Reports

In an incident report, you are actually performing the task of a reporter. Frequently, incident reports are prepared after crimes, disasters, or other problems occur. They can also be commissioned after less dramatic events, such as an argument in the workplace. As someone who is given the job of describing an unexpected event, you can use the same sorts of questions that guide journalists: Who? Why? What? When? How? The person reading your incident report should be able to understand what happened, how and why it happened, what happened as a result, and what is being done to prevent it from happening again. Imagine a pyramid or a triangle with the following parts getting more detailed as the report continues:

> Incident reports should be objective and factual, not colored by personal opinion.

▶ The summary should be just a sound bite of the incident and its outcome.

▶ The background should be a little longer to describe what led up to the incident.

▶ The facts and events section should cover as much as is necessary to give readers all they want and need to know about what happened first and then the effects of the incident.

▶ The outcome might not requires as many words, but the reader needs to be assured that the incident has been thoroughly understood, that action has already been taken, and that what has been learned will be put into place as the company or organization moves forward.

Step-by-Step Guide

Step 1: Summarize what happened.

The first step in preparing a business report is to gather information about what happened. If the incident just occurred, you can do primary research of the sort described in Chapter 6. You can interview people in your organization or in the immediate vicinity of where the incident occurred. Sometimes, though, you are called upon to report on an incident in another area, or that occurred in the past. In that case, you have to do secondary research; read newspaper or Internet news reports about the event, or go to your local library and find out all you can about what took place. Once you gather the information, write a "lead" to your report as a reporter would: summarize the what, where, when, and other pertinent details about the incident to grab the reader's interest. For example:

> On July 2, we realized that our shipments for Pyro Fireworks Company (PFC) would not reach six communities who had ordered our products. Rather than have Independence Day celebrations cancelled, which would have had grave consequences for hundreds of thousands of people, we took remedial action to retrieve the fireworks and have them redelivered. This was successful in that deadlines were met. The cost, however, was substantial. As president of PFC, I believe we had no choice.

Step 2: Provide background.

Few incidents are absolutely unpredictable. Chances are some factors led to the incident. At the very least, the people and organizations involved have backgrounds that may be pertinent to your investigation. After you summarize what happened, this is the time to take a step or two back and and describe background that might be relevant to the incident. Here is an example:

> A combination of errors and problems led to this unfortunate situation. Items included in our original order for ingredients were either held up or unavailable. We had very particular specifications, so we had to make new formulas in some cases. As you are aware, there was a job action earlier this year. Not only did we lose time on the production floor, but we lost several key employees. Problems in the warehouse led to further delays. We were also the victim of an unscrupulous trucking company.

Step 3: Describe pertinent facts and events.

This is the main body of your report. In it, you describe what happened and answer the important questions (Who? What? Where? When? Why? How?) A combination of errors and problems led to this unfortunate situation.

> Tip: Don't provide a history of your company or every detail about the individuals involved. Focus on what's relevant.

Manufacturing was slowed because of a lack of materials. Our orders for raw ingredients were held up at customs because of more strict regulations imposed by the U.S. Department of Security. Therefore, we were behind on starting the process of making the specialized fireworks that had been ordered for this landmark year. In fact, a number of substitutions had to be made because what we had specified in our original order could not pass customs at all. This caused delays and extra costs that we had not foreseen to hire specialists.

Step 4: Be objective, be factual.

> Tip: Minimize the use of adjectives and adverbs, which can make your report sound biased.

If you are describing events in which you were not involved personally, it is relatively easy to be unbiased and objective. However, even if you are writing about people you have never met, you have to take care not to let your own judgments and predispositions creep into your report. Here are some examples of descriptions of the same event. The descriptions are factually the same, but slightly different wording gives some a more opinionated tone than others.

Opinionated: When interrogated, the man who was found in the alley had obviously been drinking because we could smell the alcohol on his breath and his speech was slurred.

Objective: After the suspect was taken to the hospital, blood tests confirmed that his blood alcohol level was 50 percent over the legal limit.

Be sure you keep your opinions and judgments out of your statements.

Opinionated: The young man hit and robbed a homeless bum.

Objective: The young man attacked an elderly homeless man.

Every story has two sides. The challenge with writing incident report is to state what the two sides are without favoring one of them. This can be done by keeping your writing free of opinion and judgment. For example:

Objective: Half a dozen witnesses said they heard the manager and his assistant arguing over the payroll. Mr. Johnson allegedly hit the young man on the nose while they were arguing. We found the young man, Charles Gaylord, in the bathroom washing his bloody nose.

Opinionated: Plenty of witnesses said the manager and his assistant were fighting because the younger man had taken money out of the payroll envelope. Mr. Johnson slugged the kid in the nose because Charles had been caught doing this before. We found Charles washing severe bruises and cuts to his nose and face and a badly bruised jaw.

Favoring one side rather than the other:

   Half a dozen witnesses said the manager and the assistant argued because Charles had his hand in the payroll envelope one time too often. Charles got so mad that his supervisor lost his temper and slapped him once in the face. Charles said he had been beaten up, but he only had a bloody nose.

Step 5: Cover all the bases.

A useful and well-crafted incident report covers all the pertinent details (including who, what, where, when, why, and how) and leaves no unanswered questions. In the example above, don't stop by reporting who hit whom and why. Tell who the victim was, who reported the fight, who the witnesses were, and all the people you interviewed.

Take care to respond to all the key questions about the incident you are describing. Here are some "who" questions to answer:

- Who was most directly involved in the incident?
- Who discovered what happened?
- Who reported the incident, called police, or called supervisors?
- Who responded to what happened?
- Who did you interview on the scene?
- Did police or any investigators take evidence, or photos?
- Did anyone see or hear anything of significance?
- Who was notified when the incident took place?
- Who is insured, and who provides insurance that might have to pay compensation?

"What" questions include the following:

- What, if anything, was taken?
- What happened?
- What office or property was involved?
- What, if anything, was damaged?
- What actions did the first responders take?

▶ What equipment was damaged or taken?

▶ What evidence was collected at the scene?

▶ What was said, either during or after the incident?

▶ What was the victim's complaint, or wound?

▶ What, if anything, needs to be fixed or replaced?

"Where" questions include:

▶ Where did the incident take place?

▶ Where were you when the incident occurred?

▶ Where did the damage take place?

▶ Where did you or the first responders enter the building, or the scene?

▶ Where was evidence turned up?

"When" questions include:

▶ When did the incident occur?

▶ When was it first reported?

▶ When did first responders arrive?

▶ When did the police or other law enforcement agencies arrive?

▶ When will repairs take place?

"Why" questions include:

▶ Why did the incident happen?

▶ Was the incident an accident?

▶ Why did the people involved do what they did?

Finally, "how" questions include:

▶ How did the incident happen.

▶ How was the incident reported?

▶ How was information about the incident first obtained?

▶ How was evidence collected?

Step 6: Record property damage.

Many incidents involve some damage to property or injury to people. Here, you record the damage caused. You can't assess the damage just yet or estimate replacement cost; your job in this report is only to describe the damage.

9. Incident Reports

Step 7: What caused the incident?

You may or may not be able to assess the cause of the incident at an early stage. But if you or others are able to determine the cause, by all means report it. Noting the cause will help insurance companies and others determine liability and compensation, if needed.

Step 8: Record witness statements.

If you are fortunate enough to be first on the scene or to arrive shortly after the incident took place, you can conduct your own witness interviews to record what people saw and heard. Otherwise, you have to rely on the statements reported to the police or to others, such as reporters in the media.

Step 9: Outcome

What is the outcome of the incident? Who was affected by it, and what sorts of steps will need to be taken in order to repair damage? These are the logical statements you might include at the end of your report. Here is an example:

I very much regret the additional expenses that were incurred as a result of this situation. I have made arrangements to waive my yearly bonus as a way to make up some of the costs. I'm sure you can understand that some of the circumstances were out of our control. As president of the company, however, I assume responsibility for other errors. I have taken the following steps to make sure we are not in this situation again.

Checklist

- ❑ Did you record what happened?
- ❑ Did you answer all who, what, where, when, why, and how questions?
- ❑ Were you objective in your reporting?
- ❑ Did you describe the outcome of the incident?

Incident Report Template

Summary of Incident

Fireworks that had been ordered from our plant for the Fourth of July celebration failed to deliver due to a series of circumstances including customs problems, a strike, and a warehouse mixup. A $500,000 refund had to be sent to the customer, severely impacting the company's bottom line this year.

Background

Northwest Fireworks is one of the largest manufacturers of fireworks in the United States. Many municipalities depend on this company for their annual Independence Day celebrations. The Fourth of July this year was expected to be unusually busy due to the bicentennial. Northwest ordered 10 percent more of gunpowder and other materials from overseas suppliers. In addition, steps were taken to hire 15 new temporary employees to get orders ready for July 4th.

Pertinent Facts and Events

Manufacturing was slowed because of a lack of materials. Our orders for raw ingredients were held up at customs because of more strict regulations imposed by the U.S. Department of Security. Therefore we were behind on starting the process of making the specialized fireworks that had been ordered for this landmark year. In fact, a number of substitutions had to be made because what we had specified in our original order could not pass customs at all. This caused delays and extra costs that we had not foreseen to hire specialists.

When we were able to assemble the products, our workers went on strike. The labor negotiations were lengthy, but a new contract was finally signed. In the meantime, we had lost some experienced personnel. New hires took time to get up to speed, despite our best efforts to provide training.

Further Details

In retrospect, we discovered that a mix-up in our warehouse had caused a further delay. There is supposed to be a check-up to ensure that orders are processed in a timely fashion. However, a computer crash caused this particular shipment to be erased from the electronic memory of our system. The head of the shipping department was on vacation. So the paper forms were put in an envelope and not discovered until his return.

Then the trucking company failed to live up to its contract. Without our knowledge or approval, the main firm subcontracted to a smaller organization. That group was not prepared to meet the requirements that we had stated in our original agreement.

Under a severe time crunch, I was unable to contact the board of directors. Several individuals were out of the country on vacation and one other was dealing with a family emergency. Therefore, I made an executive decision. The trucks were instructed to go to an airport, and the products were flown to the communities involved. I also offered to deduct 15 percent from the bill of the communities to compensate for any inconvenience this problem caused.

> What was involved: 500 lbs of gunpowder, 250 firing caps, 3000
> fireworks holders, and other miscellaneous items.

Who was affected: the municipalities of Scranton, Camden, and Philadelphia.

Why did the incident occurr? A mixture of circumstances including a labor strike and unexpected customs delays.

Damage

No property was physically damaged as a result of these events, but damage of other sorts occurred. First, relations with our suppliers were hurt because of the customs problems. Relations between management and labor were severely impacted negatively due to the strike. Worst, relations with important customers in Scranton, Philadelphia, and Camden were hurt when we were unable to deliver on time, and those communities had to throw together a fireworks show quickly to make up for our failure.

Outcome

I very much regret the additional expenses that were incurred as a result of this situation. I have made arrangements to waive my yearly bonus as a way to make up some of the costs. I'm sure you can understand that some of the circumstances were out of our control. As president of the company, however, I assume responsibility for other errors. I have taken steps to make sure we are not in this situation again.

I will receive an outside review of all promises we make to clients in the future. A clause will be put into the contract allowing for reasonable substitutions. I will do everything I can to make sure that we do not bite off more than we can chew in regard to fancy fireworks and innovative designs and colors. Although we like to be on the cutting edge of our business, we should make sure we do not raise expectations higher than can be met. We also need to make sure the client will be satisfied if we are unable to produce what we originally had envisioned.

We are doing what we can to make sure our labor force is productive and content. In this difficult economy, it is now possible to hire and retain quality people. Steps are being taken to make sure that more than one person is aware of each body of knowledge. Written manuals and how-to guides are now required for each department.

A new person has been brought in to head our shipping department. I am confident that he or she will be able to keep things running more smoothly. Adaptations have been made in both the paper and electronic systems for receiving and processing shipping orders. A better safety net has been created.

We have made the trucking company aware of the seriousness of the situation. In response, we have negotiated a very favorable contract at a considerable discount. I now understand that this company had switched from being family owned and operated to a more corporate structure. While I believe that this will ultimately work in our favor, we had been caught in the labor pains of the transition. Have a more straightforward contract will give us more leverage.

Although I would certainly have never chose to endure so many sleepless nights, I believe that our company is now more streamlined than before. My goal is to pick up potential problems and remedy them so that another such crisis does not develop. I encourage workers as well as clients to bring any concerns to my attention and assure you that I will treat them with utmost seriousness. Above all I wanted to maintain the good reputation of our company. That continues to be my utmost goal.

Chapter 10

Budget Reports

No matter whether you own a business or are simply managing a volunteer group, you need to produce budget reports. Such a report lists items for which your company will incur expenses, and projects how much each will cost. It then tracks the costs and calculates how much those costs were over or under budget. Explanations for significant changes are recorded, and a summary takes stock of the financial impact of any differences.

The general types of financial statements you might need to create are:

> Balance sheet.

> Income statement.

> Cash flow statement.

Note: A special kind of budget report, a budget revenue report, examines the previous fiscal year's budget against actual revenue and expenses to gauge its accuracy.

Budget reports combine elements of all of these statements. They are different from simple budgets in that they contain analyses of significant differences in the budget. Reporting on significant differences helps higher management within the company determine where the company stands financially. Such reports are part of good fiscal practices, which help the company at tax time and when it comes time to report to shareholders.

Step-by-Step Guide

Step 1: Introduce your report.

A brief introduction tells readers who prepared the report and when it was prepared, and gives special reasons for the budget report, if applicable. For example:

As founder, president, and chief financial officer of Gandalf Bird Seed Company, I have prepared the following report to justify our expansion efforts.

Note: Even if such reports are routine and required by your company, it is helpful to provide an introduction.

Step 2: List the period you are covering.

A business can choose to keep records either according to the calendar year, which ends December 31st, or the fiscal year. In the latter, the businesses chooses a date other than December 31st to function as the end of the fiscal year. Many businesses choose a date that naturally corresponds to the end of their business cycle—June 30th, for example, or September 30th.

This budget report covers the fiscal year 2009–2010, which ends June 30th, 2010.

Step 3: List budget items and budget amounts.

This is the most basic task in budgeting. You record each item that is projected to have an expense, and you estimate how much each item will cost. If the estimate is coming from a contractor or manager within your company, record that person's name and contact information. You should also record the account number to which the expense will be charged. For example:

Item	Budget	Account	Contact
Annual report photography	$2,000	01-222356-029967	Phil Lacovara
Annual report design	$1,200	01-222356-029967	Jane Weems
Annual report printing	$6,700	01-222356-029967	Stream County Press
Annual report mailing	$700	01-222356-029967	Michael Wyans
Office supplies	$250	04-222356-029441	Barbara Sheets

Step 4: Record actual expenses.

When the budget item has been produced and all expenses have been paid, as part of the budget report you need to record the actual expense so that it can be compared to what was budgeted.

Item	Budget	Actual Expense	Account	Contact
Annual report photography	$2,000	$2,000	01-222356-029967	Phil Lacovara
Annual report design	$1,200	$1,350	01-222356-029967	Jane Weems
Annual report printing	$6,700	$6,950	01-222356-029967	Stream County Press
Annual report mailing	$700	$725	01-222356-029967	Michael Wyans
Office supplies	$250	$100	04-222356-029441	Barbara Sheets
Total	$10,850	$11,125		

In a separate document, you might record more about each expense as it comes in:

▶ The expense incurred.

▶ The type of payment made (credit card, check, or purchase order).

▶ The date of the expense.

▶ The name of the vendor.

Step 5: Record revenue.

In order for your budget to be complete, and so your company's managers can calculate the bottom line, you need to include revenue as well as expenditures. Record what came in and what was expected so decision-makers can judge whether sales ran ahead of or behind expectations. For example:

Item	Projected Income	Actual Income
Fundraising	$10,000	$8,800
Sales of new seed	$36,000	$30,000
Interest income	$3,000	$2,600
Sales of equipment	$5,500	$6,000
Total	$54,500	$47,400

Step 6: Calculate differences.

Once all expenses have been recorded, you can calculate the difference between budgeted and actual amounts. Do this not just for the totals, but for each item. If a particular project such as the annual report listed here goes over budget, managers can see which line items proved to be more expensive than projected. For example:

Item	Budget	Actual Expense	Difference	% + or -	Account	Contact
Annual report photography	$2,000	$2,000	0	0	01-222356-029967	Phil Lacovara
Annual report design	$1,200	$1,350	($150)	(12.5%)	01-222356-029967	Jane Weems
Annual report printing	$6,700	$6,950	($250)	(3.7%)	01-222356-029967	Stream County Press
Annual report mailing	$700	$725	($25)	(3.6%)	01-222356-029967	Michael Wyans
Office supplies	$250	$100	$150	40%	04-222356-029441	Barbara Sheets
Total	$10,850	$11,125	($325)	(2.9%)		

Step 7. Combine all items and add descriptions.

For the report, which is an overview that higher management will use, you'll probably want to combine income and expenses and differences in a short format that can be reviewed and evaluated quickly. The more detailed formats shown previously can be for your own records. Here is an example:

	Budget	Actual	Variance
Income			
Fundraising	$10,000	$8,800	($1,200)
Sales of new seed	$36,000	$36,000	0
Interest income	$3,000	$2,600	($400)
Sales of unneeded equipment	$5,500	$6,000	$500
Total income	$54,500	$47,400	($7,100)
Expenses			
Annual report photography	$2,000	$2,000	0
Annual report design	$1,200	$1,350	($150)
Annual report printing	$6,700	$6,950	($250)
Annual report mailing	$700	$725	($25)
Travel	$4,000	$3,500	$500

This is only a short example. For a longer version, see the Chapter 10 template.

10. Budget Reports

Step 8. Summary

The figures contained in this report show how our assets have increased with these ventures. Now we are confident that we can be successful with the Gandalf brand in other areas. For example, we will stock our birdseed to throw at weddings in white satin bags. The Gandalf logo will be subtle but visible in hand embroidery over brocade. What bird watcher can resist a powerful but economical pair of binoculars? Again, they will be identified with the Gandalf icon, which will make the bird watcher even more lucky in his quest for the most elusive of birds. And for those who like to feed birds outside, we will promote our own feeders and bird houses. They will be both beautiful and functional, with a tiny mailbox build into the design that will have Gandalf in gothic lettering. But not to forget where we started, the domestic bird will not be left out of our new ventures. A drop cloth that spells out Gandalf will be available, along with a variety of cages and bird toys and accessories. These days everyone wants a t-shirt, visor, or other wearable object to promote their hobby. Again, we at Gandalf Bird Seed Company are happy to oblige. The following budget lists startup expenses in the form of logo design and promotional campaigns. But we believe that we can make back this amount within months and that we will ultimately be selling more bird seed along with our other fine new products.

Checklist

❑ Have you introduced your report and identified yourself as the author?

❑ Have you stated the period that is covered by the report?

❑ Have you recorded budgeted amounts and actual income and expenses?

❑ Have you included contact information and account numbers if you need more information?

❑ Have you calculated differences between what was budgeted and what actually occurred?

❑ Have you consolidated income and expenses in your budget report?

❑ Have you summarized the results?

10. Budget Reports

Sample Budget Report

Introduction

As founder, president, and chief financial officer of Gandalf Bird Seed Company, I have prepared the following report to justify our expansion efforts. As you will see, income fell slightly short of expectations, and expenses ran slightly high. But as the report indicates, the differences are not huge, and justify continued expansion to build new markets for our seed products and services.

Accounting Period

This budget report covers the fiscal year 2009–2010, which ends June 30, 2010.

Budget Items and Amounts

Item	Budget	Account	Contact
Annual report photography	$2,000	01-222356-029967	Phil Lacovara
Annual report design	$1,200	01-222356-029967	Jane Weems
Annual report printing	$6,700	01-222356-029967	Stream County Press
Annual report mailing	$700	01-222356-029967	Michael Wyans
Office supplies	$250	04-222356-029441	Barbara Sheets
Travel (local)	$1,500	10-99385-38271	
Travel (out of state)	$5,000	10-99385-38271	
Consultants	$6,300	06-398383-299844	John Madison
Attorney's Fees	$24,664	06-928594-757577	Greg Corner
Rent	$10,448	10-455390-001001	
Heat	$3,668	10-455390-001001	
Utilities	$5,792	10-455390-001001	
Equipment rental	$388	10-455390-001332	
Equipment repairs	$880	10-455390-001332	
Equipment purchases	$2,199	10-455390-001332	
Insurance	$668	10-455390-001558	
Staff Development	$3,299	10-455390-001558	

10. Budget Reports

Actual Expenses

As you can see from this table, actual expenses ran slightly ahead of budgeted projections in several areas. This was due to inflation and increased fuel costs.

Item	Budget	Actual	Account	Contact
Annual report photography	$2,000	$2,000	01-222356-029967	Phil Lacovara
Annual report design	$1,200	$1,350	01-222356-029967	Jane Weems
Annual report printing	$6,700	$6,950	01-222356-029967	Stream County Press
Annual report mailing	$700	$725	01-222356-029967	Michael Wyans
Office supplies	$250	$100	04-222356-029441	Barbara Sheets
Travel (local)	$1,500	$1,600	10-99385-38271	
Travel (out of state)	$5,000	$6,330	10-99385-38271	
Consultants	$6,300	$5,237	06-398383-299844	John Madison
Attorney's Fees	$24,664	$25,800	06-928594-757577	Greg Corner
Rent	$10,448	$10,448	10-455390-001001	
Heat	$3,668	$3,700	10-455390-001001	
Utilities	$5,792	$5,899	10-455390-001001	
Equipment rental	$388	$300	10-455390-001332	
Equipment repairs	$880	$500	10-455390-001332	
Equipment purchases	$2,199	$2,000	10-455390-001332	
Insurance	$668	$700	10-455390-001558	
Staff Development	$3,299	$3,000	10-455390-001558	

10. Budget Reports

Revenue

Revenue was slightly down from projections, but we think this is because of the general slowdown in the economy, with fewer people buying pet birds. We expect demand for birds and bird seed to take off once the economy begins to improve.

Item	Projected Income	Actual Income
Fundraising	$10,000	$8,800
Sales of new seed	$36,000	$30,000
Interest income	$3,000	$2,600
Sales of equipment	$5,500	$6,000
Total	$54,500	$47,400

Differences Between Budgeted and Actual Amounts

Item	Budget	Actual Expense	Difference	% + or -	Account	Contact
Annual report photography	$2,000	$2,000	0	0	01-222356-029967	Phil Lacovara
Annual report design	$1,200	$1,350	($150)	(12.5%)	01-222356-029967	Jane Weems
Annual report printing	$6,700	$6,950	($250)	(3.7%)	01-222356-029967	Stream County Press
Annual report mailing	$700	$725	($25)	(3.6%)	01-222356-029967	Michael Wyans
Office supplies	$250	$100	$150	40%	04-222356-029441	Barbara Sheets
Total	$10,850	$11,125	($325)	(2.9)		

10. Budget Reports

Final Budget Report

	Budget	Actual	Variance
Income			
Fundraising	$10,000	$8,800	($1,200)
Sales of new seed	$36,000	$36,000	0
Interest income	$3,000	$2,600	($400)
Sales of unneeded equipment	$5,500	$6,000	$500
Total income	$54,500	$47,400	($7,100)
Expenses			
Annual report photography	$2,000	$2,000	0
Annual report design	$1,200	$1,350	($150)
Annual report printing	$6,700	$6,950	($250)
Annual report mailing	$700	$725	($25)
Travel			
Travel (local)	$1,500	$1,600	($100)
Travel (out of state)	$5,000	$6,330	($1,330)
Total travel	$6,500	$7,930	($1,430)
Payroll, Consultant, and Contract			
Consultants	$6,300	$5,237	$1,063
Attorney's Fees	$24,664	$25,800	($1,136)
Payroll	$298,023	$299,100	($177)
Total Payroll, Consultant, and Contract			

Final Budget Report (continued)

	Budget	Actual	Variance
Equipment			
Rental	$388	$300	$88
Repairs	$880	$500	$380
Purchases	$2,199	$2,000	$199
Total Equipment			
Space			
Rent	$10,448	$10,448	0
Heat	$3,668	$3,700	$2
Utilities	$5,792	$5,899	$107
Total Space			
Other			
Insurance	$668	$700	$2
Staff Development	$3,299	$3,000	$299
Postage	$3,455	$4,555	($1,100)
Telephone	$10,000	$10,468	($468)
Security	$2,300	$2,750	($450)
Miscellaneous	$4,999	$5,889	($890)
Total Other			
Total Expenditures			
Surplus (Deficit)			

10. Budget Reports

Summary

Gandalf Seed Company started out small enough, with a small supply of bird seed for domestic birds. In fact we became known as the gourmet go-to company for discriminating birds who lived in cages in the homes of folks who liked to pamper their pets. We even made special orders for pet stores where breeding and feeding of birds took place. Then we expanded to the outdoor market. We realized that millions of folks loved to watch birds in feeders in their backyards. We developed formulas that were region-specific and other formulas that followed migratory patterns. We marketed to bird watching groups, who were only too happy to try our product in the hopes of adding rare species to their life lists. Our last big venture was weddings. Some brides like to give out candy, of course. There are even a few who release butterflies during their first kiss as a married couple. But ecology experts were down on the rice throwing, saying that it upset the delicate ecological balance. With our birdseed to throw as the "just married" car leaves the parking lot, covered with shaving cream and dragging strings of tin cans, everyone is happy. The birds are especially happy because they can feast on a product that is nutritious as well as tasty.

The figures contained in this report show how our assets have fallen slightly short with these ventures. Now we are confident that we can be more successful with the Gandalf brand in other areas. For example, we will stock our birdseed to throw at weddings in white satin bags. The Gandalf logo will be subtle but visible in hand embroidery over brocade. What bird watcher can resist a powerful but economical pair of binoculars? Again, they will be identified with the Gandalf icon, which will make the bird watcher even more lucky in his quest for the most elusive of birds. And for those who like to feed birds outside, we will promote our own feeders and bird houses. They will be both beautiful and functional, with a tiny mailbox build into the design that will have Gandalf in gothic lettering. But not to forget where we started, the domestic bird will not be left out of our new ventures. A drop cloth that spells out Gandalf will be available, along with a variety of cages, and bird toys, and accessories. These days everyone wants a t-shirt, visor, or other wearable object to promote their hobby. Again, we at Gandalf Bird Seed Company are happy to oblige. The budget I have prepared lists start-up expenses in the form of logo design and promotional campaigns. But we believe that we can make back this amount within months and that we will ultimately be selling more bird seed along with our other fine new products.

Chapter 11

Evaluation Reports

Evaluation reports are usually commissioned to determine the importance of the subject, the severity of the problem, or in general, to answer the question "How significant is this?" Whereas it's a good philosophy of life in general to look on the bright side, evaluation reports often need to point out weaknesses in a project or employee. But they might also point out strengths in a job candidate or in a potential business partner. To be sure you frame those weaknesses appropriately, it's a good idea to keep the purposes of the report in mind:

▶ Track progress.

▶ Delineate responsibilities and scope.

▶ Explore skills.

▶ Explore weaknesses.

▶ Make recommendations.

In contrast to an incident report (see Chapter 9), which is supposed to be objective, an evaluation report should contain your own opinions. Those who asked for your evaluation are relying on your expertise and the research you are going to do to come up with an informed opinion. Just be sure your opinion is based on facts and observations, and not on preexisting attitudes.

Step-by-Step Guide

Step 1: Introduce the report.

As with other reports, the introduction to the evaluation report should briefly give an overview of the subject. You should also provide some basic information for those who are going to read the report but who didn't necessarily commission it, such as:

▶ Who asked for the report.

▶ What is the subject of the report.

▶ What your qualifications are.

- When the research was conducted.
- The purpose of the report.
- Your methods in evaluating the subject.

> Tip: Be sure to include a single sentence (or perhaps two) that states the main goal of the report.

Clearly state what you want the report to accomplish. It may be that you want to evaluate a high school student as a candidate for a particular college. You may want to evaluate an employee whose performance has been problematic of late. Acknowledging what you hope to accomplish right at the outset lets those who commissioned the report know that you understand their goals and concerns.

Step 2: Provide an executive summary.

If your introduction is complete enough, you don't necessarily have to include an Executive Summary, but many readers will appreciate it if you do. Here, as in other types of reports, the Executive Summary provides an overview of the report. In this case, you provide an overview of your conclusions, and you mention any recommendations you have as well. For example:

> *Despite the promise this candidate showed when he first came to the company, I must recommend his dismissal based on a thorough evaluation of his performance in his last six months in his position. I recommend he be given a generous severance package based on his early performance, however.*

Step 3: Explain your methodology.

In this section, you describe the techniques and strategies you used to conduct your evaluation. This section is especially important if your recommendation will affect someone's career or influence a major purchasing decision. It also gives management a chance to do its own evaluation—namely, of your evaluation and the way it was constructed. It is to your advantage to emphasize points like the following:

- The methods you used to collect data were carefully conducted and thoroughly thought out.
- Your evaluation was the result of a team effort, not your sole opinion.
- You collected qualitative as well as quantitative data.

Be sure to mention if you used outside consultants at any point during you research. Also identify who your information came from: coworkers, experts, or other observers. If a focus group or "comparison group" was used, describe its members and how they were chosen. This would also be a good place to mention any challenged you faced in conducting your evaluation:

The subject's demeanor and the intimidation he engendered in coworkers made this evaluation particularly difficult. Twelve coworkers were interviewed outside the office building in the hope of putting them at ease. Yet, an air of tension still hung over the discussions. Every effort was made to solicit unbiased opinions from those interviewed. Still, they were emotional as they spoke of the problems the supervisor, George Hamilton, had caused.

Step 4: Analyze qualitative and quantitative data.

Evaluation reports are different from budget reports or other types of documents in that the data you are evaluating is not just numeric or quantitative. Rather, it is also qualitative, and influenced by opinions and judgments.

When presenting qualitative data, it is important to look for patterns and recurring comments in behavior, events, or reactions from the people you interview. A single event that goes wrong or a single negative comment from a colleague should not result in a bad evaluation. Rather a pattern of problems is the key.

Because your report is meant to be shared with others, there should be some diplomacy involved. Particularly when discussing weaknesses, the goal is to create energy to move forward. It will not be helpful to be demoralizing or bring up controversy that will never be smoothly resolved. It's also okay to not be as neat and official as with some of the other reports in this book. Often there is space for a "rebuttal" from the person being reviewed or those involved with the project that is being evaluated. Nonetheless, this is about business, after all. As much as potential may be of interest, the bottom line still needs to be about profit.

Tip: Organize your data according to the patterns or themes you find. It may be useful to ask a coworker or team member help you to get a second opinion.

Step 5: Provide details of your evaluation.

This section is the core of your evaluation report. Here, you present what you have learned about the subject. Throughout the process of collecting material, writing, and distributing the report, the focus should be on determining "how it's going." What you want to be determined is whether things could be done better and whether it's time to move to the next step or level of responsibility.

In this section, you perform three tasks:

1. Organize your data.
2. Interpret your data.
3. Present your results.

11. Evaluation Reports

First, organize the information you have received so that you can make your evaluation. If you receive positive, negative, and neutral comments about a coworker, for instance, you might group them in three separate sections. You could also present examples of the comments in the form of a table.

Data analysis follows: This is the process of interpreting the information to address the aims of your evaluation. If you are an evaluating a project that contains a good deal of statistical information, you can calculate averages or percentages. For instance:

We discovered that only 30% of eighth graders in Astalitz School were able to read at a fifth-grade level.

If you are evaluating the success of a school, for instance, in order to determine whether the school should stay in operation, you should look at test scores and at dropout rates. But pay attention to qualitative information as well, such as comments from graduates, parents, and current students. Try to avoid reaching conclusions or final evaluations just yet; those come later. In this section you only report what you discovered.

Step 6: Present your conclusions.

In the conclusions section you interpret the information you gathered. In other words, this is where you actually evaluate what you have examined. Sometimes it's helpful to make an overall argument up front and then assemble relevant points to bolster your point of view. Keep in mind that your report is likely to be reviewed not only by the recipient but also by the top brass. Be sure to include the time period covered and to write introductions under heads and subheads. Your job is not only to point out weaknesses but to make constructive criticisms. Try to keep the following in mind when making your evaluation:

> Tip: At some point, you may want to invite your readers to provide feedback to tell you what they think of your opinion.

▶ Focus on the data and qualitative comments you gathered.

▶ Give particular attention to goals or milestones that were or were not met. Try to give explanations as to why the result occurred.

▶ If you found that different sources of information produced different results, try to determine why this might be the case.

▶ If you encountered anything surprising or unexpected, account for that, even if it wasn't directly related to the goals of your evaluation report.

▶ If previous evaluations were done of the same subject, compare your results to the results of those earlier reports.

> ▶ Mention whether there is something you wanted to discover about the subject of your evaluation that you did not discover from your investigation.

Tip: Above all, use groupings and structure to relate each of your points to the bottom line.

After you evaluate your subject, you might go one step further and provide your own personal views on the wider issues involved. This is not required, but those who commissioned your report could provide such views helpful in determining the best course of action to take.

Step 7: Make recommendations.

Once you have interpreted your data and evaluated your subject, you can go on to recommending appropriate action. Remember that your recommendations should presented in a straightforward way that will benefit your organization. Meaningful recommendations take into account the successes and failures, and should be intended to continue improvements to the program or organization. Recommendations should:

> ▶ Come out of your own observations and research.
>
> ▶ Reflect what you reported in earlier sections of your report.
>
> ▶ Focus on the program or subject you are evaluating.
>
> ▶ Be specific in terms of explaining what needs to be done.

Tip: Don't be afraid to use bullets and white space to make your report easy to read and understand.

Checklist

❑ Did you provide an introduction to your report?

❑ Did you include an Executive Summary?

❑ Did you explain the methods you used?

❑ Did you analyze your data?

❑ Did you organize and interpret the information you gathered?

❑ Did you present a detailed evaluation?

❑ Was your evaluation followed by your conclusions?

❑ Were recommendations needed to round out your report?

11. Evaluation Reports

Sample Evaluation Report

Introduction

Please read the following points regarding the job performance of Melissa Moors, Administrative Assistant, during the last year. This evaluation is required of all employees each year, but because of recent incidents, the administrative committee asked me to pay special attention to your job performance with an eye toward dismissal. As Director of Marketing, I am Ms. Moors's direct supervisor, so it falls to me to create this report. The investigation was conducted in January 2010. Your comments and suggestions will go into our departmental personnel files as a matter of record. They will also serve as the basis for updating each of your job descriptions this year and for better articulating the goals for the company.

Executive Summary

Melissa Moors started work at Widgets International Inc. in June 2008 as an administrative assistant. Her performance began on a positive note, with the successful launch of a new product line for our European customers. But erratic behavior throughout 2009 unsettled the staff, and a thorough evaluation finds that her negative impact on her work environment outweighs her occasional bursts of competence. It is with regret that I must recommend her dismissal.

Methodology

This report was based on results of Marketing Department projects in 2009 and interviews with 20 staff people: the 12 Marketing Department employees and eight other key staff members.

I was not alone in conducting this evaluation. Two members of the Marketing Department staff, Bill James and Rhonda Nighttower, assisted me, plus Lynn Kaspiro of the Human Resources Department.

The subject's demeanor and the intimidation she engendered in coworkers made this evaluation particularly difficult. Twelve coworkers were interviewed outside the office building in the hope of putting them at ease. Yet, an air of tension still hung over the discussions. Every effort was made to solicit unbiased opinions from those interviewed. Still, they were emotional as they spoke of the problems Melissa Moors had caused.

Data Analysis

The tragic aspect of this evaluation is the fact that Ms. Moors is, on occasion, a hard-working and competent employee. As the record illustrates, in the first year of employment Ms. Moors was commended for:

- Increased and continued work on projects with representatives of other departments.
- Balance of variety of tasks on multiple projects, both small and large.
- Contributions to smooth running of office by incorporating bodies of knowledge not always directly associated with specific projects.
- Helped rollout of product line.

- ◆ Arranged office holiday party.
- ◆ Handled stockholders' meeting well.

However, a number of incidents with which we are all familiar occurred, and they must be documented here as well:

- ◆ Ran through office in chicken costume screaming that sky was falling.
- ◆ Turned all desks toward east windows.
- ◆ Seized microphone at press conference and announced that peace with Germany was at hand.
- ◆ Randomly walked up to employees, handing them flowers and telling them they could reach a state of nirvana.
- ◆ Regularly "goosed" both male and female employees.

As you know, psychiatric counseling was provided for Ms. Moors for six months at company expense. During this period such incidents did not stop. Orange juice was mixed with the company coffee, and 27 rolls of toilet paper were found in the refrigerator on November 2, 2009.

In the hope of gathering a balanced set of data, however, the investigative team gathered the following comments from coworkers regarding Ms. Moors:

Positive	Negative	Neutral
"Keeps a neat office."	"Dresses oddly; many scarves and bracelets that cause noise when she walks."	"Never really noticed her."
"As long as she makes coffee I don't care what she does."	"Can't tell what she is going to do at any given moment."	"I, too, believe peace with Germany is at hand."
"Refrigerating toilet paper is sanitary."	"I'm tired of getting goosed when I'm carrying coffee and spilling it."	
"Did a good job on product rollout."	"I'm beginning to believe what she says and this is very worrisome."	
"Wears pantsuits well."	"She has gone from being a joke to an object of pity."	
	"She distracts everyone."	
	"She barely gets anything done any more."	
	"She holds us all back."	

The pattern in the negative comments—especially the last few—is clear. She is a distraction to others in the office. Even those who have expressed amusement at her antics now feel she is slowing down progress and causing unrest. It is this pattern of negatively impacting the productivity of the employees around her that is most significant from a job-performance standpoint.

I should add that speculation about the cause of her behavior and comments about the state of her mental health were deemed not relevant by this group and were omitted from this evaluation report.

Conclusions

Based on the data gathered, the team reached the following conclusions:

1. The six-month psychiatric evaluation period having passed with no improvement, Ms. Moors' period of employment should be terminated.

2. Counseling should be provided for employees who were traumatized by having to work with her, especially those who were physically touched by her.

Recommendations

In addition to the aforementioned conclusions, I wish to add the following recommendations:

1. Employees who joined Ms. Moors in doing a Maypole dance in front of the company building should have psychiatric evaluations as well.

2. Our relations with Germany should be scrutinized closely.

I also wish to make the personal observation that this company's tolerance of Ms. Moors is admirable, and the fact that we bent over backward to help her by providing counseling, etc. is commendable. Not many companies would have done the same. The fact that she is occasionally a productive and useful employee makes this evaluation all the more difficult. But the members of the team all stand by our conclusions.

11. Evaluation Reports

Chapter 12

Feasibility Studies

When the goal is to obtain funding or prepare a plan of action, a feasibility study will be written. Feasibility studies are especially important when the goal is costly or complicated: Conducting the study tells management if the project is worthwhile, and provides some justification of the expense and effort. In some ways it is a research report. Your potential donor or supervisor will want to know that you've defined a need, evaluated various ways of meeting that need, and suggested the best alternative for their approval.

Because feasibility studies involve funding or change of some sort, they usually involve a study of the business environment, the business location, and the technologies involved. Some study of available funds is also necessary. Therefore, a feasibility study may need to be conducted by a team that includes planning, financial, technology, and other professionals, either within your company or brought in as consultants. Examples of occasions where feasibility studies are needed include:

▶ Changing a company's or educational institutions computers from Windows to Macintosh machines.

▶ A switch in a food service company for a university or high school.

▶ Relocating the company headquarters from Washington State to Chicago, Illinois.

▶ Changing the healthcare insurance provider for a company.

In all of these cases, many employees are involved, not just a few individuals. In each case, technology may need to be changed, and in some cases competitive bids may need to be solicited. A feasibility study will indicate whether such efforts are warranted. In addition, it may point to the best way to proceed with the change.

Step-by-Step Guide

Step 1: Provide an Executive Summary.

An Executive Summary describes the problem or situation, gives a brief snapshot of each of the alternatives, and states your recommendation. It should also include the price and how quickly the costs will be recovered. For example:

On July 4, 2009, at the Community Independence Day Celebration, Clarence Goodfellow announced an important bequest to the city. He is retiring in one year and moving to a new home in Florida, leaving his mansion and the surrounding property to the City of Canalport. The mansion will be used for a combination community house, museum, and library. This report addresses the feasibility of extensively redeveloping the land.

Note: The template for this chapter introduces one way of structuring a lengthy report, as a set of sections and subsections that are each assigned numbers. For instance, the Situation Summary is numbered section 3. The subsection Business Environment is numbered 3.1, Business Locations is numbered 3.2, and so on.

Step 2: Write an introduction.

If the situation is not complex, an Executive Summary and subsequent Situation Summary may be enough of an introduction. However, in longer reports an introduction can explain topics such as who you are and what your qualifications are. Other introductory topics might include:

▶   The purpose of the study.

▶   The benefits of this project.

▶   The scope of this study.

▶   How this study relates to other studies that may have been done.

For example:

My consulting company has been advising municipalities on planned redevelopments for more than a decade. We have 400 projects under our belt. The initial reason for this study was to determine if redevelopment by the town is feasible at all, given that some city officials prefer selling to a corporation for a manufacturing or office headquarters. But we discovered quickly that redevelopment would bring extensive tax benefits to the town. This study focuses solely on redevelopment for municipal recreation and other purposes for the townspeople. An earlier study on selling the property is tangentially related and we will refer to it but only in passing because of the far different purpose.

Step 3: Summarize the situation.

The background is the history of how the problem started and what the situation is now. It introduces the current state and gives the reader an understanding of what has led up to it. In effect, it is the sales pitch that makes the reader understand the rationale for the proposal you are about to make. Your summary might start like this:

The development of Goodfellow Center and Gardens is a keystone in the revitalization of the East Side of Canalport. Although surrounded by housing, industry, and educational establishments, the East Side has been underutilized. Adopting the proposals of the committee has the potential to transform the area into a destination place that will satisfy the social, athletic, and relaxation needs of Canalportians from all parts of the city and even become a tourist attraction for the entire region.

Step 4: Identify who will manage the project.

In order for the project to get off the ground, it needs to have a manager. As part of your study, you may be called upon to recommend one. A manager may be appointed from within the organization that is commissioning the study. Or you may recommend an outside manager. After the project is complete, a manager may be needed to care for the facility or institution that has been created. For example:

Our company has actually been suggested as a manager for this project, but we got out of the business of contracting for redevelopment several years ago. The municipal Park District is the logical manager for this job. A manager will need to be hired for this new facility, however, because existing staff are busy managing existing parks and recreation sites throughout the area.

Step 5: Feasibility statement

The proposal details are the meat of the feasibility study. It can be broken into various subsections that:

1. Describe the objective criteria for an acceptable solution.

2. Suggest the solution you have found to be most appropriate.

3. Present all the alternatives, arranged in descending order of suitability. Each alternative should include a description of the solution, the result or improvement it would achieve, how it will be implemented, its advantages and disadvantages, and its cost.

12. Feasibility Studies

4. Analyze all of the possible solutions in light of established criteria. It may discuss the effects of adopting the proposed solution, adopting each of the alternative solutions, and taking no action at all. You should immediately state the criteria against which you will evaluate each method.

Step 6: Propose a system.

In order for the project you are examining to be feasible, a system has to be proposed and implemented to make it a reality. Chances are improvements will need to be made, either to a property, a building, or a house. In this section, you describe the impact of redevelopment or construction on the environment, on the site, and on existing facilities. If you are studying an existing facility or building, you need to assess network impacts as well.

Step 7: Draw up a production schedule.

In this section, you give a schedule for the implementation of the project. Part of the feasibility, after all, is the time it will take to develop the project. You may need to consult with construction engineers, IT professionals, and others to determine how long it will take to complete the project. You might need to prepare a rough schedule, no matter how simple (when contractors are actually hired a detailed schedule can be prepared):

Acquire site:	*2 months*
Clear site:	*1 month*
Construction:	*6 months*
Utilities/networking:	*3 weeks*
Furnishing/landscaping:	*3 weeks*
Total time required:	*10.5 months*

Step 8: Include a cost analysis.

The other major part of determining feasibility, along with time, is money. If your clients don't have the money to make the purchase or conduct the redevelopment, all the time in the world won't make any difference. Estimating cost is difficult at such an early stage, but you are well advised to research similar projects in other locations to determine what they cost. You can then make your own estimate, while adjusting for inflation.

Step 9: Make recommendations.

The action section elaborates on what will happen next, assuming that the proposal is approved. The style of writing should be positive and the language should be strong.

Evidence is supporting data. It contains detailed analyses, test results, drawings, and other materials that document previous statements.

Checklist

❑ Did you introduce your report succinctly and clearly?

❑ Did you summarize the situation?

❑ Have you proposed a person or group to manage the project?

❑ Have you provided a description of project feasibility?

❑ Did you propose a system to carry through the project?

❑ Does your report include a production schedule?

❑ Did you include a cost analysis?

❑ Does your report include recommendations?

12. Feasibility Studies

Feasibility Study Template

1. Executive Summary

On July 4, 2009, at the Community Independence Day Celebration, Clarence Goodfellow announced an important bequest to the city. He is retiring in one year and moving to a new home in Florida, leaving his mansion and the surrounding property to the City of Canalport. The mansion will be used for a combination community house, museum, and library. This report addresses the feasibility of extensively redeveloping the land.

2. Introduction

2.1. Author of This Study

My consulting company has been advising municipalities on planned redevelopments for more than a decade. We have 400 projects under our belt.

2.2. Purpose of Study

The initial reason for this study was to determine if redevelopment by the town is feasible at all, given that some city officials prefer selling to a corporation for a manufacturing or office headquarters.

2.3. Benefits

But we discovered quickly that redevelopment would bring extensive tax benefits to the town. This study focuses solely on redevelopment for commercial use, such as a shopping mall.

2.4. Relation to Other Studies

An earlier study on selling the property is tangentially related and we will refer to it but only in passing because of the far different purpose.

3. Situation Summary

3.1. Importance of Study

The development of Goodfellow Center and Gardens is a keystone in the revitalization of the East Side of Canalport. Although surrounded by housing, industry, and educational establishments, the East Side has been underutilized.

3.2. Potential Results

Adopting the proposals of the committee has the potential to transform the area into a destination place that will satisfy the social, athletic, and relaxation needs of Canalportians from all parts of the city and even become a tourist attraction for the entire region. Having once visited the Goodfellow Center and Gardens, a year-round schedule of programming and festivals will bring people back again and again from near and far.

4. Project Management

4.1. Steering Committee

Shortly after the announcement by Mr. Goodfellow, a steering committee was formed of city officials and neighborhood leaders. Community members were invited to three public meetings, and their ideas were solicited at these working meetings and through questionnaires. Various consultants were also hired to provide input.

4.2. Approach to Project

Response to drafts of this report elicited overwhelming support for the ideas that will make the Center and Gardens accessible and enjoyable for visitors of all ages.

4.3. Continued Community Input

To ensure continued support, community input will continue throughout the process with the assistance of local councils. With the aid of a shuttle bus and a newly formed association to plan programming, a gateway to the East Side will be provided. Local businesses, especially restaurants and coffee shops, will benefit from increased clientele. As the plan's elements are completed, the preferences of an expanded population of users will become clear. This site is ideally suited to become one of the area's premiere attractions, as it generated excitement and interest on its own as a destination.

5. Proposed System

5.1. Initial Development

The steering committee has studied various options and concluded that, for the next five years, the land should be used for year-round gardens. Other developments that may be pursued in the future include a horticulture center; a skating rink and warming house; a children's playground/garden; and water and land to promote health and healing.

5.2. Landscaping

Of course there are currently gardens and landscaping. But the steering committee is proposing planned sites for a variety of activities. Low plantings such as shrubs will surround playing fields to catch stray balls.

5.3. Athletics

Panels under athletic fields will be raised 12 to 18 inches and crowned for better drainage; turf will be improved for better field play; and manholes will be lowered flush to the turf or removed so they will not interfere with ball games. New and safer paths for jogging and bicycling will be added.

5.4. Pedestrian Facilities

Pedestrian-friendly lampposts and accent lighting will be added along main passageways. Trash receptacles and benches will be placed in high-traffic areas.

12. Feasibility Studies

Sculptures may be added in appropriate locations. Information kiosks and directional signs will guide visitors to numerous destinations. Although the goal will be to remove visual clutter, rows of existing trees will be preserved. Traffic will be halted during special events, and visitors will be transported from parking lots via trolleys.

5.5. Proposed Activities

Examples of activities include ethnic festivals, kite festivals, book fairs, story telling, and antique fairs. A grassy knoll will provide a venue for outdoor performances and the showing of movies under the stars. Although plantings will lend brightness and fragrances year-round, special attention will be given to winter plantings such as prairie grasses, evergreens, and red berries.

6. Production Schedule

We estimate that this project can be completed in less than a year. That is an ambitious schedule, and one that depends in part on good weather. However, similar developments in Station West, Mecklenburg, and Vima were completed in six, nine, and 11 months, respectively, so we feel our estimate is reliable.

Acquire site:	2 months
Clear site:	1 month
Construction:	6 months
Utilities/networking:	3 weeks
Furnishing/landscaping:	3 weeks
Total time required:	10.5 months

7. Cost Analysis

We estimate that this project will cost $200,000 to $300,000. This can be broken down into the following:

Clear property:	$20,000
Construct field house:	$145,000
Landscaping:	$25,000
Lighting:	$10,000
Seating and facilities:	$10,000
Create lake:	$20,000
Running track:	$5,000

8. Recommendations

When funds allow, the steering committee would like to propose the establishment of a horticulture center. It will be a site for garden information, planting demonstrations, gardens, and horticultural education and training, as well as a place to purchase planting and gardening supplies. Studies have shown that gardening is one of the most popular recreational hobbies. Both amateurs and professionals can be found in all classes, races, ethnicities, and income groups. The center will house classrooms, lecture halls, a library, an art gallery, an office, and retail spaces. Display and demonstration gardens will be maintained nearby. A glass tea house will offer ceremonial tea ceremonies. Master gardeners will give advise upon request, assist in neighborhood beautification projects and community gardens, inform visitors about area plants, and provide training for those who wish to pursue careers in gardening. Programs and lectures will be held on-site, and field trips will be arranged in advance.

The next vision of the steering committee is to build a warming house next to a skating rink. The rink will be a space for not only ice skating in the winter but also for summer uses that include inline skating, dancing, and theater and movie presentations. The warming house will feature fireplaces and a cafe.

A children's garden playground will require not only careful planning with the help of a team of child development specialists but also a staff of trained educators to oversee its use. The garden will incorporate concepts of mystery stability, privacy, flexibility, and discovery. All senses will be stimulated, with a special emphasis on accessibility. Children with various physical, emotional, and developmental handicaps will use their imaginations and their skills with materials, themes, and elements not found in typical playgrounds. Huge objects representing familiar things can be used for climbing and exploring. Plants will be chosen that are particularly fragrant, and water and wind chimes will add auditory interests. Care will be taken to attract butterflies and birds.

Although listed last, a space for healing and maintaining health is another priority for the steering committee. Effective outdoor design has often revolved around water, and fountains and reflecting pools will be added as funds allow. Inventive light is another way of creating a focal point, especially when combined effectively with bridges, plantings, and sculptures. The steering committee would like to build special spaces for yoga and tai chi, combined with spaces for health awareness seminars. In addition to places to relax, a perimeter walking or jogging path will have signs indicating distance markers.

From bike races to picnics, flag football to festivals, the Center and Garden will become a preferred site for a variety of activities for all citizens.

12. Feasibility Studies

Chapter 13

Business Plans

Business plans are truly "mission critical" documents. They are most often used to secure funding. But a business plan can help you and your colleagues keep a business on track by referring to it and modifying it periodically. One important goal of a business plan may be to convince investors to fund your business so it can be started in the first place. Attracting venture capital is a competitive activity, and your plan must not only inspire confidence among investors but stand out from the crowd of other plans as well. For banks, you need to address the subject of risk: why should the bank invest in your company as opposed to the many others in your field? What makes you better qualified than other entrepreneurs?

Business plans differ depending on their purpose and on the type of business being started. But certain core elements are common to every plan. The general types of plans you might need to create are listed here:

▶ Art (graphic design, photography, framing).

▶ Automotive (car dealers, repair, body work, detailing, car wash).

▶ Clothing related (dry cleaners, retailers).

▶ Computer and technical services.

▶ Construction.

▶ Consulting, public relations, marketing.

▶ Food service (restaurants, butchers, delis, grocery stores).

▶ Healthcare (pharmacies, hospitals, clinics, medical supplies, assisted care).

▶ Housing related (real estate, repair, pest control, architects).

▶ Nonprofit groups and organizations (social service agencies, zoos, museums, parks).

▶ Professional services (psychotherapy, dentistry, medicine, law, fiscal planning, insurance).

▶ Sales of collectibles or antiques.

▶ Sales of home products.

▶ Sales of personal products (beauty care,and so on).

▶ Sales of homemade items (crafts, and so on).

▶ Tourism (hotels, motels, resorts, spas, dude ranches, cruise ships, travel agencies, tour bus companies).

Step-by-Step Guide

The following is a short business plan that you can rewrite and adapt to the needs of your own company. At the beginning of each section, you'll find brief instructions. At the side of the page, you will find a brief explanation of the most important parts of the report given the products and services you want to provide. They are described briefly in the sections that follow.

Step 1: Introduce yourself and your business.

As briefly as possible, describe your company and how you envision it. You may want to say why the company was founded and how you see it evolving in the future. Also mention the purpose of this business plan: whether you are seeking venture capital, funding or new equipment, or another purpose. For example:

Grand Enterprises is a sole proprietorship with Larry Slope as the founder and sole employee. The company was formed to offer cyber staff (CS) to customers.

Step 2: Provide an Executive Summary.

In this section you summarize your long-term and short-term goals for your business. You are coming to a funding or other agency for a reason; state the reason, and provide a quick overview of how you are going to achieve your goals or why you are worthy of funding. Be brief; presenting contents in list form helps readers grasp the main points quickly. For example:

Grand Enterprises has the goal of increasing its sales revenue by 15 percent in the next fiscal year. The company has identified three market segments to target:

   ◆ *The first segment is companies of various sizes. Because of wide-scale corporate downsizing, remaining staff members are busier than ever. Projects/jobs that the current staff cannot handle are outsourced.*

- *The second customer segment is individuals. This is an attractive segment because as our daily lives become busier and busier we have less and less free time. Using a cyber staff (CS) is one way to create more free time or to pay others to do task we are unwilling or unable to do.*
- *The last customer segment is nonprofit organizations. Many hire only a few staff members on a full-time benefits-eligible basis. When extra hands are needed for special projects or busy times of the year, a CW can quickly and seamlessly take over tasks.*

Step 3: Describe your experience and expertise.

Describe quantifiable accomplishments and experience that pertains to your business and how you manage it.

Larry Slope received his undergraduate degree in business administration from the University of Illinois at Chicago. Upon graduation Larry went to work for another institution of higher learning in Chicago. Although he was mostly a writer and project manager, his responsibilities included some graphic design, accounting, and marketing. He then went into business for himself, which allowed him to be the primary parent for his two daughters.

Step 4: Describe your management team.

In this section, describe your chief executive officer and other officers. Be sure to emphasize their level of experience and expertise. Mention how long they have been working with one another. Also describe each individual's role within the company.

Larry will be the sole employee. Larry will be taking a base salary with the expectation that he will also be able to use some of the net profit once it starts accumulating. Others will be hired on a part-time, freelance basis.

Step 5: Outline your business organization.

Each business has an operating system. It consists of a variety of activities that occur systematically. Describing how the sequence of activities will occur within your business demonstrates to your funders that you have thought out your business plan thoroughly and understand how your company will operate. It is a common practice to divide the separate activities into blocks, like this:

R & D → Manufacturing → Marketing → Sales → Fulfillment → Customer Service

Once you have identified the key processes your business will perform, focus on the most critical ones. These are processes that you can do better than the competition, which gives you a competitive advantage.

Another important way to demonstrate to potential investors that your company has a well-organized structure is an organizational chart. Such a chart graphically shows the principal officers and illustrates which positions report to other ones. An example is shown in Figure 13.1.

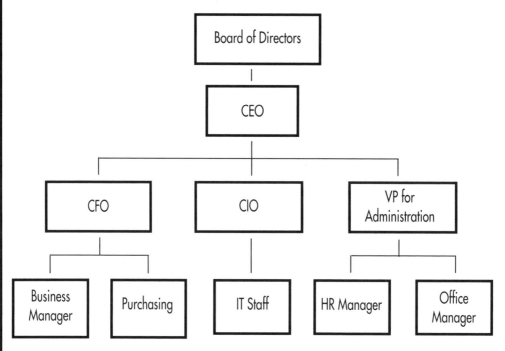

Figure 13.1. An organizational chart.

> Note: Your organization needs to be flexible, particularly if you are a start-up company. Emphasize in your report that your company is growing and the organization will changed depending on your circumstances.

Step 6: Implementation schedule

In this part of your business plan, you draw up a high-level road map for your future development. You set important milestones, and identify critical goals and when you want to achieve them. For a business plan, your goals might be months or even years down the road. A simple example is shown in the Business Plan template.

Note: A traditional way of representing an implementation schedule is known as a Gantt chart. A Gantt chart lists critical business tasks in outline form. Baseline and actual dates are given, and dependencies (whether or not one activity is dependent on the completion of another) are also indicated.

Step 7: Assess the market for your goods and services.

In the second part of your business plan you describe the state of competition in your field, and you demonstrate that there is a need for what you plan to provide. You need to base your statements not on your personal opinion, but on research backed up by third-party facts and figures. Such research will not only demonstrate to your reviewers that you deserve your support, but it will help identify the customers you want to reach and define more clearly how you will distinguish your company from the competition. Do the equivalent of a weather forecast: you see what things look like now and predict what they will be six months to a year down the road. The one-year forecast is important; banks and venture capitalists know that many companies start out strong but run into turbulent times about a year after they start. Make a case for why your company will continue to find customers a year from now.

Step 8: Describe a typical customer.

Who are you trying to reach? In this section, you describe your customers. Go into detail as far as their age, their place of residence, their profession, and other aspects of their lifestyles. The better you know your customers, and the clearer a picture you are able to draw of them, the better you will be able to tailor your goods and services to them and their needs. Consider creating profiles of three customers, with names and ages. If you are able to describe both male and female consumers, so much the better. However, for a product that is obviously oriented to one gender, such as purses or ties, focus solely on three same-sex examples.

Step 9: Present research and opinion.

Here, you identify customer segments you want to reach, and any research that describes these types of consumers. How many are within your state, or your part of the country?

Step 10: Create a competitive profile.

Knowing your competition, what they do, and what their strengths are will help you differentiate your own business. By studying the other companies who do what you do, you can pick up some ideas, and you can clearly identify how you are going to attract more customers.

Step 11: Marketing plan

Once you have analyzed your market and your competition, you need to come up with a strategic plan. Such a plan demonstrates how you will position your company to stand out from the competition and gain your share of the market. In this plan, you should be specific about how you will price your products, how you will distribute them, and how you will market your company. Show how you will become profitable and project how long this will take. Estimate the future potential of your business one, two, five, and 10 years in the future.

Step 12: Outline a financial plan/financing.

A financial plan shows a funding agency how you will use its money, and how you will manage your budget not just in the coming year, but several years down the road. You need to describe what kind of company you have, and what purchases you expect to make in the near future. For example:

Grand Enterprises has identified the following objectives:

- *To generate over $35,000 in the first year.*
- *To develop enough income to make the job a full-time position.*
- *To decrease marketing expenses after referrals and repeat customers provide sufficient work flow.*

Larry Slope has formed Grand Enterprises as a sole proprietorship. Larry will invest money of his own as well as money received from his family.

The following equipment/services will be needed for purchase to allow Grand Enterprises to begin operations:

- *Windows computer*
- *Mac computer*
- *Laser printer*
- *Broadband Internet connection*
- *Scanner*
- *Fax machine*

Step 13: Demonstrate that you are prepared for trouble.

Investors need to know that you are prepared to thrive in good times and survive the bad times. In this final section of your business plan, you describe your contingency plans in case of trouble and assess the risk your company faces if problems arise.

Contingency Plan

Once you have analyzed the market and presented both your views and those of objective third parties, you need to address one of a financier's biggest concerns: risk. You need to reassure those reviewing your plan that you have:

▶ Adequate insurance for yourself, your property, and your employees.

▶ Adequate reserve capital in case of financial shortfalls.

▶ Adequate computer security, including firewalls, virus protection, and backups.

▶ Physical security: locks, alarm systems, and so forth.

Risk Assessment

Lenders want to know how much of a risk they are taking when they invest their money with you. You can reassure their fears by telling them that your assumptions are not written in stone and that you have allowed for a reasonable margin of error. Also explain:

▶ What the basic risks are (competition, market forces, technological changes, attacks) that your business faces.

▶ How you will face these risks.

▶ What your business would look like in five years under best-case and worst-case scenarios.

If possible, draw up best-case and worse-case scenarios showing that you have a thorough understanding of both your business opportunities and the risks you face. This gives funding agencies the ability to judge whether your plan is realistic or not, and to assess how risky their investment is.

13. Business Plans

Business Plan Template

Introduction

Grand Enterprises is a sole proprietorship with Larry Slope as the founder and sole employee. The company was formed to offer cyber staff (CS) to customers. Grand has been in business for the past six years. During that time we have been able to refine our product line and improve our marketing efforts substantially. Our membership and revenue have increased 20 percent in the past year. We have also instituted efficiencies in the manufacturing process that enable us to cope with the current economic slowdown and at the same time be in place for the increase in sales we are anticipating in the short term.

Executive Summary

Grand Enterprises is seeking funding so it can expand its manufacturing capacity. The company has the goal of increasing its sales revenue by 15 percent in the next fiscal year. The company has identified three market segments to target:

▶ The first segment is companies of various sizes. Because of wide-scale corporate downsizing, remaining staff members are busier than ever. Projects/jobs that the current staff cannot handle are outsourced.

▶ The second customer segment is individuals. This is an attractive segment because as our daily lives become busier and busier, we have less and less free time. Using a cyber staff (CS) is one way to create more free time or to pay others to do task we are unwilling or unable to do.

▶ The last customer segment is nonprofit organizations. Many hire only a few staff members on a full-time, benefits-eligible basis. When extra hands are needed for special projects or busy times of the year, a CW can quickly and seamlessly take over tasks.

Grand Enterprises offers a wide range of services:

▶ Services at the lower level are administrative in nature (for example, data entry, mailing list updates).

▶ Services in the middle require planning and organization, but not necessarily a high level of expertise (for example, concierge services and travel arrangements).

▶ Services that are billed out near the top of the range require higher levels of skills (for example, accounting, marketing, and graphic design).

Experience and Expertise

We want to assure you that funds received as a result of this application will be well managed and your investment will be worthwhile. The CEO of Grand

Enterprises, Larry Slope, has been in the field for 20 years. He received his undergraduate degree in business administration from the University of Illinois at Chicago. Upon graduation Larry went to work for another institution of higher learning in Chicago. Although he was mostly a writer and project manager, his responsibilities included some graphic design, accounting, and marketing. He then went into business for himself, which allowed him to be the primary parent for his two daughters.

Management Team

Larry will be the sole employee. Larry will be taking a base salary with the expectation that he will also be able to use some of the net profit once it starts accumulating. Other contractors will be hired on a part-time freelance basis.

Business Organization

The fact that our company has been in business for more than a decade means we have stability and a well developed managerial structure that enables us to weather difficult economic challenges. We have three senior vice presidents supporting our chairman and CEO; each SVP has two vice presidents, and each of them has managers handling marketing, sales, and administration. Though there has been some turnover in recent years, our CEO has been in place since the company was formed in 1999. And six other members of upper-level management have been on board nearly as long.

Implementation Schedule

Our company has remained in business despite a sharp economic downtown and decrease in sales. Sales have leveled off in the past three weeks. We plan to get a loan from a bank for $100,000. We plan to cut five positions to save $250,000. We plan to more aggressively market our most successful product line and cut out our least successful one.

Implementation Schedule

Task	Projected Completion Date	Dependent on...
A. Acquire property	4/09	-
B. Furnish and set up office	8/09	A
C. Complete hiring	9/09	A, B
D. Acquire hardware	11/09	A, B
E. Produce product 1	1/10	C, D
F. Sales $10,000	6/10	E
G. Sales $100,000	12/10	F

Table 13.1

13. Business Plans

Market Report

Currently Grand Enterprises has virtually no competition in the Midwestern part of the U.S. Some sites on the Internet sell the same products, however. But 90 percent are located in Europe and the Far East.

Customer Profile

James Craybill, 24, is a busy young professional who is entering his first job with a while-collar company. He has a golden retriever dog named Rocket, and he drives a Honda Insight. He works as an assistant account manager for an advertising agency in the Chicago Loop. He needs to dress well to make a good impression and to fit in with the corporate culture. Yet, he does not want to look like everyone else. He lives in an apartment in the Lakeview area of Chicago—trendy, busy, and hip, and not expensive. He wants a wardrobe that will help him present a professional demeanor but not make him resemble those in his parents' generation.

Research and Opinion

Grand Enterprises has divided the market into three customer segments that are each attractive and distinct: companies, individuals, nonprofits. Market research indicates that these are the most likely consumers of remote administrative assistants. Although the CS concept is fairly new, it is proliferating along with the Internet. Membership records within the larger virtual assistant associations indicate that there are typically 10–15 virtual assistants within each state.

Competitive Profile

The majority of CS services are secretarial and can be handled by an administrative assistant. In addition to the more menial tasks, Grand Enterprises is able to offer clients a wide range of more technical skills (for example, QuickBooks Pro for accounting issues, Photoshop and PageMaker for graphic design, and well-honed marketing and research skills). This is a competitive edge because once clients have found a CS they have an economic incentive to continue to use them as opposed to finding someone else (assuming that they are happy with the level of service and the work product). The problem occurs when the client is happy with the CS but needs work on a project that requires skills that are beyond the range of the CS. An advantage is created when the CS (Grand Enterprises) has a wider and more complex range of skills, which makes them of more value to the client.

Grand Enterprises is an exciting application of the cyber staff (CS) business model. By providing a wide range of customer services from a remote location, the power of the Internet is leveraged. This is very efficient business model will provide Larry with reasonable income and the flexibility to handle the jobs when and how he chooses. The sales forecast indicates revenue will rise for year two and year three along with corresponding net profit increases.

Financial Plan

Grand Enterprises has identified the following objectives:

+ To generate over $35,000 in the first year.

+ To develop enough income to make the job a full-time position.

+ To decrease marketing expenses after referrals and repeat customers provide sufficient work flow.

Larry Slope has formed Grand Enterprises as a sole proprietorship. Larry will invest money of his own as well as money received from his family.

The following equipment/services will be needed for purchase to allow Grand Enterprises to begin operations:

+ Windows computer

+ Mac computer

+ Laser printer

+ Broadband Internet connection

+ Scanner

+ Fax machine

+ Copier

+ Software (for example, Adobe Acrobat, Photoshop, and PageMaker; Microsoft Office, Word Perfect, and QuickBooks Pro)

+ Attorney services to develop a standard contract template for clients.

Start-up Expenses

Legal	$1,000
Website Development	$5,000
Insurance	$50
Rent	$150
Total Start-up Expenses	$6,200

Start-up Assets

Cash Required	$16,800
Othis Current Assets	$0
Long-term Assets	$7,000
Total Assets	$23,800
Total Requirements	$30,000

Start-up Funding

Start-up Expenses to Fund	$6,200
Start-up Assets to Fund	$23,800
Total Funding Required	$30,000

Assets

Non-cash Assets from Start-up	$7,000
Cash Requirements from Start-up	$16,800
Additional Cash Raised	$0
Cash Balance on Starting Date	$16,800
Total Assets	$23,800

Liabilities and Capital

Liabilities

Current Borrowing	$0
Long-term Liabilities	$0
Accounts Payable (outstanding Bills)	$0
Other Current Liabilities (interest-free)	$0
Total Liabilities	$0

Capital

Planned Investment	
Larry	$20,000
Family	$10,000
Additional Investment Requirement	$0
Total Planned Investment	$30,000
Loss at Start-up (Start-up Expenses)	($6,200)
Total Capital	$23,800
Total Capital and Liabilities	$23,800
Total Funding	$30,000

Contingency Plan

Grand Enterprises has a contingency fund of $12,000 in case of emergencies.

We have an alarm system wired to a central office, and a sprinkler system in case of fires.

Our files are backed up to a "cloud" service on the Internet.

Meetings and Procedures

PART IV

Chapter 14

Business Trip Reports

Most business trip reports are written by individuals or groups to pass along information to their supervisor. In contrast to travel diaries written as a personal record or letters that recount trips to friends or family, business travel reports are frequently done to record economic and social conditions or to evaluate business opportunities in a remote location. Typically, the situation is that a person has temporarily left his or her usual place of work to do something somewhere else. Some examples include:

▶ Taking a fact-finding trip to evaluate a vendor, client, or competitor, both in terms of both where and how it operates.

▶ Installing, modifying, or repairing off-site equipment or instruments.

▶ Participating in a group process or educational event, such as a retreat, class, conference, or workshop.

Writing in the first person is the acceptable style because you are not only recounting your personal observations, but you are also providing business interpretations defined by your experience. Here are the components of the report, which may be modified for each specific trip:

▶ A summary might be what you'd tell someone on an elevator about where you went, what you did, and why you thought it was a good idea in the first place.

▶ The background is pretty much cut-and-dried facts. You should describe the purpose of the trip, mention who approved it, and list such other circumstantial details and names, dates, and places.

▶ In the trip activities, you get into more detail about whether what you expected actually happened. It's important to mention why a plan was not carried out and to include other unanticipated events.

▶ The outcome both looks back to results that were achieved and looks forward to follow-up action that will be required.

Note: Keep your audience in mind and what they want to learn most from your trip, and focus on it. Leave sightseeing and entertainment news for talk around the water cooler.

Step-by-Step Guide

Step 1: Executive Summary

Begin with a brief statement about where you went, what you did, when you traveled, and why you or your superiors thought the trip was a good idea in the first place. Also provide a brief (one- or two-sentence) overview of what you discovered. For example:

As founding members of the Genial Gourmet catering group, we are looking for a rural setting to hold training sessions, as well as to introduce potential clients to the advantages of our wares. A trip was taken in August 2009 by a group of staff members to evaluate Low Bridge, a small community originally located on a canal. We discovered firsthand that Low Bridge is an exceptional place for an educational experience.

Many organizations provide staff with standard forms they fill out to report travel expenses incurred on business trips. This chapter, however, describes a different kind of report: one in which the purpose of the travel was to promote the business or to look toward a new future for your company, either with a foreign trading partner, a new location, or new business clients who are located overseas.

Step 2: Background

After summarizing your entire report, take a step back. Describe the purpose of the trip, mention who approved it, and list other circumstantial details and names, dates, and places.

We had received a video of the site, and we had talked extensively via conference calls to the seller as well as to members of the chamber of commerce. Based on comparisons with other similar sites, we felt Low Bridge was a good possibility. However we believed that we need to view the facility in context as well as to obtain "a feel" for the environment that could only be obtained in person. It was unusual to take such a large group on an initial visit. However, after consulting with our major funder, it was believed that we all needed to experience the site as a group without being prejudiced by a subjective report by a "scout." So on August 8, 2009, the following group left for a long weekend: a project manager, an in-house writer/editor, a designer, a production artist/manager, and an image specialist. Each person will contribute in varying extents to the launch of this project. The trip was approved by senior staff and the board of directors, several of whom joined us for at least part of the time.

Step 3: Trip Activities

In this section, you provide details about whether what you expected actually happened and about unanticipated events. Make sure the events pertain to the purpose of the report. For a business travel report, you would logically focus on:

▶ How expensive it is or how easy/difficult it is to get to the destination.

▶ What sorts of accommodations are available, either for your company representatives, or for clients or partners who would come to visit you should you locate to the destination.

▶ Local customs that travelers from your country should know about.

▶ Meetings you held with local representatives.

▶ Interviews you did with local businesspeople that are relevant to the goal of the trip.

While you are traveling be sure to take good notes. These days, it's easy to take along a digital camera or video camera to document your excursion. Your video content can supplement or illustrate the written part of your report. For instance:

At the beginning of the project, our goals and objectives were to find a site that would:

1. *Communicate information about our company and products to regular and prospective customers*

2. *Convey the high quality of an experience provided by our catering group and identify new endeavors to increase that quality*

3. *Demonstrate the marketability of an enhanced catering line and its development of food and extras*

4. *Offer opportunities for client participation in and contact with the catering process*

The purpose of the trip was to determine if Low Bridge would meet these criteria.

> Tip: Be sure to keep receipts, not only so you can be reimbursed for travel expenses, but to remind you of where you went and what you did when you write your report.

14. Business Trip Reports

Step 4: Describe the outcome of your trip.

Look back to results that were achieved and look forward to follow-up action that will be required.

All members of the group voted enthusiastically that we proceed with our plans with Low Bridge as our new venue. We believe that Low Bridge has the potential to be developed in the direction we wish to go. Although some remodeling will be necessary, the facilities are structurally sound. We are starting with a good foundation, and we can develop in the way we wish to go. Promotional literature will be developed by our creative staff so that, through narratives and graphic images, it will be easy for prospective clients to identify with satisfied customers and to imagine themselves enjoying similar special events. Our goal is to develop an advertising blitz that will portray the winning combination of learning about catering with cutting-edge technology from world-class professionals and other customers in a beautiful and culturally rich environment. We want to encourage visits to the Low Bridge neighborhood by presenting a positive and forthright picture of a unique rural community on the economic upswing.

> Tip: You might supplement your travel report by including an informal bibliography—a list of Websites, books, or articles that will provide your colleagues with more information about the area should they need it..

Checklist

❑ You have summarized where you went, what you did, and the original purpose for the trip.

❑ You have identified the personnel who approved the trip, and provided circumstantial details.

❑ You have elaborated on whether the goals were met and mentioned unanticipated events.

❑ You made every effort to keep extraneous details out of the trip report.

❑ You have given a wrap-up of what was accomplished and a preview of follow-up action that is needed.

Trip Report Template

Executive Summary

As founding members of the Genial Gourmet catering group, we are looking for a rural setting to hold training sessions, as well as to introduce potential clients to the advantages of our wares. A trip was taken in August 2009 by a group of six staff members to evaluate Low Bridge, a small community originally located on a canal. We discovered firsthand that Low Bridge is an exceptional place for an educational experience, and we enthusiastically recommend it for training and client visits.

Background

As you know, Genial Gourmet depends on cooking classes and sales to a small and select group of "foodies." A location that will serve as a "destination" to attract dedicated customers is essential to our future growth. After much research online and at the library, we settled on three sites. After some discussion, we decided to take our first trip to Low Bridge as it seemed the most promising candidate.

We had received a video of the site, and we had talked extensively via conference calls to the seller as well as to members of the Chamber of Commerce. Based on comparisons with other similar sites, we felt Low Bridge was a good possibility. However, we believed that we needed to view the facility in context as well as to obtain "a feel" for the environment that could only be obtained in person.

It was unusual to take such a large group on an initial visit. However, after consulting with our major funder, it was believed that we all needed to experience the site as a group without being prejudiced by a subjective report by a "scout." We were given a $2,000 travel budget. So on August 8, 2009, the following group left for a long weekend: a project manager, an in-house writer/editor, a designer, a production artist/manager, and an image specialist. Each person will contribute in varying extents to the launch of this project. The trip was approved by senior staff and the board of directors, several of whom joined us for at least part of the time.

Trip Activities

At the beginning of the project, our goals and objectives were to find a site that would:

1. Communicate information about our company and products to regular and prospective customers

2. Convey the high quality of an experience provided by our catering group and identify new endeavors to increase that quality

3. Demonstrate the marketability of an enhanced catering line and its development of food and extras

4. Offer opportunities for client participation in and contact with the catering process

We feel that a few facts and figures about the trip will indicate the success of Low Bridge in meeting these goals:

Cost of trip	$1,236
Accommodations	Bridge View Motor Inn
Travel	Minivan.
Representatives we met	Chamber of Commerce executives; City Manager of Low Bridge; head of the local "food club"
Distance to nearest airport	48 miles
Rental car companies at airport	Hertz, Avis, Budget
Cost to rent van	$179

The purpose of the trip was to determine if Low Bridge would meet these criteria. As a result of our on-site visit, we were able to see first-hand the exceptional quality of the educational experience that would be possible, continue to consolidate details about the program options, and get a glimpse of the advantages of this particular location.

Interviews Conducted:

- The Chamber of Commerce said office space would be available should we wish to set up a training area. A building at 1200 High Street was shown to us, and a 1,500 square feet vacant space seemed suitable.
- The City Manager said he would waive the usual business fee as an incentive for having us relocate.
- Several food enthusiasts suggested local farms that could supply us with fresh meat and dairy products.

The weather was particularly hot and muggy so that not a lot of time was spent outside of doors. But this brought to awareness the need for ample air conditioned facilities, as well as for comprehensive mosquito abatement. We might also schedule main events at times that are cooler and drier.

Sources of information:

Low Bridge Website: *www.lowbridge.org*

Chamber of Commerce: *www.lowbridgecofc.org*

Zagat Guide to Low Bridge, published 2009

Chapter 15

Meeting Minutes

You've probably been taking or reading minutes ever since the days of scout meetings. But now, a record of meeting minutes may well be an official document that is required by your group's bylaws or your company's policies and procedures. The obvious items you need to include are the date, location, names of those in attendance, and name of the organization. But by listing budget information, old and new business, and other components, you can remind those who were there of what they promised to do and inform others who weren't there of past, present, and future issue.

In other words, effective meeting minutes do much more than summarize a gathering. Done properly, they can be the driver for an organization by being an accurate record of progress made on important issues. They can identify who the decisive force behind important decisions was (and who was asleep at the switch). Minutes are not just for folks who were there. In fact, they can be even more relevant to those who did not attend. So be sure that links are provided to relevant materials that may have been distributed at the meeting by distributing the minutes electronically. Subcompartments should focus on:

▶ What participants should have learned or accomplished by attending the meeting.

▶ What the organizers of the meeting promised would be covered.

▶ What happened as a result of the dynamic among those attending the meeting.

Step-by-Step Guide

Step 1: Include the meeting particulars.

Briefly, indicate time, place, attendance, and introductory comments. For a small group, these details need to only occupy a few lines. But for the board meeting of an international corporation or a workshop held by an important nonprofit group, some background may be helpful. For a big group, you might mention how long it has been since the group's last session, any special guests who were invited, and of course the central goal of the meeting. Here is a brief example:

Board Meeting Minutes
Stellar Building Management Company
November 19, 2009
3 p.m.; Company Headquarters, Chicago, Illinois

Note: Meetings of boards can be important legally. They are regarded as legal documents in the courts and by the Internal Revenue Service. It's essential to keep them complete and accurate.

It has been three months since the management company's last board meeting. This meeting was especially important because it was the first since the porch collapse that injured three people. After inspection by the city, bids have gone out to contractors, and this meeting was to discuss the bids and select a contractor to do the repairs.

Also report whether a quorum was achieved, when the meeting ended, and who wrote the meeting minutes.

Step 2: Summarize the reports.

Although every meeting is different and groups don't follow a uniform set of steps, most meetings contain reports of one sort or another. In board meetings, one of the first reports is a review of the minutes taken at the previous meeting. Any changes to the previous meeting's minutes should be amended to the minutes and a new version submitted before the next meeting where the new version is reviewed to be accepted. Summarize reports by standing committees and/or other relevant entities. Here is an example:

Chief Executive's Report:

- *Recommends that if we are not able to find a new facility by the end of this month, the organization should stay in the current location over the winter. After brief discussion, Board agreed.*

- *Staff member Jackson Browne, and Swanson attended the National Practitioner's Network meeting in Atlanta last month and gave a brief extemporaneous presentation. Both are invited back next year to give a longer presentation about our organization. After brief discussion, Board congratulated Swanson and asked her to pass on their congratulations to Browne as well.*

Finance Committee report provided by Chair, Sandra Toler:

- *Toler explained that consultant, Susan Johnson, reviewed the organization's bookkeeping procedures and found them to be satisfactory, in preparation for the upcoming yearly financial audit.*

- *Long-range plan is needed, as well as shift of money to Calvert account. MOTION to accept financial statements; seconded and passed.*

> Note: A written version of your minutes needs to be distributed to board members before the next meeting for members' review.

Step 3: Summarize agenda items.

Perhaps the main part of a meeting minutes report, and the part people will jump to first, is this section, where you provide notes on old, new, and other business.

Old Business:

Final inspections on porch rehabilitation to be made by architects and owners. Complaints have been received regarding wooden boards that have not been replaced and are not painted properly. Other structures are rotting away where tree branches are making contact.

New Business:

Water bills for several properties have notably increased. Investigations need to be made in regard to running water, leaks in units, and/or problems with meters.

Other Business:

Departmental secretary has now returned from maternity leave. Interim temporary worker is no longer on staff.

Step 4: Assess the meeting and report on follow-up.

In this section, you give particulars for next meeting as well as who is responsible for completing assignments by what deadlines. For a meeting that is particularly eventful or important to the company's future, you may also be called upon to provide personal observations about the success of the meeting or the progress of critical agenda items. You should discuss such reporting with your superiors beforehand, because they are not part of the standard meeting minutes report. A basic report will simply give the facts of what occurred. But for board members who were unable to attend, or for executives who want a record of what transpired, a personal assessment can prove highly valuable. For example:

This meeting was striking for the amount of cooperation between residents, who have been hostile to one another since the accident. This observer feels the project has "turned a corner" and a major improvement to the building is about to take place.

Step 5: Conclusion

In this wrap-up section, you identify the person who took notes (namely, you, unless you are writing the report based on notes taken by a secretary or other staff member), and give any final details.

15. Meeting Minutes

Meeting adjourned at 5:30 p.m.
Minutes submitted by Secretary, Hannah Carver

Checklist

❑ You indicated particulars about the meeting (time, place, attendance) and introductory comments.

❑ You summarized reports by standing committees and/or other relevant entities.

❑ You provided notes on old, new, and other business.

❑ You gave particulars for the next meeting and designated individuals who are responsible for completing assignments, as well as deadlines.

❑ You signed my name and gave appropriate final details.

15. Meeting Minutes

Meeting Minutes Template

Introduction

Board Meeting Minutes
Stellar Building Management Company
November 19, 2009
3 p.m.; Company Headquarters, Chicago, Illinois

It has been three months since the management company's last board meeting. This meeting was especially important because it was the first since the porch collapse that injured three people. After inspection by the city, bids have gone out to contractors, and this meeting was to discuss the bids and select a contractor to do the repairs.

Board Members:

> *Present:* Jon Alitto, Paula Bear, Hannah Carver, Elizabeth Frisch, Douglas Gordon, and Sandra Toler
>
> *Absent:* Roslyn Kuhl
>
> *Quorum present?* Yes
>
> *Others Present:* Exec. Director: Anita Stewart
>
> Other: Susan Johnson, Consulting Accountant

Proceedings:

- ▶ Meeting called to order at 3:00 p.m. by Chair, Elizabeth Frisch
- ▶ (Last month's) meeting minutes were amended and approved

Meeting ended at 4:35 p.m.

Minutes recorded by Cecilia Wycliffe

Report Summaries:

Chief Executive's Report:

- ◆ Recommends that if we are not able to find a new contractor by the end of this month, the residents should stay with the usual remodeling company to begin work on the project over the winter. After brief discussion, Board agreed.

- ◆ Staff member Jackson Browne, and Swanson attended the National Practitioner's Network meeting in Atlanta last month and gave a brief extemporaneous presentation. Both are invited back next year to give a longer presentation about our organization. After brief discussion, Board congratulated Swanson and asked her to pass on their congratulations to Browne as well.

- ◆ Drucker asserts that our organization must ensure its name is associated with whatever materials are distributed at that practitioner's meeting next year. The organization should generate revenues where possible from the materials, too.

- ◆ Swanson mentioned that staff member Sheila Anderson's husband is ill and in the hospital. Motion to send a gift to Anderson's husband, expressing the organization's sympathy and support; seconded and passed.

Finance Committee Report provided by Chair, Sandra Toler:

- ◆ Toler explained that consultant Susan Johnson reviewed the organization's bookkeeping procedures and found them to be satisfactory, in preparation for the upcoming yearly financial audit.
- ◆ Long-range plan is needed, as well as shift of money to Calvert account. Motion to accept financial statements; seconded and passed.

Consulting Accountant's report:

- ◆ Amount held in co-op accounts: $55,000
- ◆ Estimated cost of repairs: $66,000
- ◆ Assessment needs to increase by $143 per month for two years for all residents to pay for repairs.

Agenda Items

Old Business:

- ▶ Final inspections on porch rehabilitation to be made by architects and owners. Complaints have been received regarding wooden boards that have not been replaced and are not painted properly. Other structures are rotting away where tree branches are making contact.

- ▶ New interior lights were installed in all buildings to be in compliance with green initiative. Electrician needs to inspect buildings for possible problems with circuits, fuses, and/or wiring. He/she should also evaluate exterior lights and give price for repair and/or provide prices for other options.

- ▶ Possible lawsuits related to injuries sustained in porch collapse were discussed briefly.

New Business:

- ▶ Water bills for several properties have notably increased. Investigations need to be made in regard to running water, leaks in units, and/or problems with meters.

- ▶ Seasonal landscaping and tree maintenance need to be scheduled.

Other Business:

- ▶ Departmental secretary has now returned from maternity leave. Interim temporary worker is no longer on staff.

- ▶ Nameplates for new staff members have been ordered and will be installed in mail room.

Assessment and Follow-Up

▶ Because of sale of Bank Office Building, current landlord needs to provide closing statement to assume ownership. Stewart will conduct inquiry and provide report.

▶ Representatives will be asked to attend the next meeting, on January 10, 2010, at which time officers will be elected. Frisch was appointed head of nominating committee.

▶ This meeting was striking for the amount of cooperation between residents, who have been hostile to one another since the accident. This observer feels the project has "turned a corner" and a major improvement to the building is about to take place.

▶ Despite this cooperation, the meeting ended on a negative note, when the Chair noted that three people were late when the meeting started. He urged all members to be on time in the future.

Conclusion

After scheduling the next meeting, this meeting adjourned at 5:30 p.m.

Minutes submitted by Secretary, Hannah Carver

15. Meeting Minutes

Chapter 16

Summary Reports

Just because your project is completed doesn't mean your work is done. If you are writing a report for your supervisor, you need to make sure you get credit for your accomplishments and that you state that you took appropriate actions along the way. If you are directing your comments to a client, your goal is to get repeat business and referrals by explaining that any cost over-runs were necessary.

Remember that your summary report is important; it is not a throwaway. Rather, it gives you a chance to make a good first impression and sets the tone for the full report to come. A summary that is well-structured and coherent tells reviewers that the subsequent full report will be worth reading as well.

This report need not be long, but it should be complete and objective. It is often submitted on letterhead with your name and title at the bottom. It should be dated. Although it is usually addressed to the primary recipient, others involved in the project should also receive a copy. The parts are as follows:

▸ The summary is the bare-bones part of the report. It should identify the project and state when it was completed. It should also briefly mention any recommendations of action for the reader.

▸ The background should include relevant particulars. It should state who authorized the project, the initial agreement, and the original schedule.

▸ The highlights should again spell out the goals but should also elaborate on how they were accomplished. It is important to be as specific as possible so the reader will understand the quality and complexity of the work.

▸ A report on most projects will include a section for exceptions. Most projects require adjustments in schedule and cost. Previous progress reports should have communicated the situation as progress was being made so that nothing will be a surprise. Apologies are not productive, but it's okay to mention the consequences of not making changes. This is the place to describe discoveries that make additional time necessary or required other changes in specifications. Be as complete as you can in detailing when a problem arose, what solutions were agreed upon, and who authorized the action.

▶ Action beyond this point is recommended in the next section. If a review is needed, you should spell out exactly what should be evaluated. If you are asking for a response, give a timetable and instructions for the form of the reply.

Step-by-Step Guide

Step 1: Title of Report

List the title of your report so people will know what to expect and what will be discussed.

Step 2: Identify your project, state the completion date, and a give brief recommendation.

Should a summary report have an Executive Summary? The answer for all but the shortest summary reports is yes. Boiling down the main points of your report so that busy managers can grasp your main point quickly is always a good strategy. Once you have written a description of your innovative curriculum project, it helps to summarize it as per the Project Summary Template so that it becomes clearer to you and easier for the reviewer of the projects. It also serves the same purpose as an "Abstract" does (puts all essential elements in a nutshell) in a scientific paper.

An Executive Summary is a perfect place to mention the most unusual or noteworthy feature about your project. This might be an innovation, a discovery, or a milestone. It will grab the reader's attention and encourage him or her to read on. It also makes your project out from others and puts the subsequent project description in a different and better perspective for the reader. For example:

> Note: Some summary reports are less than a page in length; you might not need an Executive Summary for such reports. But be sure to encapsulate your main conclusion in a sentence or two.

This report marks the five-year anniversary of the Bittersweet Chocolate Company, a time when profits have reached an all-time high and a new line of Golden Ticket candy bar is about to be launched.

Step 3: State who authorized your report, the initial agreement, and the original schedule.

Because you are summarizing, you only need to state this basic information in a sentence or two, or perhaps a paragraph. Tell readers who you are, who commissioned the report, what the purpose is, and when it was conducted.

This report was prepared by Magnus O'Shaughnessy of the marketing department for the board of directors, who wanted to conduct a five-year in-depth assessment of BCC's progress and standing in the industry. It was conducted in December 2009. As you no doubt will recall, we were happy on our five-year anniversary to be in the enviable position of being profitable. As part of our way of sharing our good fortune with the community, we sponsored a series of social events in venues around town that included games, food, and, of course, free samples of our product. We conducted several focus groups during these events, collected questionnaires, and conducted more informal verbal surveys. A committee reviewed and analyzed the results. Members included the president, the chairman of the board, a departmental director, and three staff members.

Step 4: Elaborate on how your goals were accomplished.

Elaborate briefly on the goal of the report mentioned in the Executive Summary. In this section, you aren't necessarily summarizing all of the goals of your company or organization. Focus solely on the goals or the project of your report. Consider answering questions such as:

▸ Were all of the activities you planned actually carried out, or does much remain to be done?

▸ What is the level of participation in the company? Is everyone working as efficiently as possible?

▸ What methods did you use to reach your conclusions?

Public service and volunteerism are flourishing at BCC, as this report makes abundantly clear. Numerous examples have been documented on how BCC employees have channeled their skills and knowledge, as well as their energy and enthusiasm, into programs designed to improve the quality of life in the local area. Here is a summary of some of the programs:

◆ *Many of the outreach programs (nearly 20) are aimed at disadvantaged youth. A large number are educational in nature, but others emphasize physical fitness and healthcare.*

◆ *Other programs (more than 15) serve the community at large, often with a focus on beautification, civic pride, and neighborhood events and festivals.*

16. Summary Reports

> ◆ *As many as 400 to 500 BCC employees volunteer their time on a weekly basis in a community-based public service activity. The total estimated time commitment of all volunteers is more than 1,500 hours per week.*

Step 5: Describe problems and solutions.

In this section you detail problems you encountered conducting your report. Perhaps all the employees you wanted to talk to were not present at the time the report was conducted. Or perhaps your assumptions need to be reassessed.

If the company, organization or project you are examining has fallen short of its own goals, be sure to mention them in this section as well, along with any solutions you uncovered as a result of your research:

> *While there is much to be proud of in the success of the programs launched last year, an important roadblock remains. It is the strong belief of members of the Community Involvement Committee that more needs to be done to welcome the community to our physical facility. Rumors remain of unsafe working conditions and negative environmental impacts. We propose that special events and regular programs be held on site that would be open to the public. These should be both cultural and recreational in nature, and they should be held both in our facilities and in our open land. For example, our company gymnasium and pool could be open to visitors once a month.*

Step 6: Be straightforward about costs.

Often, a summary report is used to provide a quick overview of a highly technical project or a complex undertaking that involves machinery or new technologies. What are the cost impacts of implementing the new systems? You don't need to go into detail about the actual, final costs in the summary. Summarize the impact here, and explain further in the full report.

> *The implications of the new line of candy are significant. They will consume a sizeable percentage of last year's profits. But the expected revenues are worth the outlay, as described in the detail in the full report.*

Step 7: Give timetable and instructions for reply and other necessary action.

To round out your summary, give a rough schedule for the time it would take to implement the changes or complete the project about which you are reporting. Also mention:

▶ When readers need to respond.

▶ What sort of feedback you want to receive.

▶ Any other necessary actions that need to be taken as a result of your report.

We ask that a subcommittee be formed within the next month to study the feasibility of enlarging the scope of community involvement. We would need an indication within the next two weeks of how many of the current subcommittee are willing to renew their membership.

Checklist

❑ Have you identified the project, stated when it was completed, and briefly stated recommendations at the beginning of the report?

❑ Have you indicated authorization, the initial agreement, and the original schedule?

❑ Have you spelled out the goals and described how they were accomplished, giving indications of the quality and complexity of the work?

❑ Have you included details on problems that arose, solutions that were agreed upon, and who authorized the action?

❑ Have you recommended further action to take, giving specifics and deadlines for responses that you are requesting?

❑ Did you mention each significant component of your project?

❑ Did you mention costs, or summarize them briefly?

16. Summary Reports

Summary Report Template

Title of Report

A Sweet Five Years: Options for Future Growth for BCC

Executive Summary

This report marks the five-year anniversary of the Bittersweet Chocolate Company, a time when profits have reached an all-time high and a new line of candy bar is about to be launched.

One year ago, to celebrate its fifth year of moving to the town of Safe Haven, the Bittersweet Chocolate Company (BCC) launched an initiative for community involvement. We are happy to be successful in not only completing this report in a timely fashion as tasked but also to be able to include in the report so many accomplishments of which we can be justifiably proud. We want, however, to be clear in our intention that the launch is only the beginning. In particular, it is important that an ongoing quantifiable assessment continue to be made on a quarterly basis of how the BCC is attempting to fulfill its obligation to be a good neighbor.

Background

This report was prepared by Magnus O'Shaughnessy of the marketing department for the board of directors, who wanted to conduct a five-year in-depth assessment of BCC's progress and standing in the industry. It was conducted in December 2009.

As you will recall, we were happy on our five-year anniversary to be in the enviable position of being profitable. As part of our way of sharing our good fortune with the community, we sponsored a series of social events in venues around town that included games, food, and, of course, free samples of our product. We conducted several focus groups during these events, collected questionnaires, and conducted more informal verbal surveys. A committee reviewed and analyzed the results. Members included the president, the chairman of the board, a departmental director, and three staff members. They reported that we were well liked by those who actually had direct contact with the company. However, there remained more potential problems from outsiders that ranged from indifference to suspicion. Another subcommittee was formed and given the direction that, within twelve months, we should submit this report. The report should track ways that company staff were already contributing to the well-being of the residents who leave near our facility and to report on the results of the launch of at least six new initiatives to encourage at least 80 percent of the staff to find an enjoyable way to volunteer. The purpose of this summary is to help both the town residents and the company employees become aware of the scope of community involvement and to help assess the cumulative impact of individual programs.

Highlights

Public service and volunteerism are flourishing at BCC, as this report makes abundantly clear. Numerous examples have been documented on how BCC employees have channeled their skills and knowledge, as well as their energy and enthusiasm, into programs designed to improve the quality of life in the local area. Here is a summary of some of the programs:

- Many of the outreach programs (nearly 20) are aimed at disadvantaged youth. A large number are educational in nature, but others emphasize physical fitness and healthcare.

- Other programs (more than 15) serve the community at large, often with a focus on beautification, civic pride, and neighborhood events and festivals.

- As many as 400 to 500 BCC employees volunteer their time on a weekly basis in a community-based public service activity. The total estimated time commitment of all volunteers is more than 1,500 hours per week.

These conclusions were reached using a variety of research methods:

- A matrix to demonstrate key competencies and skills of individual employees.

- A survey of work groups within the company to assess efficiencies, including:

  - Highly structured interviews for department managers.

  - Feedback surveys handed out to rank and file.

  - Feedback surveys mailed to contractors.

The data generated from the surveys and questionnaires were combined with the matrix to judge the level of success at the five-year period.

Exceptions

While there is much to be proud of in the success of the programs launched last year, an important roadblock remains. It is the strong belief of members of the Community Involvement Committee that more needs to be done to welcome the community to our physical facility. Rumors remain of unsafe working conditions and negative environmental impacts. We propose that special events and regular programs be held on site that would be open to the public. These should be both cultural and recreational in nature, and they should be held both in our facilities and in our open land. For example, our company gymnasium and pool could be open to visitors once a month.

A group of perhaps twenty could register in advance for a tour, followed by time to work out or simply enjoy some leisure. Our childcare facility could be open once a month during off hours (on a Sunday afternoon, perhaps) to celebrate the birthdays of up to thirty non-staff children who, again, would

16. Summary Reports

register in advance. Accompanied by an adult caregiver, we could provide food, games, and a magic show. A community-wide picnic could be held each year on the anniversary of our founding. Tents and tables could be set up on our front lawn with family-friendly entertainment. Free cake could be distributed, and local restaurants could set up booths to offer samples our their specialities at a reasonable price.

Interviews with managers, contractors, and rank and file employees resulted in a number of other suggestions:

- Sponsoring a special day at Navy Pier.
- Giving out chocolate at the big annual rock concert, Lollapalooza.
- Taking out a booth at the annual Candy Show for the industry.
- Expanding the Website to include contests and quizzes.
- Creating a page on Facebook and Twitter.

Financial Implications

The implications of the new line of candy are significant. They will consume a sizeable percentage of last year's profits. But the expected revenues are worth the outlay, as described in the detail in the full report.

Recommendations

We ask that a subcommittee be formed within the next month to study the feasibility of enlarging the scope of community involvement. We would need an indication within the next two weeks of how many of the current subcommittee are willing to renew their membership. We would also like to receive within the next two months responses to a questionnaire from board members and staff that will give us feedback on our current efforts and suggestions for other ideas to possibly implement. But our most emphatic conclusion is a salute to the volunteers who believe in the obligation of public service and who know that their efforts really can make a difference in the betterment of Safe Haven. We dedicate this report to them and hope it inspires others to join in these ventures.

Chapter 17

Policies and Procedures

Every office has a set of policies and procedures—rules of communication, behavior, and process that all employees are expected to follow. The problem for many organizations is that those policies and procedures are only communicated verbally. They aren't codified in the form of a written document. Having such a document covers you in case of dispute, and it empowers employees, who are able to refer to the file when needed without necessarily needing to consult management.

> Note: Publish your policies and procedures not only in print but on the office network so all employees can access them easily.

What you have to say when you are writing a report based on policies and procedures must be serious, realistic, specific, and factual. Being well researched and well thought out is the only way to avoid errors and misunderstandings that can lead to a few dollars wasted at the least and a huge disaster at the worst. Just to make sure we all understand our terms, I'm using "policies" to mean general statements of how things should be and "procedures" to mean the step-by-step definitions of what to do to implement those policies. Here are only a few examples of when such a report would be useful:

Legal: how to be sure you're in compliance with the laws or other important rules, and what to do when violations occur.

Money: how, when, and to whom money must be paid; who has the authority to approve expenditures; and when credit will be extended.

Employees: one of the many subsets would be benefits (for example, how to get raises, time off, education funds, and retirement vesting).

Occupying space: whether a single-family dwelling, office complex, or dormitory, residents need to know everything from acceptable noise levels to where to put their trash.

Step-by-Step Guide

Step 1: Provide introductory material.

In the introductory section, you should include the title of your document, its purpose, and a history of revisions. A history of revisions lets readers know whether or not they have the current version at hand. For example:

Title: *Hyde Park Condominium Association Policies and Procedures*

Purpose: *To provide rules of behavior and procedures for meetings and maintenance for co-owners.*

Revision history: *Version 1: 3/11/02*

                    Version 2: 6/05/05

                    Version 3: 1/1/09

                    Version 3a: 1/15/09

                    Version 4: 4/12/10

Step 2: State your policies and their importance.

Policies are rules of usage and communication that employees need to follow in order to maintain the orderly working of your office, maintain your public image, and maintain a high level of morale among fellow employees. Policies can be wide ranging. They might include the following:

- *Computer use: Computers are only to be used for business purposes. Employees are prohibited from surfing the Web during work hours.*

- *Email: A work email account is only to be used for work-related communications. Employees should use their personal accounts for personal e-mails.*

- *Cell phones: Employees may use their personal cell phones in a closed office, in the stairwell, or outside the building.*

- *Smoking: There is no smoking in the building.*

- *Sexual harassment: Inappropriate nicknames or remarks are forbidden; touching is forbidden; see the Human Resources Department's Sexual Harassment guidelines for more.*

- *Interoffice mail: Use this service whenever possible to save postage and cut back on messenger service.*

- *Dress code: This is a "business casual" office except on days specifically designated "casual days."*

- *Staff directory: Everyone is required to have a listing in the staff directory. However, inclusion of personal details such as marital status, address, and home phone are optional.*

Step 3: List procedures you want employees, residents, or members to follow.

Procedures refer to business or other tasks that need to be completed. Each organization has standard forms and procedures to follow, and this is where you spell them out for your constituents. For example:

Competitive bids: Any printing or maintenance must be the result of three competitive bids.

Purchasing: For projects over $5,000, you must go through the Purchasing Dept. rather than soliciting bids yourself.

Office supplies: Must be obtained through the Purchasing Dept., which gets discounts from preferred suppliers.

Step 4: State advantages and disadvantages of each procedure.

Some procedures, like conflicts and lawsuits, are risky for many reasons. You or your company might be liable for damages, and you might face a lengthy dispute in the civil courts. In such cases, you should provide pros and cons that will give employees "thinking points" so they can make informed decisions. For example:

Suing for breach of contract is fraught with danger. There are several downsides to this method of action. In the past, we have had owners who have managed to avoid service for years. We've also had to pay a lot for post-judgment procedures. All of this takes time, and typically owners manage to disappear, file for bankruptcy, get into even worse financial shape, and even allow mortgage foreclosure actions to happen. Unfortunately a number of our owners have no cars, no jobs, and few other assets that we can collect. Sadly, the process of lien foreclosure has all these disadvantages, plus the problem that we would have to have the money to purchase the unit. We could sell the unit to a third party. But we would also be subject to mortgage liens, which means the mortgage company might foreclose on us because the title was transferred without its consent. That leaves the forcible entry and detainer action.

Step 5: Give suggestions for which options would work best and the reasoning behind them.

Policies and procedures should be clear. But in some instances, there are "gray areas." In the case of a procedure that presents the employee with multiple options, you can add a section that describes what to do. For example:

In case of a marital dispute in which one spouse tries to enter without the permission of the other spouse, procedures are not always clear. The circumstance for each owner's situation varies. We need to evaluate on a case-by-case basis in order to be fair on the one hand but also to accomplish

17. Policies and Procedures

our goals on the other hand. Overall, however, we believe that a forcible entry and detainer action would be best for most owners. We recommend it over the others because it costs less, is quicker, and is usually more effective.

Step 6: Summarize your report and try to end on positive note.

Finish up by summarizing your report and ending on a positive note that encourages employees, members, or residents to follow the specified policies and procedures:

We very much regret having to submit this report. In many cases, these individuals are not only our neighbors but also our friends. However we all have a financial stake in our property. A bankruptcy will prevent us from taking action to collect what is owed to us, and a foreclosure will eliminate our ability to collect the assessment from the sale of the property itself by either a lien foreclosure or forcible entry and detainer action. If both occur, our lien is completely wiped out. We are sorry for those who have fallen on financial hard times and wish to do everything we can to lend them a helping hand. However, we do not want to overstep what is morally right or fiscally responsible to the point that more of us end up facing financial difficulty. With this in mind, it is our fervent wish that stating these policies and procedures will lead to a more happy ending for all involved (besides the lawyers).

Checklist

☐ Have you stated the policy and its importance?

☐ Have you listed main possible procedures?

☐ Have you described each relevant procedure?

☐ Have you stated advantages and disadvantages of the procedures?

☐ Have you given suggestions for which one is likely to work best in most situations, and your reasoning?

☐ Have you concluded my report in a positive way by giving a summary?

17. Policies and Procedures

Policies and Procedures Template

Introduction

Title:

Hyde Park Condominium Association Policies and Procedures

Purpose:

To provide rules of behavior and procedures for meetings and maintenance for co-owners.

Revision history:

Version 1: 3/11/02

Version 2: 6/05/05

Version 3: 1/1/09

Version 3a: 1/15/09

Version 4: 4/12/10

Policies

Assessment bills are mailed on the last day of each month to each owner of a condominium unit in the Home Sweet Home assessment. Those who have signed up for direct deposit will have funds deducted from their designed bank account on the first day of the next month. Other owners must mail or hand-deliver their payment to the office of the property manager; it must be received by the property manager on or before the 15th of each month. Our budget is dependent on these funds being available in a timely manner for our vendors to be paid. However, because of the bad economy, the Home Sweet Home condo association has been faced with a higher percentage than usual of delinquent assessments. Many condo owners have lost their jobs. Others have moved to find better-paying jobs and rented out their units, without continuing to pay their assessments. One condo owner is now deceased with no known survivors. The purpose of this report is to outline our options of procedures for collecting.

Garbage: Will be thrown in green containers.

Recyclables: Will be placed in blue containers.

Bulk trash: Will be left in back; call city for pickup.

Noise: This building will have "quiet time" after 11 p.m. each night.

Parties: Party room can be used if you sign up one week in advance.

Meetings: Condo board will meet once each quarter.

Gardening: Residents have space for their own gardens on east side of building.

17. Policies and Procedures

Parking: No resident parking in alley or behind building. Only street parking is available.

Painting: Any redecorating of hallway will be subject to approval by the condo board.

Procedures

Competitive bids: Any printing or maintenance must be the result of three competitive bids.

Purchasing: For projects over $5,000, you must go through the Purchasing Dept. rather than soliciting bids yourself.

Office supplies: Must be obtained through the Purchasing Dept., which gets discounts from preferred suppliers.

Suggestions: Should be given to Office Manager.

Complaints: Should go to the Human Resources Dept.

Parking spaces: Are obtained by applying to the Parking Office for the building, 4-8832.

Disputes: Consult with legal department; your main choices are to sue for breach of contract, the process of lien foreclosure, and a forcible entry and detainer action.

Pros and Cons

Our first choice is to sue for breach of contract. Our complaint will be filed and forwarded to the county sheriff, who will serve the owner with our complaint. If this is unsuccessful, we can hire a special process server. When this is accomplished, we can proceed with our lawsuit with a court date. We are confident that a judgment would be entered in our favor, even if a counter claim needs to be addressed. The best-case scenario is that the judgment will be paid voluntarily. If not we will need to determine what assets are available and go on to collect our delinquency.

Another way to go is the process of lien foreclosure. In this case, our first step would be to file the lien in the county's recorder's office. If the owner still doesn't pay, we can file a lawsuit to foreclose the lien, which means we will own the unit. Then we would file a complaint and service of the complaint on the owner, which would lead to a trial. We would win if a judgment is entered, followed by a direction that execution issue. What's an execution? It's an order signed by the clerk of the court that renders the judgment directing the sheriff to sell the property to pay off our judgment. The sheriff would then deliver a copy of this execution to the owner. Then there is a levy. This is a formal and technical step in which the sheriff sets apart and appropriates a particular part of the property to satisfy the command of the execution. Usually this just means that the sheriff would make a statement to that effect and describe the real estate. Then the sheriff can publish notice of the coming sale and post copies in public places.

On the sale date, the sheriff would auction the unit to the highest bidder. We would then own the unit by bidding up to the amount of the judgment without producing any case other than the sheriff's cost.

The last choice covered in this report is a forcible entry and detainer action. We recommend going with it because it costs less, is quicker, and is usually more effective. Our first step is to send a notice to the owner saying that they have to pay the entire delinquent assessment in 30 days or their right to possession of the unit will be terminated. We would send it both as a certified letter and through the regular U.S. postal service. We don't have to have proof that the owner received the letter; we just have to verify that we sent it to the right address with the correct amount of postage. If we don't get payment in 30 days, we can file the action. No counter claim is allowed, except in a separate lawsuit. Our lawyer will include disclosures that are required. Again, there are supposed to be complaints filed and served on the owner. However if this is unsuccessful, in this case we only have to post forms indicating that we're taking action against the unit. If we win and get a judgment, we can take possession based on an order. We won't have actual ownership and there are more time periods granted to the owner to pay. Not only will they have to pay the past due assessments but also the attorney fees and court costs. If they don't we will get a writ to remove the owner. The owner will get a notice of that. However the next step is to evict the owner, with sheriff's movers putting all personal possessions outside. We'd have to change locks to prevent the owner from returning. The good news is regarding our units that the owner has rented. In these units, we can just require that the renter give rent payments to us.

Recommendations

The circumstance for each owner's situation varies. We need to evaluate on a case-by-case basis in order to be fair on the one hand but also to accomplish our goals on the other hand. Overall, however, we believe that a forcible entry and detainer action would be best for most owners. We recommend it over the others because it costs less, is quicker, and is usually more effective.

Conclusion

We very much regret having to submit this report. In many cases, these individuals are not only our neighbors but also our friends. However we all have a financial stake in our property. A bankruptcy will prevent us from taking action to collect what is owed to us, and a foreclosure will eliminate our ability to collect the assessment from the sale of the property itself by either a lien foreclosure or a forcible entry and detainer action. If both occur, our lien is completely wiped out. We are sorry for those who have fallen on financial hard times and wish to do everything we can to lend them a helping hand. However, we do not want to overstep what is morally right or fiscally responsible to the point that more of us end up facing financial difficulty. With this in mind, it is our fervent wish that stating these policies and procedures will lead to a more happy ending for all involved (besides the lawyers).

HUMAN RESOURCES

PART V

Chapter 18

Employee Assessments

Many employees, when they hear the words *employee assessment*, simply think about whether they'll get a raise, or if there is a possibility they will be demoted or even fired. But evaluations of workers can also influence the goals and role of an entire company. By making the most of employee evaluation and tying it in to the company's overall objectives, you can help employees develop personally and professionally, and measure the organization's progress toward its long-term progress.

Employee evaluations can also be as a tool to develop an individual's skills and work performance in a way that will prove beneficial to both the staff person and the employer. Discussions that are conducted as part of employee evaluations serve as an opportunity for supervisors and staff to establish goals, set standards for performance, plan for future compensation increases, and come up with a plan for managing time.

The general types of plans you might need to create are listed here:

1. Compliance with the Americans with Disabilities Act, EEO and affirmative action, and employee privacy rights.
2. Compensation and benefits.
3. Union organizing and bargaining.
4. Eldercare and childcare.
5. Flexible staffing and scheduling; family leave; vacations, holidays, and sick time.
6. Contingent workers and employment at will.
7. Workplace violence and other emergencies.

In some government agencies, employee assessments are required by law, and not being in compliance with the law can lead to disasters not only within your staff but also extend to the community at large. The problem is that court cases are being resolved on a daily basis, and ignorance that they are in effect will not help mitigate the potential impact on your business. By organizing information in an effective way and conveying it to those both in and outside your company, you'll be able to focus on why you started your business in the first place: to provide a good or service.

Step-by-Step Guide

Step 1: Provide background, if necessary, and assess the employee's current performance.

In some cases, employee assessments are a matter of routine, and you don't need to explain why they are being performed. But if there is a special reason for employee assessments, provide background as to why they are occurring. Encourage employees to play role in the process by examining their own performance and projecting goals for the future. Help staff understand what's involved in the evaluations and why, and make sure they know the procedure is designed to help both employees and the company to grow, and not merely to find fault with or punish those who have performed poorly. For example:

> As of the end of 2009, the Acme Widget Company had 300 paid filled positions. There were 32 vacant positions. Thirteen workers were within 30 days of completing their working test period. A round of performance evaluations has been scheduled so that benefits of permanent employment can be extended. Six employees are on leaves of absence. Five employees have passports, visas, or work permits on file that will expire in the next 90 days. In response, a report was run that determined that three of those had citizenship status, country of citizenship, and visa records that contained discrepancies.

Note: You may want to consider hiring an outside consultant to evaluate employee performance, as many companies do. This frees up your HR staff for other tasks.

Step 2: Include standard HR terms in your assessment.

A number of standard terms are used by human resources officers to prepare employee assessments. Using the standard terms makes sure you discuss the important topics: continued development of job skills, time management, and so on. Make the reports standardized and including the same terms in each so that no single employee feels singled out. Terms you may want to use include:

1. Compensation management. This is sometimes referred to as pay-for-performance; it is the process of planning goals and linking increases in salary to them. Compensation management can serve as an incentive for employees to work effectively and efficiently to increase their productivity. Organizations can also benefit from compensation management by retaining stellar employees, because their paycheck reflects their hard work.

2. Time management. As you might expect, this is the process of completing multiple tasks and getting the required amount of work done in the time available. Giving employees time-management training will help them to work more efficiently and effectively, which will result in increased productivity for your organization. You might encourage employees, as part of the assessment, to prioritize tasks, maintain job logs, and overcome procrastination.

3. Goal-setting management. This is a process of examining current goals, refining those goals to conform to processes and objectives within the organization, and setting new goals. Processes within the company that might be examined include better cooperation, improved record keeping, and automation.

4. Performance management. This process includes an evaluation of how an employee is progressing towards established goals.

5. Learning and development. Continued learning and development opportunities to employees are critical to the success of any organization, not only to keep competitive in the industry but also to retain employees by helping them to advance in their careers and boosting their morale.

6. Succession planning. This involves the foresight of an organization to plan for future situations that may arise when an employee leaves. This process requires that an organization identify an employee's strengths and provide training opportunities to that individual to increase his or her versatility within the organization.

Step 3: Have the employee perform a self-evaluation.

This step is optional, but sometimes the most revealing comments and best suggestions of improvements can come from the employee who is being evaluated. Standard self-evaluation forms that ask a few simple questions can solicit valuable material that you, the supervisor, can use as a basis for discussion when your own evaluation occurs. A complete template is included at the end of this chapter, but you might ask questions such as:

18. Employee Assessments

▶ What are your most significant accomplishments or contributions of the past year?

▶ How well have you met the goals/objectives outlined in your previous review?

▶ To improve your professional development, what are one or two things you need to learn or study in a class?

▶ Name one or two career goals for the coming year and indicate how you plan to accomplish them.

Step 4: Specify improvements required of the employee.

Employee evaluations really gain benefit for the company by pointing the way to improvement and growth on the job for individual employees. Make it clear that improvements can help lead the company forward. Use employee assessments to help staff set goals, and then align those goals with the progress of the company. For example:

This employee has been very good at accomplishing a few major tasks such as publications, which have turned out to be of high quality. But jobs tend to take more time than expected because the employee does not delegate adequately. By trying to handle minor as well as major projects, all jobs get delayed. Better delegation of routine tasks to subordinates will keep the whole office moving more productively because major projects will be on time.

Step 5: Set goals for future job performance.

After you identify the employee's strengths through the assessment, you can use the assessment to build a plan for future goals and improvements. Whatever system you choose, whether simple employee evaluation forms or making use of complex performance-evaluation software, make sure it can help you outline an action plan. For example:

The employee, in conjunction with her supervisor, identified five goals for the coming year:

1. Better delegation of major jobs

2. More regular meetings with superiors

3. Better advance planning

4. More use of resources throughout the office

5. More on-time arrivals

Checklist

❑ If there is a special reason for the report, did you provide it?

❑ Did you thoroughly and objectively assess the employee's current performance?

❑ Did you include standard HR terms and concepts?

❑ Did you give the employee a chance to evaluate him/herself?

❑ Did you specify improvements the employee needs to make?

❑ Did you tie employee improvements to the progress of the overall goals of the company?

❑ Did you set goals for future job performance?

Employee Assessment Template

Current Performance

As of the end of 2009, the Acme Widget Company had 300 paid filled positions. There were 32 vacant positions. Thirteen workers were within 30 days of completing their working test period. A round of performance evaluations has been scheduled so that benefits of permanent employment can be extended. Six employees are on leaves of absence. Five employees have passports, visas, or work permits on file that will expire in the next 90 days. In response, a report was run that determined that three of those had citizenship status, country of citizenship, and visa records that contained discrepancies.

Your performance in the past year has been good. You have accomplished a great deal, and the public image of the company has improved for it. You have created an improved annual report; you have established a Facebook presence for the company; you have improved the Web site with video; you have established better contacts with faculty; you have streamlined the admissions publications.

Standard Topics

- *Compensation management.* If you are able to meet goals specified you will receive the standard 5 percent pay raise.

- *Time management.* You do need improvement in this area; you are encouraged to prioritize tasks and maintain job logs.

- *Goal-setting management.* The company needs a new catalog for the left-handed product line to be produced by September 1. A new magazine should come out in December.

- *Performance management.* Your process toward established goals has been excellent.

- *Learning and development.* You need more training in writing for the Web and in working with video.

Self-Evaluation

Please fill out the following self-evaluation form and return it to your supervisor by _____

Performance Assessment Period _____

Supervisor Name _____

Employee Name _____ Date _____

Job Title _____ Office _____

Your thorough and timely participation in the assessment process will help facilitate a fair and comprehensive review of your progress and accomplishments since the last performance review.

18. Employee Assessments

Supervisors: Attach completed Self-Assessments to the Employee's Performance Appraisal and return to HR.

1. Describe your most significant accomplishments or contributions in the last year.

2. How do your accomplishments support the goals/objectives outlined in your previous review?

3. In the past year, have you successfully performed any new tasks or additional duties outside the scope of your regular responsibilities? If so, please specify.

4. What activities have you initiated, or taken part in, to encourage a spirit of teamwork within your group and/or the company as a whole?

5. Describe your personal development in the past year. Mention whether or not you performed on-site training, peer training, management coaching or mentoring, on-the-job experience, or had more better exposure to challenging projects.

6. List areas where you think you need improvement in terms of your professional capabilities. Describe how you will achieve this improvement and/or the resources you need to accomplish this.

7. What suggestions would you have for improving the company's client and/or employee satisfaction and retention?

8. List one or two career goals for the coming year and describe how you plan to accomplish them.

18. Employee Assessments

Assess your job performance since your last assessment. If a category does not apply to you, write "N/A." Use the following scale:

4 - Outstanding

3 - Very Competent or High Level

2 - Satisfactory

1 - Inexperienced or Improvement Needed

Category	Self-Assessment	Category	Self-Assessment
a. Technical skills		i. Interpersonal skills	
b. Technical knowledge: are you up-to-date on new technologies and processes?		j. Communication skills	
		k. Innovation or creativity	
c. Quality of work		l. Collaboration/ teamwork	
d. Level of productivity		m. Knowledge of employee policies	
e. Business development			
f. Project management abilities		n. Leadership skills	
g. Computer skills		o. Punctuality and attendance	
h. Time management and organization		p. Overall job performance	

Improvements

This employee has been very good at accomplishing a few major tasks such as publications, which have turned out to be of high quality. But jobs tend to take more time than expected because the employee does not delegate adequately. By trying to handle minor as well as major projects, all jobs get delayed. Better delegation of routine tasks to subordinates will keep the whole office moving more productively because major projects will be on time.

Goals for the Future

The employee, in conjunction with her supervisor, identified five goals for the coming year:

1. Better delegation of major jobs.
2. More regular meetings with superiors.
3. Better advance planning.
4. More use of resources throughout the office.
5. More on-time arrivals.

18. Employee Assessments

Chapter 19

Disciplinary Reports

Perhaps some other types of reports in this book could be defined as "FYI." But a disciplinary report is a whole lot more than "For Your Information." It must be expertly drafted and meticulously executed. And it's really a problem if the documentation falls through a crack in your crack filing system. A lawsuit for alleged wrongful discharge is a lose/lose situation, both for your companies and your employees. A better goal is to make the experience a learning tool that will lead the employee to more work satisfaction and to improved productivity—in other words, a win/win situation. A list of a the possible reasons a disciplinary report would be written would be too long (and discouraging) to add to this chapter. But here are just a few typical examples:

▶ Inadequate, insufficient, or late work.

▶ Being absent or tardy, leaving work station without permission, sleeping.

▶ Misuse of company property or electronic documents.

▶ Inappropriate dress or bad hygiene.

▶ Being insubordinate, rude, or abusive.

▶ Infractions involving drugs, alcohol, guns, or smoking.

Step-by-Step Guide

Step 1: Indicate other infractions that would have a possible bearing on the case.

Begin your report by providing background to readers who aren't familiar with the person being disciplined. Summarize other violations of a similar nature that have occurred in the past. If the individual's supervisors have exercised a progressive discipline process, describe the violations or incidents that led to the previous disciplinary measures. This will clarify for the employee and those evaluating the case why the particular level of discipline was imposed. For example:

On May 26, 2009, Don Powers was brought before the Panel on Unlawful Harassment convened by the Hynes Potato Chip Factory. No formal charge had previously been leveled against Mr. Powers. However, after the current allegation was made, four letters were received from other women who claimed that they had been the target of inappropriate behavior by Mr. Powers. Two were unsigned and claimed that he had touched them inappropriately. One was signed by a woman who said he continued to ask her out despite her repeated refusals. One signed letter included a printout of a "spam" e-mail allegedly forwarded by Mr. Powers that included an off-color "joke."

Step 2: Describe the allegations in the current incident.

Some work needs to be completed in advance of your report. You need to conduct a thorough investigation of the current incident. Your investigation may include primary research (interviews with those affected, or with the employee personally) or secondary research (reports of the incident). You may even want to prepare an investigative report to back up the recommendations in this disciplinary report.

Even if you do not conduct a full-fledged investigation, be certain you have gathered the relevant facts. The scope of your investigation typically depends on the nature and seriousness of the incident. For example, an investigation of a theft of office equipment will be more thorough than an investigation relating to someone who consistently parks in the wrong parking space. For the sake of all involved, your inquiries should be completed promptly, and the discipline should be imposed promptly. In writing the facts, stick to the most important points and avoid coloring your report with your own opinions. For example:

The female secretary of Mr. Powers had accused him of offensive sexually related workplace conduct that included unwelcome comments, touching, and leering. She said his behavior persisted although she had ignored him, calmly asked him to stop, yelled at him, sent him a written request (which he provided copies of), and threatened to file a complaint.

See Chapter 24 for instructions on how to write an investigative report, and this book's report templates for an example of such a report.

It's a good idea to include copies of any evidence or documentation that indicate what happened and point to the consequence of the employee's action. Without explaining the effects of the incident, neither the employee nor a jury will understand why the level of discipline or discharge is justified. Though the facts alone show that the employee did something wrong, they don't demonstrate how serious the infraction was.

Step 3: Include statements from witnesses.

Part of the investigation you conduct before your report is the gathering of statements from witnesses to the incident. These ideally are interviews you conduct yourself (ideal because primary research has more credibility than secondary research). Witness statements are important because they indicate the personal consequences of what the employee did. They also take away from you the entire burden of describing the offense, so that your report doesn't appear to be personally motivated in any way. For example:

Another secretary who worked in the adjoining office (who described herself as a friend of the secretary of Mr. Powers) submitted a written statement. She said she had overheard his secretary reacting negatively when Mr. Powers asked her on a date, told her he liked the sweater she was wearing, asked how she liked to be kissed, and so on. Another woman wrote a statement saying she had found the secretary crying in the women's restroom on two occasions, saying that the behavior of Mr. Powers was upsetting her.

Step 4: Summarize the response of the accused employee.

There are two sides to every story, and it is important to get the views of the employee accused of the incident as well as statements from witnesses. Because you are writing the report and presumably recommending disciplinary action, it might be useful to conduct the interview with the employee along with another staff member who can provide an independent opinion. In any case, ask standard questions (the same questions you would ask anyone in the organization) such as:

▶ What is your view of what happened?

▶ What is the reason this happened?

▶ What do you see as the effects of the incident?

▶ What disciplinary action do you think is appropriate for this incident?

For example:

The employee said he is not the only man in the office who finds the secretary attractive, and because he recently broke up with a longtime girlfriend he has been lonely and under stress. He apologized for the incident and said he realizes how it might disturb the woman. He was not sure what kind of disciplinary action he would find appropriate. But he did mention that if perhaps the secretary did not dress in a provocative way, he would not react as he did.

It's always a good idea to keep your personal emotions out of the interaction.

Step 5: State the disciplinary action to be taken.

Clearly state the disciplinary action that will be taken so no one is in doubt about what will happen. In some situations, the infractions and appropriate actions will be spelled out in your company policies and procedures manual. If that is the case, be sure to state what rules or procedures have been broken. If the discipline results in suspension, give the start and end dates of the suspension, the date the employee is expected to return to work, and to whom the employee should report when he returns to work. For example:

Mr. Powers signed a written apology to the secretary and an acknowledgement that he is on indefinite probation. The secretary has been reassigned.

See Chapter 17 for instructions on preparing policies and procedures for an office if you don't have them already.

Step 6: Specify any deadlines that were set.

Ignoring the past infraction after the disciplinary action has been exercised opens up the possibility that it will occur again. To prevent this, set a follow-up meeting. Tell the employee that you will meet in (for example) a month or two and assess whether behavior has improved. If it has not, spell out the consequences. For example:

Mr. Powers was told that a follow-up meeting will be held three months from now, on June 17. If any infractions or offensive behaviors have occurred in that time, he will be subject to further disciplinary action.

Step 7: Give what will happen if goals are not met.

Make it clear that should the infraction of offensive behavior occur again, further disciplinary action will be taken. Clearly spell out what that action will be. For example:

The employee should also clearly understand what may happen if there's another violation. Because most employers' discipline policies give the employer the flexibility to impose discipline at any level they deem appropriate, the discipline document may identify the next step in the discipline process but also warn that the discipline imposed could be up to or including discharge.

Checklist

☐ You have indicated other infractions that would have a possible bearing on the case.

☐ You have described allegations in current incident.

☐ You have included statements from any witnesses.

☐ You have summarized response of the accused employee.

☐ You have given action to be taken.

☐ You have specified any deadlines that were set.

☐ You have given what will happen if goals are not met.

Disciplinary Report Template

History of Past Infractions

On May 26, 2009, Don Powers was brought before the Panel on Unlawful Harassment convened by the Hynes Potato Chip Factory. No formal charges had previously been leveled against Mr. Powers. However, after the current allegation was made, four letters were received from other women who claimed that they had been the target of inappropriate behavior by Mr. Powers. Two were unsigned and claimed that he had touched them inappropriately. One was signed by a woman who said he continued to ask her out despite her repeated refusals. One signed letter included a printout of a "spam" e-mail allegedly forwarded by Mr. Powers that included an off-color "joke."

Allegations in Current Incident

The female secretary of Mr. Powers had accused him of offensive sexually related workplace conduct that included unwelcome comments, touching, and leering. She said his behavior persisted although she had ignored him, calmly asked him to stop, yelled at him, sent him a written request (which he provided copies of), and threatened to file a complaint.

Statements of Witnesses

Another secretary who worked in the adjoining office (who described herself as a friend of the secretary of Mr. Powers) submitted a written statement. She said she had overheard his secretary reacting negatively when Mr. Powers asked her on a date, told her he liked the sweater she was wearing, asked how she liked to be kissed, etc. Another woman wrote a statement saying she had found the secretary crying in the women's restroom on two occasions, saying that the behavior of Mr. Powers was upsetting her.

Comments of Employee

Mr. Powers refused to provide a written statement. When interviewed by the panel, he refused to answer most questions by saying he didn't remember or wasn't aware. When pressed, he said words to the effect that he was sorry his behavior was misunderstood and that he thought the secretary was mutually interested in him.

Mr. Powers added that he is not the only man in the office who finds the secretary attractive, and because he recently broke up with a longtime girlfriend he has been lonely and under stress. He apologized for the incident and said he realizes how it might disturb the woman. He was not sure what kind of disciplinary action he would find appropriate. But he did mention that if perhaps the secretary did not dress in a provocative way, he would not react as he did.

Action to be Taken

Mr. Powers signed an apology to the secretary and an acknowledgment that he is on indefinite probation. The secretary has been reassigned.

Time Line for Improvement

Within three months, Mr. Powers is required to attend a three-day program on sexual harassment and other boundary issues. Mr. Powers was also told that a follow-up meeting will be held three months from now, on June 17. If any infractions or offensive behaviors have occurred in that time, he will be dismissed.

Consequences

As required by our company's policies and procedures for employees, Mr. Powers signed a last-chance agreement that has notified him that his employment will be terminated if another complaint is received. The agreement was also signed by the director of human resources, and copies have been placed in the permanent file of Mr. Powers as well as of the secretary.

OTHER REPORTS

PART VI

Chapter 20

Inspection Reports and Situation Summaries

Inspection reports, which are also sometimes called situation summaries, are important in a variety of fields: agriculture, the restaurant business, and construction, to name just a few. When inspection reports are conducted by government agencies, they follow a well-defined format that includes interviews, data collection, and more. Whether you are inspecting a business for a group that performs oversight, or you are doing an in-house inspection of one of your company's own facilities, the purpose of the report is to provide documentation for the files and to make sure that proper steps are taken going forward. Some situations where such an inspection/situation report would be appropriate in a business environment include:

▶ After a product is delivered, a record should be made that notes if the right number of items was received, if the right items were received, and if the quality is acceptable.

▶ While a product is being manufactured and, particularly, before a delivery is made, the product should be inspected to make sure the specifications are being followed (for example, size or color) and that the quality is acceptable.

▶ On a construction or manufacturing site, the adequacy of the equipment and/or materials should be evaluated to make sure the desired result will be achieved.

▶ When the product will not be shipped (as in the case of a bridge, building, or sculpture installation), an inspection must be made on-site not only when the project is completed but also throughout the process.

Both a situation summary and an inspection report accomplish the same task: They summarize the state of a project and provide findings, deficiencies, and an outcome.

Step-by-Step Guide

In many cases, it is helpful to provide a form to those making the inspection before they leave for the site. That way they can make notes in a consistent way "on the spot" that can later be transcribed into a written report after their return. A writing structure called an "inverted pyramid" is used in the parts of the inspection report or situation summary, meaning that the sections of the report start out small and focused but increase in size and scope as data are gathered.

Step 1: Summarize your findings.

Here, as in other situations, it's useful to begin with an Executive Summary. The summary is a brief synopsis of what has been found out. It should be written based on the outcome. Stick to the facts; don't include your opinions. Try to keep this section to a sentence or two, or a paragraph at most. For example:

Department of Public Works

Bay City, Minnesota

Inspection Report

Alterations to Restore Mirror Lake

Repairs to and reconstruction of shoreline to restore Mirror Lake after it was drained by flood.

Except for some repairs to the walkway around the shoreline, the reconstruction of the shore of the lake and the strengthening of the area around the dam are complete. The lake can be filled in on April 1 as originally planned.

A summary statement immediately tells readers what they need to know when the job is complete.

Step 2: Provide information about the company/facility you examined.

In this section, you provide reviewers with a brief listing of the company you examined. If the facility has a number (a vendor number, an ID number, or other identifier) you would list it here. This section includes:

▶ Company name.

▶ Identifying number.

▶ Responsible official.

▶ Ownership details.

Step 3: Give the date and location of your inspection.

State the location of the inspection and the date it was conducted.

Step 4: List all those who participated.

Give the names, ID numbers, and job titles of anyone who participated. That includes you, anyone in your own group who assisted you, and members of the company or group that was being inspected and who gave you access and accompanied you.

Step 5: Describe the goals and objectives of your inspection.

This section describes the purpose of the inspection and the circumstances that led up to it. It isn't always straightforward; there may be more than one objective you are trying to achieve or bit of information for which you are looking. For instance:

This inspection was conducted to assess the work done to repair and shore up the dam around Mirror Lake. Because of the danger to surrounding communities should the dam collapse, inspectors were ordered to pay special attention to the quality of the repairs, the length of time they are likely to last, and surrounding structures to see if any more faults exist.

Step 6: Describe the inspection and what you found.

In this section you describe what you found as a result of your inspection. Details can be presented in the form of a list or table. If the extent of the information warrants, you can break the description into Findings and Deficiencies sections.

Findings typically begin with summary of the inspector's conclusions. ("The contractor has done an acceptable job.") This part of the report continues with conditions found at the site, which describes what the inspector noticed. If instructions have been followed, it is not necessary to detail exactly what has been done. You only have to say that the job been completed in an acceptable manner. When problems exist, they must be described in detail in the following section.

Inspections typically begin and end with brief conversations or meetings between inspectors and those whose facilities are being inspected. Brief descriptions of those opening and closing conferences are frequently included in inspection reports, and they would go in this section.

Opening Conference

Mention who attended the conference and what was discussed in advance of the inspection. Were those being inspected cooperative? Were there disagreements over what was to be inspected? State as much here.

Findings

The findings section should have two subsections: conditions found and deficiencies. In conditions found, the emphasis is on quality; attention should be given to the facility, to the items, and to the workmanship. A deficiency can be an unacceptable condition, work that needs to be done, or a missing item. In most cases, it is sufficient to briefly note that specifications have been met if this is the case. If there has been a deviation from specifications, however, each item that has not been properly done must be spelled out completely. Or if there was a reason to make a switch to a different kind of material, for example, that must also be thoroughly explained.

Deficiencies

Account for deficiencies. What is included in the deficiency list will determine much of the outcome. In this section in particular, it is helpful to use the first person ("I") so that a strong and confident image will be conveyed. It is important to be a clear as possible about what action needs to be taken and who should be responsible for implementation and approval. If a client is involved, a procedure must be in place to communicate the results.

> Each deficiency that needs to be remedied is described clearly in a numbered list for easy reference.

Closing Conference

After the inspection has been conducted, those who met at the beginning should meet at the end to discuss what will happen next: Will a follow-up visit be required? When will the report be released?

Step 7: Assess outcome.

In the final section, an assessment is given on whether the work is acceptable and the job can be considered complete. Next steps are also listed, such as whether a follow-up inspection should be conducted, further repairs or changes need to be made, and so on.

Checklist

❑ Did you begin by summarizing your findings?

❑ Did you introduce the topic of your report completely?

❑ Does your report identify the company or organization being inspected?

❑ Did you list the date and location of the inspection?

❑ Did you list the participants by name?

❑ Does your report clearly state the inspection objective?

❑ Does your inspection description include findings and deficiencies?

❑ Did you describe opening and closing conferences, if they were held?

❑ Did you finish with an Outcome section that includes recommendations and follow-ups?

Template Inspection Report/Situation Summary

Executive Summary

Department of Public Works

Bay City, Minnesota

Inspection Report

Alterations to Restore Mirror Lake

Repairs to and reconstruction of shoreline to restore Mirror Lake after it was drained by flood.

Except for some repairs to walkway around the shoreline, the reconstruction of the shore of the lake and the strengthening of the area around the dam are complete. The lake can be filled in on April 1 as originally planned.

Company Background

Company Name:	Reliable Water Construction 1300 Water Street Poughkeepsie, New Jersey
ID Number:	Vendor No. 10-63972
Responsible Individual:	Mark Gradema, President
Ownership Details:	Reliable Water Construction was directly responsible but hired Northwest Cement of Camden, New Jersey as a subcontractor.

Date and Location of Inspection

Date of inspection:	March 25, 2010
Location of inspection:	North shore of Mirror Lake, at end of Route 32

Participants

Inspector:	Gary Wendeemus, City Inspector, City of Mirror Lake
Also present:	Jim Williams, City Manager, City of Mirror Lake
	Mark Gradema, President, Reliable Water Construction
	Julio Martinez, Crew Chief, Reliable Water Construction

Inspection Objectives

This inspection was conducted to assess the work done to repair and shore up the dam around Mirror Lake. Because of the danger to surrounding communities should the dam collapse, inspectors were ordered to pay special attention to the quality of the repairs, the length of time they are likely to last, and surrounding structures to see if any more faults exist.

Torrential rains caused Mirror Lake to overflow its banks on May 16, 2008. Although the dam held, the area just west of the dam was structurally inadequate and fell apart. All the water of the lake flowed into Muddy River. A contract for rebuilding the part of the lakewall that collapsed was awarded to Aqua Construction, Inc. on September 10. The contract detailed the work to be done and specified a completion date of April 1, 2009. The contractor informed the city on March 10 that the work was complete. I was ordered to inspect the worksite on March 16.

Inspection Summary

Opening Conference

An opening conference was held the morning of March 25. Those present are listed in the Participants section of this report with the exception of Jim Williams, who was not present for this meeting but who attended the inspection. We were shown a boat that we would take to the building site. We discussed the length of time the repairs took and the fact that the grade of cement had to be changed twice during the project when cracks developed. This bit of information raised concerns in my mind about the quality of earlier repairs. I asked the two contractors' representatives if the poor-quality cement used initially was removed completely before subsequent repairs were made.

In my judgment the president of Reliable was cooperative with questions and invited us to go to the site to inspect all stages of the repairs. We inspected from the shore and at the site itself, getting right up to the edge of the dam using the boat supplied by Reliable.

Findings

When we arrived at the site it became clear that several layers of repairs had been completed at several stages. The early repairs done with Grade 1 cement have a distinctive gray color that does not match the color of the original dam. Some of this gray cement was clearly visible above the water line. An underwater camera was used to view underneath, and I was pleased to see that none of the early cement was visible. Later repairs done with Grade 2 cement have a beige color that more closely resembles the dam, and this was visible under the water line where repairs are most important. Those repairs are judged to be acceptable.

Deficiencies

I noted several deficiencies that the contractor must remedy immediately.

1. The gap between the concrete wall and the dam plugged with silicone or another substance.
2. The top of the concrete wall needs to be smoothed out so it is suitable for pedestrians.
3. The walkway leading up to the dam needs to be cleaned and covered with gravel.
4. The lighting that was knocked out needs to be replaced.

Closing Conference

There was some discussion between Reliable and the inspectors about the extent of repairs we are ordering. They inquired as to why the walkway needs to be repaired, when that was not (as they claimed) part of the original job description. We said we would review the original description, and upon review, the walkway was not mentioned. Reliable will charge $2,500 for walkway repairs and we recommend they be completed even though this is an addition to the original budgeted expenses.

Outcome

The contractor has done an acceptable job. The area around the dam has been extended with a concrete wall 50 feet on either side. The surrounding soil has been replaced and sod has been planted. The quality of the work seems to be acceptable.

The preceding deficiencies will not prevent the mayor from holding the celebration on April 1, although the streetlamps should be replaced and the pavement should be smoothed out for safety reasons. Other deficiencies should be remedied before the lake is refilled with water.

My recommendation is that a second inspection be conducted before the contractor receives the final payment.

Gary Wendeemus

City Inspector

City of Mirror Lake

Chapter 21

Marketing Research Reports

For many businesses, marketing (the process of publicizing an organization in order to build goodwill and attract business) is a time-consuming and costly operation. A marketing report can serve several functions and take several forms. It can serve as a planning document, to describe marketing efforts in the coming year; it can report on a special publicity effort, such as the promotion of an open house or lecture; it can report on the amount spent on publicity; it can report on the types of marketing efforts that have been conducted in a particular time period, and how successful (or unsuccessful) they are.

The general types of plans you might need to create are:

▶ News releases.

▶ Feature stories.

▶ Budgets.

▶ Planning documents.

▶ Press clipping reports—examples of articles that mention your business.

▶ Public service announcements.

> Tip: If you want to gather press clippings, you might want to subscribe to one of the services that gather press clippings and send them to your company in print form.

Step-by-Step Guide

Step 1: Summarize your market research: what you found, and what you recommend.

An Executive Summary gives busy managers the most important parts of your report in a single paragraph. It's a good chance for you to quickly make your case for an improved marketing effort. For example:

An examination of the marketing efforts of the Messy Face Candy Company reveals that publicity strategies are stuck in the 1990s. The company needs to move to Facebook, Twitter, the Web, and blogs to reach a new generation of candy lovers for less than the cost of a ton of chocolate.

Step 2: Provide readers with background: how past publicity efforts have worked, and what problems remain.

Summarize the background that leads to your central findings. Explain in the next paragraph or two exactly how the topic in question has been dealt with in the past, what those results have been, and why earlier approaches did or didn't work. Building a new market research effort on failed former attempts is a great way to develop support for your efforts. For example:

In the past five years the Messy Face Candy Company has placed a total of 25 articles in local and national newspapers. Fifteen of these were in papers that cover the immediate three-county area. Two radio ads were produced. The company has developed a static and out-of-date Website that fails to gather more than a few hundred visits per month.

Here is an example of typical publicity efforts:

The president of Messy Face Company attended a church social held at the cozy cottage of Mr. and Mrs. Filbert. Proud parents that they were, they were bubbling over with enthusiasm for their daughter, Candace. On spring break at the time, Candace put in a personal appearance. Even a nonparental unit couldn't help noticing that Candace was as cute as a chocolate-covered cherry. And she was obviously very articulate, as well as full of energy and initiative. A public relations representative was assigned to prep Candace for her interview with a feature writer for the local newspaper, Woodward Bernstein. Mr. Bernstein arrived the next day. The public relations representative took numerous photographs and also videotaped the interview. This was excellent publicity, but it only lasted two days, and then it was gone. And the circulation of the local newspaper is no more than 8,000 people.

The problem: *Messy Face is losing business to larger candy companies, and people who grew up with the company have moved away. A new generation of sweet-toothed potential customers needs to find out about its offerings on the Internet.*

Step 3: Report on recent marketing efforts and trends.

The next section of your marekting report should address what you found as a result of your research. It's helpful to present different types of marketing options in an organized format with subheadings so it is easy to digest. Don't be afraid to use footnotes or citations to give the information credibility. You may also wish to include a short statement describing the methodology you used to conduct your market research.

Press Clippings

The Messy Face Candy Company placed 15 articles in local papers, including:

- *"New Easter Offerings Have Customers Hopping,"* Springfield Observer, *June 10, 2010, p. 4.*

- *"Chocolate Turns White for Holidays,"* New Solon Shopper, *July 22, 2010, p. 1.*

- *"Mother's Day Boxes Take on a New Face,"* Springfield Observer, *August 3, 2010, p. 10.*

- *"Messy Face Marks 25 Years in Booneville,"* Springfield Observer, *August 18, 2010, p. 2.*

- *"Candy Company Founders Started with Single Gumdrop,"* East Marine Chronicle, *August 22, 2010, p. 5.*

- *"Candymakers Continue to Employ Local Teens,"* New Solon Shopper, *September 20, 2010, p. 3.*

- *"Kids Flock to New Ice Cream Parlor at Messy Face,"* East Marine Chronicle, *October 17, 2010, p. 1.*

- *"When It Comes to Chocolate, Messy Face Has It Covered,"* Kenison Tribune, *November 1, 2010, p. 27.*

Publicity

In the past, Messy Face has relied on press releases for its publicity. The company issues a press release whenever a new line of candy has been created. Occasionally, around important holidays or days like Valentine's Day, a release will be issued to tell customers what is being offered. There is no guarantee that such releases will be picked up by the local media. On rare occasions they will be reposted by one of the larger metropolitan daily papers. But this is increasingly uncommon, especially given the shrinkage of the larger papers.

What Works

- *On average, 63% of press releases issued by the company have been accepted. It must be acknowledged that a certain amount of success has been achieved by Messy Face using its old-fashioned methods.*

- *Billboards located on the interstate highway are believed to draw in 100–200 out-of-town visitors per year, though this is difficult to quantify.*

- *Word of mouth, passed from one resident to another, is believed to be the most effective means of marketing the candy company.*

21. Marketing Research Reports

What Hasn't Worked

- *Attempts at getting the Web page to attract business seem not to be successful because the page has barely been undated in the past three months.*
- *A rare attempt at sending a video clip to a television station was virtually ignored.*

Trends

The trend these days is to create a Facebook page for a business and attract "fans." Facebook pages and Web pages can offer giveaways such as discount coupons to customers. The success of these efforts can be immediately calculated, as customers bring the coupons in to the business for redemption.

- *A new site called Groupon gives local consumers one deep discount per day on restaurants, spas, and other businesses.*
- *A revamped Website that is updated at least once every two to three days is a must have for any business, anywhere.*

Step 4: Describe options you recommend for new and more successful marketing.

In this section you present marketing recommendations that build on your report's introduction, background, and findings. Refute challenges that some might make to your conclusions by presenting the questions you would ask if you were in the reader's place. If you include "pros and cons" with your suggestions, this will show readers that you have looked at the subject from all angles and produced a market research report that is both comprehensive and analytical. For example:

- *Paying for advertising is pretty much a fact of life for any business. But what if you could spread goodwill and promote your business all at the same time without paying a penny? After all, it's much more effective to have someone else touting your wares than promoting your own goods and services. That's where you only have to remember two words: social networking. Getting your story published in one outlet is only the beginning. With just a little more effort on your part, your interest in your material has the potential snowball until you're potentially appearing online all the time. Consider the following press release created by the Messy Face Company located on Fingerlickin Island.*
- *If Messy Face could be covered on Groupon with 50% off a candy purchase, it would boost business considerably.*
- *A Website that includes graphics showing candy offered, and a way to purchase candy through an online catalog, would open the business up to potential customers from around the company.*
- *A Twitter feed from Messy Face would help to build community among local users and those who have moved away but remember the company fondly and want to keep in touch with this icon of the local economy.*

Step 5: Draw your conclusions and outline your marketing plan.

Readers of a marketing research report want to rely on a professional to make informed recommendations. In this final section, you present your recommendations in the form of a list and invite feedback and questions.

We suggest that future press releases should be written in the form of already-completed press releases like this example:

Sweet Tooth
Pays Off
for Student

CAMPUSTOWN, XY—When Candace Filbert left her beloved Fingerlickin Island, where she had been born and raised, to attend Brigadoon College, she was homesick. The only thing that would cheer her up was a care package prepared by her doting mother. Whatever else it contained, there was always an ample supply of specialty products created by Messy Face Candy Company.

"My college community was a virtual wasteland when it came to confection," said Ms. Filbert. "I'd have to hide my stash or it would disappear before I barely had time to unwrap it."

In fact, Messy Face Company has made Fingerlickin Island famous, according to the local chamber of commerce. "Of course we'd like folks to vacation here for weeks or even months," said Irving Potter, chamber president. "But a lot of time we get tourists who come over on the ferry just to buy Messy Face candy and then take the next boat back to the mainland. We call them 'Messes.'"

So Ms. Filbert didn't have a tough sell when she decided to open up a business selling Messy Face goodies. In fact, the business was built on some of her earlier failures. "Shelving books in the library put me to sleep and washing dishes in the cafeteria made me nauseous," said Ms. Filbert. "So I tried hydroponic gardening and pulling a rickshaw. But the candy is what has made it possible for me to pay my tuition bills."

Yet Ms. Filbert claims that it's not even all about the money. "I'm learning a lot about business," she says. "What's more, I'm not so homesick when I know I'll never run out of Messy Face Fudge."

Spin-Off Coverage

Once a press release has been placed in the campus newspaper as well as the daily on Fingerlickin Island, the Messy Face Candy Company public relations department can do several things to follow up:

- *Distribute the tear sheets to various other magazines and newspapers (along with a fresh sampler of the product). This way, local television stations can pick up the story.*

- *Post a video clip of a candy factory tour on YouTube.*
- *Create a fan page on Facebook.*
- *Create a special treat box with the Brigadoon College logo, suitable for including in a care package similar to the one that had kicked off the whole process.*
- *Create a WordPress blog in which Brigadoon students could vote for their favorite flavor, with a participant randomly selected once a week to receive one of the aforementioned treat boxes. Once a month a participant receives an all expenses paid weekend on Fingerlickin Island.*
- *The Websites of the island chamber of commerce, Messy Face Candy Company, and Brigadoon College should all have links to each other, as well as to the various social media sites.*
- *Candace Filbert should have her own Website where people can find out about her and how she started the company.*

Checklist

- ❑ Did you present an Executive Summary that includes your main conclusions and recommendations?
- ❑ Did you provide background information about past marketing efforts (and hopefully, how they can be improved)?
- ❑ Did you give examples of spin-off coverage?
- ❑ Did you present your findings?
- ❑ Did you list options for better marketing?
- ❑ Did you recommend a new marketing effort based on the background, research, and findings already presented?

Marketing Research Report Template

Executive Summary

An examination of the marketing efforts of the Messy Face Candy Company reveals that publicity strategies are stuck in the 1990s. The company needs to move to Facebook, Twitter, the Web, and blogs to reach a new generation of candy lovers for less than the cost of a ton of chocolate.

Background

In the past five years, the Messy Face Candy Company has placed a total of 25 articles in local and national newspapers. Fifteen of these were in papers that cover the immediate three-county area. Two radio ads were produced. The company has developed a static and out-of-date Website that fails to gather more than a few hundred visits per month.

Here is an example of typical publicity efforts: The president of Messy Face Company attended a church social held at the cozy cottage of Mr. and Mrs. Filbert. Proud parents that they were, they were bubbling over with enthusiasm for their daughter, Candace. On spring break at the time, Candace put in a personal appearance. Even a nonparental unit couldn't help noticing that Candace was as cute as a chocolate-covered cherry. And she was obviously very articulate, as well as full of energy and initiative. A public relations representative was assigned to prep Candace for her interview with a feature writer for the local newspaper, Woodward Bernstein. Mr. Bernstein arrived the next day. The public relations representative took numerous photographs and also videotaped the interview. This was excellent publicity, but it only lasted two days, and then it was gone. And the circulation of the local newspaper is no more than 8,000 people.

The problem: Messy Face is losing business to larger candy companies, and people who grew up with the company have moved away. A new generation of sweet-toothed potential customers needs to find out about its offerings on the Internet.

Findings

Press Clippings

The Messy Face Candy Company placed 15 articles in local papers, including:

- "New Easter Offerings Have Customers Hopping," *Springfield Observer*, June 10, 2010, p. 4.

- "Chocolate Turns White for Holidays," *New Solon Shopper*, July 22, 2010, p. 1.

- "Mother's Day Boxes Take on a New Face," *Springfield Observer*, August 3, 2010, p. 10.

- "Messy Face Marks 25 Years in Booneville," *Springfield Observer*, August 18, 2010, p. 2.

- "Candy Company Founders Started with Single Gumdrop," *East Marine Chronicle*, August 22, 2010, p. 5.

- "Candymakers Continue to Employ Local Teens," *New Solon Shopper*, September 20, 2010, p. 3.

- "Kids Flock to New Ice Cream Parlor at Messy Face," *East Marine Chronicle*, October 17, 2010, p. 1.

- "When It Comes to Chocolate, Messy Face Has It Covered," *Kenison Tribune*, November 1, 2010, p. 27.

Publicity

In the past, Messy Face has relied on press releases for its publicity. The company issues a press release whenever a new line of candy has been created. Occasionally, around important holidays or days like Valentine's Day, a release will be issued to tell customers what is being offered. There is no guarantee that such releases will be picked up by the local media. On rare occasions they will be reposted by one of the larger metropolitan daily papers. But this is increasingly uncommon, especially given the shrinkage of the larger papers.

What Works

- On average, 63% of press releases issued by the company have been accepted. It must be acknowledged that a certain amount of success has been achieved by Messy Face using its old-fashioned methods.

- Billboards located on the interstate highway are believed to draw in 100–200 out-of-town visitors per year, though this is difficult to quantify.

- Word of mouth, passed from one resident to another, is believed to be the most effective means of marketing the candy company.

What Hasn't Worked

- Attempts at getting the Web page to attract business seem not to be successful because the page has barely been undated in the past three months.

- A rare attempt at sending a video clip to a television station was virtually ignored.

Trends

The trend these days is to create a Facebook page for a business and attract "fans." Facebook pages and Web pages can offer giveaways such as discount coupons to customers. The success of these efforts can be immediately calculated, as customers bring the coupons in to the business for redemption.

+ A new site called Groupon gives local consumers one deep discount per day on restaurants, spas, and other businesses.

+ A revamped Website that is updated at least once every two to three days is a must have for any business, anywhere.

Options

Paying for advertising is pretty much a fact of life for any business. But what if you could spread goodwill and promote your business all at the same time without paying a penny? After all, it's much more effective to have someone else touting your wares than promoting your own goods and services. That's where you only have to remember two words: social networking. Getting your story published in one outlet is only the beginning. With just a little more effort on your part, your interest in your material has the potential snowball until you're potentially appearing online all the time. Consider the following press release created by the Messy Face Company located on Fingerlickin Island.

+ If Messy Face could be covered on Groupon with 50% off a candy purchase, it would boost business considerably

+ A Website that includes graphics showing candy offered, and a way to purchase candy through an online catalog, would open the business up to potential customers from around the company.

+ A Twitter feed from Messy Face would help to build community among local users and those who have moved away but remember the company fondly and want to keep in touch with this icon of the local economy.

Recommendations

Since a competing candy company in Lugston revamped its Website, candy sales have increased 30 percent last year. A graphic designer was hastily hired to design a range of products touting the candy, island, and college. Business has been brisk, both through brick and mortar stores at the three locations and online. The most striking benefit has been an increase in tourist visits to the island.

+ Tours of the candy factory are very popular and should be held every weekend.

+ A festival will be held at the end of May each year to celebrate the birthday of Candace Filbert.

+ Results of the voting on the blog have provided valuable marketing data.

+ The president of Messy Face Company has resolved to attend more church socials.

We also suggest that future press releases should be written in the form of already-completed press releases like this example:

Sweet Tooth
Pays Off
for Student

CAMPUSTOWN, XY—When Candy Filbert left her beloved Fingerlickin Island, where she had been born and raised, to attend Brigadoon College, she was homesick. The only thing that would cheer her up was a care package prepared by her doting mother. Whatever else it contained, there was always an ample supply of specialty products created by Messy Face Candy Company.

"My college community was a virtual wasteland when it came to confection," said Ms. Filbert. "I'd have to hide my stash or it would disappear before I barely had time to unwrap it."

In fact, Messy Face Company has made Fingerlickin Island famous, according to the local chamber of commerce. "Of course we'd like folks to vacation here for weeks or even months," said Irving Potter, chamber president. "But a lot of time we get tourists who come over on the ferry just to buy Messy Face candy and then take the next boat back to the mainland. We call them 'Messes.'"

So Ms. Filbert didn't have a tough sell when she decided to open up a business selling Messy Face goodies. In fact, the business was built on some of her earlier failures. "Shelving books in the library put me to sleep and washing dishes in the cafeteria made me nauseous," said Ms. Filbert. "So I tried hydroponic gardening and pulling a rickshaw. But the candy is what has made it possible for me to pay my tuition bills."

Yet Ms. Filbert claims that it's not even all about the money. "I'm learning a lot about business," she says. "What's more, I'm not so homesick when I know I'll never run out of Messy Face Fudge."

Spin-Off Coverage

Once a press release has been placed in the campus newspaper as well as the daily on Fingerlickin Island, the Messy Face Candy Company public relations department can do several things to follow up:

- Distribute the tear sheets to various other magazines and newspapers (along with a fresh sampler of the product). This way, local television stations can pick up the story.
- Post a video clip of a candy factory tour on YouTube.
- Create a fan page on Facebook.
- Create a special treat box with the Brigadoon College logo, suitable for including in a care package similar to the one that had kicked off the whole process.

- Create a WordPress blog in which Brigadoon students could vote for their favorite flavor, with a participant randomly selected once a week to receive one of the aforementioned treat boxes. Once a month a participant receives an all-expenses-paid weekend on Fingerlickin Island.

- The Websites of the island chamber of commerce, Messy Face Candy Company, and Brigadoon College should all have links to each other, as well as to the various social media sites.

- Candy Filbert should have her own Website where people can find out about her and how she started the company.

Chapter 22

Liability Reports

Of all the examples in this book, the liability report can have the most extreme significance for a business because it can involve legal actions and possible financial settlements or fines. Those who might be called upon to prepare a liability report include:

▶ Production or traffic managers.

▶ Drivers or operators.

▶ Inspectors before the accident.

▶ Inspectors after the accident.

It is a serious matter when equipment is damaged or destroyed. The prospect of litigation is frightening. But nothing is more important than preserving the health and welfare of workers. Liability reports must be complete, clear, and true.

Developing and using a standardized form is a good way to ensure that various critical questions are answered by your report. It is vital that an account of what happened be presented in a way that allays suspicion and serves as a reference. Responsibility should be assigned in a matter-of-fact way without dwelling on blame or judgment. But it is most crucial that the contents of the report contribute to preventing a similar tragedy in the future.

Even directly following the incident, notes should be readable and without abbreviation. What is evident in the moment will be hard to follow as time goes on. In many cases, a sketch map should be made at the scene. If the weather is bad or materials aren't available, this document must be produced as soon as possible.

Step-by-Step Guide

Step 1: Begin with a synopsis of damage done.

Do not spare the details on both permanent features of the scene and components that are artificial and/or temporary. Statements should be gathered from all involved in the incident, as well as from witnesses. Interviews should be conducted immediately. As soon as possible, formal text should be typed and then signed and dated with the time that the signature was affixed. For example:

> This report is an addendum to the Illinois Motorist Report (HP 216892) from Rose Lebovitz, 5985 S. Greenwood Ave., Chicago, IL 60637, regarding collision of delivery truck (owned by our company, Daring Delivery Services, and driven by our employee Stanley Taylor) and a privately owned car (driven by Abigail Ducharme) at Main and 8th Streets, prepared by Homer Conover, head investigator of Daring Delivery Services. Mr. Taylor is claiming injury to his neck and emotional trauma. Representatives of Ms. Ducharme's insurance company claim that Mr. Taylor was at fault for the accident. Ms. Ducharme is not claiming physical or emotional injury.

Step 2: Outline facts as clearly and objectively as possible.

It's helpful to begin this section with a list stating the location and time of the incident for which your company may be liable. Then, briefly state the who, what, where, when, why, and how of the incident. If you can, do as much primary research as possible by visiting the scene, taking photos, and interviewing witnesses. If you are conducting your report well after the fact, photos are still valuable, but you may need to conduct secondary research, and review and report on police and news accounts of the incident.

> Date of incident: Sept. 10, 2009
>
> Location: Main and 8th Streets, Mirror Lake
>
> Time of incident: 8:30 a.m.
>
> Individuals involved: Stanley Taylor, Melanie Ducharme
>
> When I arrived on the scene at approximately 8:30 am, 3-10-09, Mr. Taylor was loudly berating Ms. Ducharme. There had been no broken glass, and both vehicles could be driven away. The left-hand front of the delivery truck had scraped the passenger side of the car. No tickets were issued by police.

Step 3: Provide additional background that may have bearing on the case.

Take a step back from the incident. Do research to investigate any circumstances that may have caused the incident or had a bearing. If it is a traffic accident, is the intersection clearly marked? Are there stop signs all around? What was the weather when the incident occurred? If it is an industrial accident, are there previous accidents that are similar? Were there complaints leading up to the incident? Think like the lawyers who may sue your company; they will do the same investigation and try to come up with the same questions. At the very least, you need to be ready for such questions. At best, you may be able to come up with reasons why your company or organization is not liable for what occurred.

> *Mr. Taylor admits he was late making a delivery. He came out of a parking lot, which is why Ms. Ducharme didn't see him when she first checked her side-view mirror. However, he claims he had a right to be in his lane and that he hit Ms. Ducharme because she swerved to avoid the other truck. He later claimed he was injured. However, even if Mr. Taylor was at fault, it should also be noted that the intersection has a history of traffic accidents (12 previous ones this year) and should be reconfigured for better safety.*

Step 4: Provide statements of witnesses.

As you have learned in previous chapters (such as Chapter 6 on Research Reports), primary research is best if you are able to conduct it. When possible liability is involved, it's especially important to gather witness statements. That way, your conclusions aren't based either on opinion or on secondhand information.

Each witness should start at the beginning by identifying his or her position and any other relevant details. Then evidence should be explained in chronological order with an indication of the passing of time when possible. Begin with the name of the witness or participant, his address and occupation, and his position in the company if he is on staff. Hearsay and colloquialisms should be avoided. Be sure that all persons mentioned are referred to with their first initial and surname. It is not appropriate to use first names or nicknames because disciplinary or legal proceedings may be forthcoming. Be sure to differentiate between fact and opinion. If expert opinion is included, credentials and status must also be noted. All interviews should be conducted in formal and official ways. For example:

> *Three witnesses were reported by the police, and I was able to contact all three and talk to each in person, either by phone or on a visit to the person's home. Humes reported that she was standing at the northwest corner of Main and 8th when the accident occurred. She said the weather was clear, and Taylor was backing out of the light. She believes it is impossible for anyone backing out of the lot to see traffic proceeding down Main Street.*

Step 5: Based on evidence, give judgment on who was at fault.

Supplement any witness statements with police reports, news reports, or other items that are pertinent to the case. Then, taking all statements and reports into account, draw your informed conclusions.

My conclusion is that Mr. Taylor could have avoided the accident because he knew what Ms. Ducharme was doing and could see that she was avoiding the other truck. It should have been clear to Mr. Taylor that Ms. Ducharme wasn't aware of his presence until she heard and felt his truck scraping her car. She was not playing music or talking on the cell phone, so she would have heard his horn if he had honked it. There was not even much of a jolt because they were going so very slowly.

Step 6: Assess what action needs to be taken, including payments to be made.

If you are not liable, state as much, and recommend what response or statements need to be made to those who are questioning whether or not your company is liable for the incident. If you are liable, make a suggestion of appropriate compensation. For example:

Based on the evidence I have gathered, the insurance company of Ms. Ducharme is within its rights to expect our insurance company to pay for the repair of her car. Our insurance company will also be advised that they should pay for the damage to our truck. When sick leave accrued by Mr. Taylor runs out, he will be told that any further time off will be taken without pay. Our medical insurance will cover any medical or therapy bills he has accrued, but he will be responsible for the copay and for any further treatment.

Step 7: Conclude with suggestions for further action to be taken.

If any further actions need to be taken with regard to the incident, recommend them here. For example:

If Mr. Taylor wants to return to work, I suggest that he be given a desk job. My fear is that he is emotionally unstable, and that he has conjured up these charges to take advantage of the situation. I highly recommend that he be given very strict guidelines for conduct that is expected in the office, and that his work be monitored closely. Documentation should be on file if he displays attitude problems or does not choose to produce work of satisfactory quality. My guess is that he will quit in frustration over the close supervision or that we will soon be able to accrue evidence that will make it possible to fire him with sufficient cause.

Checklist

☐ Did you provide an assessment of damage done and give a quick review of situation?

☐ Did you outline facts as clearly and objectively as possible?

☐ Did provide additional background that may have bearing on the case?

☐ Did you, based on evidence, give judgement on who was at fault?

☐ Did you assess what action needs to be taken, including payments to be made?

☐ Did you make suggestions for further action to be taken?

22. Liability Reports

Liability Report Template

Description of Damage

This report is an addendum to the Illinois Motorist Report (HP 216892) from Rose Lebovitz, 5985 S. Greenwood Ave., Chicago, IL 60637, regarding collision of delivery truck (owned by our company, Daring Delivery Services, and driven by our employee Stanley Taylor) and a privately owned car (driven by Abigail Ducharme) at Main and 8th streets, prepared by Homer Conover, head investigator of Daring Delivery Services. Mr. Taylor is claiming injury to his neck and emotional trauma. Representatives of Ms. Ducharme's insurance company claim that Mr. Taylor was at fault for the accident. Ms. Ducharme is not claiming physical or emotional injury.

Presentation of Facts

Date of incident: Sept. 10, 2009

Location: Main and 8th Streets, Mirror Lake

Time of incident: 8:30 a.m.

Individuals involved: Stanley Taylor, Melanie Ducharme

When I arrived on the scene at approximately 8:30 am, 3-10-09, Mr. Taylor was loudly berating Ms. Ducharme. There had been no broken glass, and both vehicles could be driven away. The left-hand front of the delivery truck had scraped the passenger side of the car. No tickets were issued by police.

The intersection is where two one-way streets meet (Main going south and 8th going west). Main in effect dead-ends into 8th, which is divided going around a high-rise apartment building. There is a stop sign at each corner. Although Main is one-way southbound, it is effectively a single lane because it is narrow with cars parked on both sides (especially when there are some piles of snow still remaining). There is no parking by the intersection, so it is possible for two cars to turn at once (The usual practice is for cars to wait patiently in single file and not try to get in front of each other; 8th has two (unmarked) lanes going in each direction, but it is confusing there because the lanes are not marked for two cars to be turning at the same time and because folks are coming around curves; you have to cross over both lanes and turn left after a short distance in order to turn right to proceed south on Main.

Ms. Ducharme lives only a few blocks from the accident, and claims she had brushed the snow off her windows before starting out. She reports that she came to a complete stop at the stop sign and waited her turn because there was quite a line-up of cars going westbound on 8th. After she waited for a pedestrian, she says another truck driver did not yield to her, even though she clearly had the right of way. That is what she was intending to do; judging by the damage to her car, she was already well into her turn. She assumes she was staying to the left even as she was slowly turning right. She admits that her attention was focused on the other truck in the intersection and she did not double-check her side-view mirror at the last minute to realize that Mr. Taylor had come up quickly behind her and then was trying to pass her on the right. So the result was that Mr. Taylor, despite being a professional driver, sideswiped Ms. Ducharme while trying to cut her off.

Mitigating Circumstances

It was a cold and gray day, with some icy drizzle and a few actual snowflakes. There was still snow from the last storm piled against the curb.

Mr. Taylor admits he was late making a delivery. He came out of a parking lot, which is why Ms. Ducharme didn't see him when she first checked her side-view mirror. However, he claims he had a right to be in his lane and that he hit Ms. Ducharme because she swerved to avoid the other truck. He later claimed he was injured. However, even if Mr. Taylor was at fault, it should also be noted that the intersection has a history of traffic accidents (12 previous ones this year) and should be reconfigured for better safety.

Witness Statements

Three witnesses were reported by the police, and I was able to contact all three and talk to each, either by phone or on a visit to the person's home:

> Marian Humes, 1124 W. Belmont
>
> Jerilynn Maxwell, 1700 W. Fletcher
>
> Mickey Zippi, 3860 N. Clark

- ◆ Marian Humes reported that she was standing at the northwest corner of Main and 8th when the accident occurred. She said the weather was clear, and Taylor was backing out of the lot. She believes it is impossible for anyone backing out of the lot to see traffic proceeding down Main Street.

- ◆ Jerilynn Maxwell was a passenger in Ms. Ducharme's car. She reports that Ms. Ducharme honked her horn but the truck did not seem to notice and backed into them. She adds that they were trapped by surrounding traffic and could not get out the way.

- ◆ Mickey Zippi was a customer in a nearby Starbuck's coffee shop. He said the truck did signal to move and he thinks the truck honked. He did not notice Ms. Ducharme's car honking.

Statement of Responsibility

My conclusion is that Mr. Taylor could have avoided the accident because he knew what Ms. Ducharme was doing and could see that she was avoiding the other truck. It should have been clear to Mr. Taylor that Ms. Ducharme wasn't

22. Liability Reports

aware of his presence until she heard and felt his truck scraping her car. She was not playing music or talking on the cell phone, so she would have heard his horn if he had honked it. There was not even much of a jolt because they were going so very slowly.

Compensation

Based on the evidence I have gathered, the insurance company of Ms. Ducharme is within its rights to expect our insurance company to pay for the repair of her car. Our insurance company will also be advised that they should pay for the damage to our truck. When sick leave accrued by Mr. Taylor runs out, he will be told that any further time off will be taken without pay. Our medical insurance will cover any medical or therapy bills he has accrued, but he will be responsible for the copay and for any further treatment.

Recommendations

If Mr. Taylor wants to return to work, I suggest that he be given a desk job. My fear is that he is emotionally unstable, and that he has conjured up these charges to take advantage of the situation. I highly recommend that he be given very strict guidelines for conduct that is expected in the office, and that his work be monitored closely. Documentation should be on file if he displays attitude problems or does not choose to produce work of satisfactory quality. My guess is that he will quit in frustration over the close supervision or that we will soon be able to accrue evidence that will make it possible to fire him with sufficient cause.

Chapter 23

Annual Report

The concept of the annual report began to form in the middle of the 19th century, and things have changed a lot since then. It's still true that the basic idea is that once a year a corporation, nonprofit, or government unit summarizes activities. This document is, in effect, an accounting to various publics how funds have been managed. But ways to distribute information and the groups of readers who might be interested have expanded. Labor unions and governmental entities have become very powerful. Other factions who believe they should have a say, in addition to stockholders, might include customers and community members. The last thing a company or organization wants to convey is the notion that something is being held back. Therefore the current philosophy is to tell as many people as possible as much as possible.

If your group is a nonprofit, your annual report may include an honor roll of last year's donors and will certainly provide information to make it easy to make further donations. Readers also want to be entertained. Writers are often hired to cover topics of interest to all possible audiences, making the annual report a major part of the public relations program of most corporations. Graphic designers and photographers make sure the report looks as good as it sounds, being appealing as well as informative. The approval process is formidable, with care being taken to present the group in the best possible light even as accuracy is checked to make sure both text and numbers are reliable. Far from being just page after page of charts and numbers, the effective annual report will be a coffeetable publication that warms the heart as it assures the reader of fiscal responsibility.

Some of the following components may be included:

▶ Wages and fringe benefits for workers.

▶ Lists of trustees, officers, and staff with highlights of significant new hires and promotions.

▶ Products, including research and development on new products.

> ▸ Overall policies, such as steps to improve environmental impact.

> ▸ Prizes and awards won by the company and/or individual staff members.

> ▸ Construction projects completed or approved.

> ▸ Financial statements of profit and losses.

> ▸ A letter from the president or top executive.

Other reports in this book may focus on analysis and problem-solving. The annual report, on the other hand, is likely to stick more closely to facts. But annual reports are important to an organization for many reasons. They inform shareholders; they reassure board members; they can boost a company's image among the general public.

Note: If your organization depends on outside funding, an effective annual report can directly affect the amount of support you receive. Show that investors' dollars are being used in a judicious way.

Step-by-Step Guide

Step 1: Give your company or organization's name, year, address, phone, Website, etc.

Because this is just introductory material designed to be presented either on the front or back covers or a title page, you should keep the information to a minimum. Subsequent sections will present your organization's mission and other important information. For example:

> *Society for Children Inc.*
> *1234 S. Main St., Suite 999*
> *Wonderland, CA 26262*
> *tel. 630.639.4289*
> *fax 630.879.2108*
> *societyforchildren@abcglobal.org*
> *www.societyforchildren.org*
> *Annual Report*
> *Fiscal year 2008–09 Annual Report: July 1, 2008, to June 30, 2009*
> *"We never met a child we didn't like."*

> Note: Many annual reports are presented in the form of a booklet, often printed on glossy paper and in color. Consider spending the money to achieve the best presentation possible.

Step 2: Identify your organization by its core values.

Include your company's or organization's mission statement. If you don't have one already, you should strongly consider coming up with a one-paragraph statement of your core values. It is a useful communications tool for employees, investors, and the general public. For example:

The mission of Society for Children Inc. is to provide the best quality of life possible for children in need throughout the world. We seek to provide services that rise above the competition in regard to treating the whole child: physical, emotional, and spiritual. Recognizing that many children cannot afford to pay to allieviate their suffering, we sponsor many fundraisers to make sure benevolence monies are available. We will turn away no child in need.

Step 3: Include a personal letter from the director, chair, or president.

Nearly all annual reports contain a greeting from the person who heads the organization. This communication is usually in the form of a letter. It should serve as a friendly greeting to all constituents, and it should refer to recent significant developments or highlights. The letter should take a positive tone and acknowledge difficulties while not dwelling on them. Most such letters finish on a positive note and look forward to future efforts to further the group's mission. For example:

Dear Friends,

As many of you know, I have not yet completed my first full year as the director of Society for Children. Although I knew this position would be challenging when I was hired last July, I could never have anticipated the highs and lows that have made up the last fiscal year. The changes in the economy present us with needs we could not have anticipated.

Clearly, there is no place like the organization that I now head. I ask that you read the pages that follow with an open mind, an open heart, and, most importantly, an open wallet. We are proud of our accomplishments and hope that you will celebrate with us all that we have done to forward our cause. But truly the trees are yet heavy with fruit that is ripe for the plucking. All we need are the tools to bring in the harvest. Please learn all you can from the information that is presented for your edification and enjoyment. And then join us in our efforts to move forward the cause of the children in need around the world.

Sincerely,

Sheila Jordon
Executive Director

Step 4: Draw up a table of contents.

This section, although optional, will help readers navigate to the most important contents. It is especially important for reports that are five to six pages or more in length. For example:

Table of Contents

> *1 Mission Statement*
>
> *2. Message from the Executive Director*
>
> *3. History*
>
> *4. Profile*
>
> *5. Highlights of the Year*
>
> *6. Financial Statements*
>
> *7. Awards and Grants*
>
> *8. Personnel*
>
> *9. Future Plans*

Step 5: Include relevant construction projects, awards, and other news.

Summarize the year's events for your shareholders, board members, and other interested parties. This is where your organization needs to "blow its own horn." Any awards, accomplishments, workshops, new products, technical advances, new facilities, or any positive developments need to be mentioned. Photos would be helpful wherever possible. For example:

New Hope in Preventing Child Obesity

With a generous grant from Farmers Markets Association, a study was conducted to prevent child obesity. The reassuring finding is that the concept of child obesity has been overfed by infused statistics. A simple change of diet is recommended by most physicians in order to prevent obesity. A farmer's market held outside our corporate headquarters attracted attention from local media and called attention to the need for better nutrition among children.

Secretary Awarded Prize
for Child Compassion

As a first person encountered when a child enters our facility, Amelia Boggart was overwhelmingly voted our most popular employee. Testimonials were obtained via exit interviews as well as on our popular blog. We congratulate Ms. Boggart on this well-deserved recognition.

23. Annual Reports

Off-Site Facility to Offer
Neighborhood Support

Although we are always looking for ways to increase traffic into our main headquarters, it has become increasingly clear that we need to take our services to the streets where children actually live when they are in foster care or in need of specialized medical attention. We are excited to have broken ground for our first satellite clinic, which will make it possible to treat the formerly untreatable.

Step 6: Provide a financial statement of profit and loss.

Statement of Activities

Total Assets $250,000
    Current Assets $200,000
    Property and Eqiupment $50,000
Total Liabilities $25,000
Revenue Sources
    Service Fees $500,000
    Donations $75,000
    Total $575,000
Expenses
    Programs $700,000
    Administration $60,000
    Total $760,000

Step 7: List any awards and grants your organization received.

This section may not be relevant for a for-profit company or corporation. But if you are preparing an annual report for a nonprofit group, it's essential to recognize donors and other funding sources. Giving those who support you proper recognition is essential for your future success:

Awards
    Felicia Biddlebrook Award for Child Welfare ($19,000)
    Child Welfare League of America ($25,000)
Grants
    MacArthur Foundation Fellowship ($100,000)
    UNESCO Grant ($59,000)
    City of Middle Lake Foster Care Program ($5,000)

23. Annual Reports

Adoption Promotion League ($3,850)

Step 8: List trustees, officers, and staff, with notation of significant new hires and promotions.

This section, too, is optional, but publicizing the names of the directors in your organization puts a personal face on the group and lets people know who to contact if they have donations to make or questions of importance.

Executive Director	*Shiela Jordon*
Chairman of Board	*Rachel Griffiths*
Board Members	*Howard Grant*
	Ernest Pyle
	Leticia Mortenson
	Kathy Jacobs
	Emilio Casanova

Step 9: Describe your future plans.

Take a look forward to the next 12 months, and briefly outline your goals and objections. Do you seek new sources of funding? Do you have new projects you are undertaking? Are you breaking ground on a new building? This is the place to describe such projects.

Checklist

❏ On the title page, did you indicate name, year, address, phone, Website, and so on?

❏ Did you identify your organization by its core values, including your mission statement?

❏ Did you obtain, or ghostwrite with approval, a personal letter from the director, chair, or president?

❏ Did you make newsbriefs to highlight relevant construction projects, awards, and other news?

❏ Did you provide a financial statement of profit and loss?

❏ Did you list major awards and grants received, if applicable?

❏ Did you list trustees, officers, and staff, with notation of significant new hires and promotions?

❏ Did you make an effort to describe your organization's future plans?

Annual Report Template

Introduction

Society for Children, Inc.

1234 S. Main St., Suite 999

Wonderland, CA 26262

tel. 630.639.4289

fax 630.879.2108

societyforchildren@abcglobal.org

www.societyforchildren.org

Annual Report

Fiscal year 2008–09 Annual Report: July 1, 2008 to June 30, 2009

"We never met a child we didn't like."

Printed April 2010

Table of Contents

1 Mission Statement

2. Message from the Executive Director

3. History

4. Profile

5. Highlights of the Year

7. Financial Statements

8. Awards and Grants

9. Roster

10. Future Plans

Message from the Executive Director

Dear Friends,

As many of you know, I have not yet completed my first full year as the director of Society for Children. Although I knew this position would be challenging when I was hired last July, I could never have anticipated the highs and lows that have made up the last fiscal year. The changes in the economy present us with needs we could not have anticipated.

Clearly, there is no place like the organization that I now head. The Society for Children has expanded its operations to 24 countries on four continents, and is expanding all the time. Children face new challenges of hunger, poverty, and loss of parents through illnesses such as AIDS, political persecution, imprisonment, or other causes.

I ask that you read the pages that follow with an open mind, an open heart, and, most importantly, an open wallet. We are proud of our accomplishments and hope that you will celebrate with us all that we have done to forward our cause. But truly the trees are yet heavy with fruit that is ripe for the plucking. All we need are the tools to bring in the harvest. Please learn all you can from the information that is presented for your edification and enjoyment. And then join us in our efforts to move forward the cause of the children in need around the world.

Sincerely,

Sheila Jordon

Executive Director

Financial Statement

Statement of Activities

Total Assets	$250,000	
Current Assets		$200,000
Property and Eqiupment		$50,000
Total Liabilities	$25,000	
Revenue Sources		
Service Fees		$500,000
Donations		$75,000
Total		$575,000
Expenses		
Programs		$700,000
Administration		$60,000
Total		$760,000

Awards and Grants

Awards

Felicia Biddlebrook Award for Child Welfare ($19,000)

Child Welfare League of America ($25,000)

Grants

MacArthur Foundation Fellowship (100,000)

UNESCO Grant ($59,000)

City of Middle Lake Foster Care Program ($5,000)

Adoption Promotion League ($3,850)

Personnel

Executive Director	Shiela Jordon
Chairman of Board	Rachel Griffiths
Board Members	Howard Grant
	Ernest Pyle
	Leticia Mortenson
	Kathy Jacobs
	Emilio Casanova
Chief Executive Officer	Ronald Coleman
Chief Financial Officer	Theda Bara
Chief Technical Officer	Leon Marx

Future Plans

In the coming 12-month period, the Society for Children looks forward with great anticipation. We plan to open offices in three new countries: in Beijing, China; Kuala Lumpur, Malaysia; and Lima, Peru.

We plan to initiate a program of child nutrition throughout the world, in conjunction with renowned television chef Jamie Oliver, who has a television show urging American children to change their diets and reduce obesity.

We are scheduled to address a Congressional committee discussing the welfare of children who are being adopted from other countries, such as Russia, in light of recent controversial adoption cases.

Chapter 24

Investigative Reports

You may automatically get anxious when you look at the title of this chapter. If an investigation is necessary, it often means that something bad has happened. Indeed, in this electronic age, the types of incidents requiring a report rarely are of a cat-stuck-in-a-tree nature. Indeed, some businesses need to have ongoing surveillance measures in place, ranging from a security camera on the parking lot to software of their employees' computers to detect unacceptable activity. You don't need me to tell you that people are poised to sue at the drop of a hat. So if, knock on wood, you are in the position of needing to do a report for a serious problem, the first step would be to consult an attorney. But that said, there are still guidelines to keep on the backburner of your mind. So I offer a more tongue-in-cheek example, not to make light of a serious situation but to outline the ways to proceed. The general steps apply, after all, no matter what the circumstance. Though some of the other reports included in this book are, in effect, written anonymously, the investigative report may have a large number of contributors, including:

▶ Those with viewpoints that are different from one another.

▶ Witnesses.

▶ A chairperson.

Investigative reports can be very complex. Frequently the subject has wide-ranging philosophical and moral implications. One of the first major challenges might be to restrict the area of the investigation. Often there is a time pressure, causing the turn-around time to be very brief. Another goal is to set a schedule that includes a process for requesting an extension. To produce the text, often there are interviews of witnesses or participants. Analysis may be provided by various experts.

Step-by-Step Guide

Step 1: Give a brief description of the incident.

Although many investigative reports are ordered as a result of a single significant incident, they may also be called upon to examine a series of events or a trend that is occurring. In any case, begin with a brief overview of the subject you are investigating. Here, as in other reports, it's important to put your personal reactions aside and stick to the facts of the situation—the who, what, where, when, why, and how of what happened. Be sure to mention:

▶ The date of the event.

▶ The location of the event.

▶ The time of the event.

▶ What happened.

▶ Who was affected.

Here is an example:

> *Located in the midst of thousands of acres of gently swaying corn fields, Tipsytown rarely is the center of anything. The third Saturday of May was no exception. Some folks had come into town for their weekly shopping. A group of committed volunteers was putting up bunting in preparation for Memorial Day remembrances. Suddenly a crowd converged on the village green. They arrived from all directions via car, truck, motorcycle, skateboard, and rollerblade. Within moments, they had formed an orderly line. With no apparent leader, they marched three times around the courthouse, chanting "Where's the beef?" And then, as quickly as they had arrived, they vanished, leaving not a trace.*

Step 2: Identify concerns that were raised.

By its nature, an investigation involves controversy. Often, the subject being discussed is contentious. Other times, an incident occurred that affected people. Any trends or incidents that led up to the incident, or any protests and questions that were raised by what happened, should be listed here. Be sure to answer questions such as:

▶ Who discovered what happened?

▶ Who reported the incident?

▶ Who was the first person on the scene?

▶ How did emergency personnel respond?

▶ Was the response well-coordinated? Slow? Efficient?

For example:

> *Although a few excitable citizens started spreading false rumors about Tipsytown being under siege by a peculiar strain of terrorists, hardly any level-headed person would have concluded that there was immediate danger. It was possible that the group had come to gather information and would return to cause havoc at a future date. But our main concern was to determine who our short-term visitors were, why they had chosen Tipsytown, and what we could do to get them to spend money they next time they came to Tipsytown.*

24. Investigative Reports

Step 3: Summarize what was done immediately after incident.

Sometimes, the reaction or response to an incident is as significant and problematic as the event itself. Be sure to describe the initial response to the event or sequence of events you are investigating. Are notification procedures adequate, or do they need improvement? Your investigation should answer this question, if applicable:

A siren was sounded to summon our volunteer fire department, and one generous citizen, who prefers to be anonymous, paid Bobby Sears $5 to pedal on his bicycle as fast as he could to summon the sheriff. Mostly folks came out of the stores, barber/beauty shop, and restaurants to ask each other, "Did you see that?" Because the marchers had left without a trace, there was no evidence to be collected on the scene.

Step 4: Give an overview of your information-gathering methods.

After describing the incident, in this section you discuss your own investigation and how it was conducted. Mention who commissioned your report, and how many people, if any, assisted you with it. Also describe the investigative methods you used—whether you were able to conduct personal interviews and a personal observation of the effects of what happened, or whether you are relying on secondhand sources such as news reports. For example:

This report was written by a committee composed in haste by the chamber of commerce of Tipsytown. As luck would have it, a quorum of the chamber of commerce had already gathered for mid-afternoon refreshments at the Brew 'n' Stew Pub, conveniently located on the corner of the village green. After brief consultation, we chose as our chairman Rodney Reed. Actually Mr. Reed was vehemently alarmed by the proceedings and had already begun his own investigation before we caught up with him. As one of the citizens who had been pinning bunting to the courthouse door, he had a personal stake in the event. As soon as he could get down from his ladder, he chased after the participants. The misfortune of one marcher, who had fallen off his skateboard and sprained his ankle, was our good fortune because it allowed him to be caught. Mr. Reed was unable to get much information out of him, however, as he was mostly moaning in pain. Finally Mr. Reed delivered him to the emergency room after receiving only a vague mention about receiving a posting on an Internet blog.

Step 5: Indicate witnesses and other persons of interest who were contacted and what was learned from interviews.

Interviews with witnesses form an important part of many reports that examine events after they occurred. An investigation is no exception. The focus here, however, is different than with an Incident Report. In an investigative report, you don't necessarily interview witnesses. You talk to anyone who has knowledge of the subject and its effect on people. In the case of a company whose toxic waste emissions allegedly caused illness in the surrounding community, you would speak to alleged victims, doctors, scientists, and representatives of the company itself, as well as officials in the municipality where the emissions took place.

Mr. Reed then returned to the village square to interview other eyewitnesses. Some had already retired to the aforementioned Brew 'n' Stew and claimed no knowledge of the event. Mrs. Muriel Booker was still on the bench where Mr. Reed had observer her throughout the proceedings. She, however, claimed no knowledge of what had happened and became quite indignant at being woken up from "a nice long nap."

Step 6: Provide a wrap-up of information, putting details into context.

In this section, you pull all of the data you gathered together and draw conclusions based on comments and conditions observed either firsthand or from reliable sources.

Ultimately the mystery was solved by the nephew of a committee member, who muttered "flash mob" as he walked past a meeting in progress that was being held in his uncle's living room. A subcommittee was formed to ask the computer teacher at the high school to do further research. It was determined that there is little hope of assembling the same group in the future. The conclusion was also reached that "Where's the beef?" was a phrase that was picked at random by the organizers of the event. For that matter, Tipsytown itself was chosen only because it had a village green and a fine courthouse to march around.

Step 7: List suggestions for remedial action to be taken.

If actions need to be taken to compensate victims or prevent similar incidents from occurring in future, you should recommend them here. You have authority to make suggestions based on your research and your knowledge of what occurred.

Because it is so remarkable that anything so exciting could happen in Tipsytown, we decided to build on the momentum that was created by this incident. A contest was held to come up with a Website to promote Tipsytown as the best location to go to for beef. We created a work/study position for a young Webmaster to put links on all possible sites that might be frequented by those who visited us so very briefly last May. In fact a new restaurant has opened on the village green named "Flash Mob" that specializes in juicy hamburgers with all the trimmings.

Checklist

❑ Did you give a brief description of the incident?

❑ Did you identify concerns that were raised?

❑ Did you summarize what was done immediately after incident?

❑ Did you give an overview of strategy that was determined to be most effective in gathering information?

❑ Did you indicate witnesses and other persons of interest who were contacted and what was learned from interviews?

❑ Did you provide a wrap-up of information, putting details into context?

❑ Did you list suggestions for remedial action to be taken?

24. Investigative Reports

Investigative Report Template

Introduction

Located in the midst of thousands of acres of gently swaying corn fields, Tipsytown rarely is the center of anything. The third Saturday of May,2009 was no exception. Some folks had come into town for their weekly shopping. A group of committed volunteers was putting up bunting in preparation for Memorial Day remembrances. Suddenly a crowd converged on the village green. They arrived from all directions via car, truck, motorcycle, skateboard, and rollerblade. Within moments, they had formed an orderly line. With no apparent leader, they marched three times around the courthouse, chanting "Where's the beef?" And then, as quickly as they had arrived, they vanished, leaving not a trace.

Concerns

Although a few excitable citizens started spreading false rumors about Tipsytown being under siege by a peculiar strain of terrorists, hardly any level-headed person would have concluded that there was immediate danger. It was possible that the group had come to gather information and would return to cause havoc at a future date. But our main concern was to determine who our short-term visitors were, why they had chosen Tipsytown, and what we could do to get them to spend money they next time they came to Tipsytown.

Report of Immediate Action

A siren was sounded to summon our volunteer fire department, and one generous citizen, who prefers to be anonymous, paid Bobby Sears $5 to pedal on his bicycle as fast as he could to summon the sheriff. Mostly folks came out of the stores, barber/beauty shop, and restaurants to ask each other, "Did you see that?" Because the marchers had left without a trace, there was no evidence to be collected on the scene.

Outline of Strategy

This report was written by a committee composed in haste by the chamber of commerce of Tipsytown. As luck would have it, a quorum of the chamber of commerce had already gathered for mid-afternoon refreshments at the Brew 'n' Stew Pub, conveniently located on the corner of the village green. After brief consultation, we chose as our chairman Rodney Reed. Actually Mr. Reed was vehemently alarmed by the proceedings and had already begun his own investigation before we caught up with him. As one of the citizens who had been pinning bunting to the courthouse door, he had a personal stake in the event. As soon as he could get down from his ladder, he chased after the participants. The misfortune of one marcher, who had fallen off his skateboard and sprained his ankle, was our good fortune because it allowed him to be caught. Mr. Reed was unable to get much information out of him, however, as he was mostly moaning in pain. Finally Mr. Reed delivered him to the emergency room after receiving only a vague mention about receiving a posting on an Internet blog.

Interviews

Mr. Reed then returned to the village square to interview other eyewitnesses. Some had already retired to the aforementioned Brew 'n' Stew and claimed no knowledge of the event. Mrs. Muriel Booker was still on the bench where Mr. Reed had observer her throughout the proceedings. She, however, claimed no knowledge of what had happened and became quite indignant at being woken up from "a nice long nap."

Conclusions

Ultimately the mystery was solved by the nephew of a committee member, who muttered "flash mob" as he walked past a meeting in progress that was being held in his uncle's living room. A subcommittee was formed to ask the computer teacher at the high school to do further research. It was determined that there is little hope of assembling the same group in the future. The conclusion was also reached that "Where's the beef?" was a phrase that was picked at random by the organizers of the event. For that matter, Tipsytown itself was chosen only because it had a village green and a fine courthouse to march around.

Recommendations

Because it is so remarkable that anything so exciting could happen in Tipsytown, we decided to build on the momentum that was created by this incident. A contest was held to come up with a Website to promote Tipsytown as the best location to go to for beef. We created a work/study position for a young Webmaster to put links on all possible sites that might be frequented by those who visited us so very briefly last May. In fact a new restaurant has opened on the village green named "Flash Mob" that specializes in juicy hamburgers with all the trimmings.

Chapter 25

Technical Specifications

Technical specifications are reports that define important technical terms and describe characteristics and processes in a way that a non-technical audience can understand. Often, such reports are provided by contractors to explain what they did when they completed a project, or in advance of the project as a planning tool. When a project is in progress, workers and supervisors will be able to evaluate initial findings and make any necessary adjustments. When explaining a process, it is important to give examples and to define your terms. If supervisors know what goes into making a decision, they are more likely to be pleased with the result and to trust you to use your best judgment.

Step-by-Step Guide

Step 1: Describe the challenges of selecting a vendor for technical services.

In this section, you provide introductory information about the problem, situation, or immediate need that required a technical solution. You explain how the need determined the selection of a vendor, and what particular qualities, abilities, or experience the vendor required. For example:

When it comes to choosing a printer, it's helpful to think of a three-legged stool. We evaluate a printer in the following three areas: service, cost, and quality. Our company produces publications for many different audiences for many different purposes. Let's say, for example, that we want a flyer to encourage employees to bring their families to our annual Independence Day Picnic. We'd want something fun and attractive that would get their attention, appealing to their school-aged child as well as to the grandparent. But we wouldn't expect it to be laminated and saved for posterity in a keepsake booklet. On the other hand, we're all familiar with the annual report. For that we'd have very high expectations. Therefore, the next section will examine the four categories of printing quality. Before we begin, please note that we're not being critical or fawning. We are simply classifying a product so that we can work with departments and clients to produce a result that is appropriate to the message.

Step 2: Present the criteria on which decisions are made.

In this section you describe, for a non-technical audience, the qualities you were looking for in a vendor. You also elaborate on the technical challenges facing your organization and how a vendor would help you meet them. For example:

Basic printing gets the job done reasonably well without losing legibility. Using only one ink color limits design, and although photographs are recognizable they may lose detail from the originals. These printers require a lot more hand-holding on our part. Usually there is no customer service representative. We expect to do press checks on both printing and binding, although our main goal is to make sure nothing has gone missing. We can become rather pesky as we check and recheck to see that all copy and artwork are there and positioned correctly, that the paper stock is what we wanted, and that our job hasn't been forgotten altogether.

When we have a one- or two-color flier or a brochure that will probably be a "throw-away," we're happy to go with a good printer. We don't expect perfect registration, but it should be pretty tight. Images should be crisp, and colors should be strong. Although we check in on a regular basis, we expect them to tell us if they encounter a problem.

Step 3: Make sure readers understand relevant terms.

By its nature, a solution that involves technical issues has jargon that the general public doesn't understand. Computer and networking projects, in particular, use terms like *middleware, Ethernet,* and *firewall* that businesspeople need to understand, especially when they discuss the status of the project with contractors. In this section, you help your colleagues by defining terms that apply to the situation at hand so they can understand what is being done and discuss the topic authoritatively. Here is a brief example:

Accordion. Series of parallel folds that each open opposite the next.

Antique. Natural random finish imparted by felts in the manufacturing process.

Artwork. Photographs, drawings, paintings, hand lettering, and the like, prepared to illustrate printed matter.

Basis weight. The weight of one ream (500 sheets) of paper when cut to the industry standard for that specific paper grade. Example: 500 sheets of 20" x 26" cover paper weighing 80 pounds is Basis 80 cover paper.

Bind. Join pages together with thread, wire, adhesive, or other means; to enclose in a cover.

Black and white. Distinguished from multicolor by originals and reproductions being in single color.

Bleed. Image that extends beyond the time edge of the page.

Blueline. Photoprint made from stripped up negatives or positives, used as a proof to check position or image elements.

Color separation. Process of separating full color originals into the primary printing colors, in negative or positive form, with one piece of film for each color.

Cover paper. Heavy, durable paper used as covers for literature.

Dummy. An exact, handmade format sample created with blank papers to show the desired size, shape, weight, and general appearance of a project prior to production.

Dylux. Fast, self-fixing photographic proofing paper that is sensitive on both sides.

Note: A more complete set of definitions is included in this book's Technical Specifications Template.

Embossed. Overall design or pattern impressed in paper when passed between metal rolls engraved with the desired pattern.

Four-color process. Full-color reproduction is obtained by printing successive images from photographic plates in yellow, magenta, cyan, and black inks.

French fold. Sheet folded twice, with the second fold at right angles to the first.

Step 4: Show a typical technical specification sheet.

In order to help readers understand the issues involved in the technical project being considered, include a typical specification sheet that shows what the contractor will be called on to do. For example:

Quantity: 1,500 or 2,000; no overs

Size: 5-1/2" × 8-1/2" bind on 8-1/2"

Number of pages or panels: 100 or 104 pages, plus cover

Binding: Perfect

Paper: Body 70#; Cover 80#; please provide dummies

Ink: Black and PMS 202. 2/0 on cover; 1/1 on body. Bleeds on cover; no bleeds in body.

Artwork: InDesign CS3. 98 b & w halftones (95) approx. 2" × 1.125", (3) approx. 3" × 2"

Composition: Direct to plate from furnished disk

Proofs: Digital Dylux 2 sets of Random Epson proofs

Binding and Finishing: Fold and perfectbind

Packing and Shipping: Shrink wrap in convenient cartons delivery; inspection samples in advance to publications office; balance to client.

Step 5: Give an example of how a vendor might respond.

It's important to provide actual or sample vendor responses so staff can understand how much the job might cost. Including specifications in actual responses is preferred because it gives your coworkers a chance to review the work that is to be done and verify that the specifications are correct. For example:

1500 Cougar: 100 page = $4,480; 104 page = $4,538

2M Cougar: 100 page = $4,947; 104 page = $4,997

1500 Finch Fine: 100 page = $4,344; 104 page = $4,666

2M Finch Fine: 100 page = $5,195; 104 page = $5,297

Step 6: Conclude with a summary of who was selected and what will be done.

In the final section, you describe the work that will be done and who will do it. One goal is to inform management on how such technical decisions are made:

We choose Lane County as the vendor, partly because they had the lowest bid, and partly because they have delivered high-quality printing work in the past.

We are very careful to keep details records of why we selected the printer for each job and the results. However, we are always looking for new vendors. In addition to samples, equipment lists, and other indications of their capabilities, we always conduct an on-site visit before the first job is awarded. We are particularly interested in print shops owned by minorities, and we also want to know in advance about those that specialize in unusual requests. We ask to be updated when equipment is phased out or new equipment is purchased. Often this is an opportunity to get a good price on a cutting-edge technology. Often we get rush jobs that are important. We want to have done our homework in advance so we are prepared to move quickly with confidence. We also think ahead to jobs that are likely to be reprinted. In those cases, we would want to go to a premium-quality printer with computerized presses that can be reset to original levels. When we know that we will be doing press checks, it is useful to factor in the distance to the printer's location. Our selection process is time consuming, but we believe the benefits are, as they say, priceless. Our reputation is on the line whenever we produce a printed piece. We are eager to save money, but we also want the best possible reflection on our company.

Checklist

- ❑ Did you briefly describe the challenges of selecting a vendor?
- ❑ Did you outline the criteria on which decisions are made?
- ❑ Did you define relevant terms?
- ❑ Did you give an example of a specification sheet?
- ❑ Did you give an example of a bid?
- ❑ Did you summarize the process?

Technical Specifications Template

Overview

When it comes to choosing a printer, it's helpful to think of a three-legged stool. We evaluate a printer in the following three areas: service, cost, and quality. Our company produces publications for many different audiences for many different purposes. Let's say, for example, that we want a flyer to encourage employees to bring their families to our annual Independence Day Picnic. We'd want something fun and attractive that would get their attention, appealing to their school-aged child as well as to the grandparent. But we wouldn't expect it to be laminated and saved for posterity in a keepsake booklet. On the other hand, we're all familiar with the annual report. For that we'd have very high expectations. So let's look at the four categories of printing quality. Before we begin, please note that we're not being critical or fawning. We are simply classifying a product so that we can work with departments and clients to produce a result that is appropriate to the message.

Options

Basic printing gets the job done reasonably well without losing legibility. Using only one ink color limits design, and although photographs are recognizable they may lose detail from the originals. These printers require a lot more hand-holding on our part. Usually there is no customer service representative. We expect to do press checks on both printing and binding, although our main goal is to make sure nothing has gone missing. We can become rather pesky as we check and recheck to see that all copy and artwork are there and positioned correctly, that the paper stock is what we wanted, and that our job hasn't been forgotten altogether.

When we have a one- or two-color flier or a brochure that will probably be a "throw-away," we're happy to go with a good printer. We don't expect perfect registration, but it should be pretty tight. Images should be crisp, and colors should be strong. Although we check in on a regular basis, we expect them to tell us if they encounter a problem.

When we have a four-color brochure, a poster, or a more important piece, we want to go up to the level of premium printing. If your eye isn't too discriminating, you aren't likely to find much to complain about in their product. We can focus on details, for example tweaking the colors to match our expectations. A customer service representative becomes almost like a trusted friend. We mutually develop a good relationship over the years. Yet we expect him or her to spend a lot of time with us at the get-go, ensuring that everyone understands the desired outcome. He or she will advocate on our behalf with those involved in all stages of the job, consulting us if he or she foresees a glitch. The rep wants our long-term business. So if there is an occasional error, he or she is quick to make it right either with a reprint or a hefty discount.

A showcase printer is a rare and unique joy. These are artisans who give the most scrupulous attention to detail. Even the most experienced person in our office will defer to their judgment because they are far more demanding that we can ever hope to be. Only the finest machines and materials are worthy of their consideration. They are the ones asking the tough questions to make sure they understand what we want. If there is a problem, we never know about it because they resolve it among themselves. It's a beautiful thing.

Definition of Terms

The following technical terms are likely to be used in the course of this project, and knowledge of their definitions will help you understand and talk about the project:

Accordion. Series of parallel folds that each open opposite the next.

Antique. Natural random finish imparted by felts in the manufacturing process.

Artwork. Photographs, drawings, paintings, hand lettering, and the like, prepared to illustrate printed matter.

Basis weight. The weight of one ream (500 sheets) of paper when cut to the industry standard for that specific paper grade. Example: 500 sheets of 20" x 26" cover paper weighing 80 pounds is Basis 80 cover paper.

Bind. Join pages together with thread, wire, adhesive, or other means; to enclose in a cover.

Black and white. Distinguished from multicolor by originals and reproductions being in single color.

Bleed. Image that extends beyond the time edge of the page.

Blueline. Photoprint made from stripped up negatives or positives, used as a proof to check position or image elements.

Color separation. Process of separating full color originals into the primary printing colors, in negative or positive form, with one piece of film for each color.

Cover paper. Heavy, durable paper used as covers for literature.

Dummy. An exact, handmade format sample created with blank papers to show the desired size, shape, weight, and general appearance of a project prior to production.

Dylux. Fast, self-fixing photographic proofing paper that is sensitive on both sides.

Embossed. Overall design or pattern impressed in paper when passed between metal rolls engraved with the desired pattern.

Four-color process. Full-color reproduction is obtained by printing successive images from photographic plates in yellow, magenta, cyan, and black inks.

French fold. Sheet folded twice, with the second fold at right angles to the first.

Gatefold. Four-page insert with fold-outs on either side of a center spread.

Halftone. Reproductions of black and white continuous tone subjects can be achieved in one impression with black, the most typical ink color. Other halftone techniques include duotones and tritones using additional halftone impressions in a second and third color to enhance tonal values and introduce a specific color value.

Linen. Overall embossed paper resembling the look and feel of linen cloth.

Out of register. Pages on both side of the sheet that do not back up accurately; two or more colors not exactly aligned when printed.

Overprinting. Copies printed in excess of the specified quantities.

Perfect binding. Flexible adhesive used to hold each page in place after folds along the spine have been cut off.

Quality standards. Specified acceptable variations and inspection routines.

Reprint. Print again from standing negatives, with or without corrections.

Ring binder. Metal housing to which heavy wire rings are attached that open in the center.

Scoring. Letterpress scoring prior to folding is important for cover weight papers and heavy text papers. Stock is creased with a blunt blade along the line of the fold.

Sheet fed press. Printing press that prints on individual sheets of paper (as opposed to web press that prints in a continuous roll).

Shrink wrap. Clear plastic covering, heat shrunk to fit tightly.

Single color press. Printing press capable of printing only one color at a time.

Smooth. Paper surface free from textures and irregularities created when paper passes through a series of rollers on a paper machine prior to drying.

Spiral binding. Wires in spiral form are inserted through holes punched along the binding side.

25. Technical Specifications

Stapling. Binding a book or loose sheets with one or more wire staples.

Text. A paper of fine quality manufactured in white and colors from chemical wood pulp or cotton fiber content furnishes.

Trim. Cut away folded or uneven edges to form a smooth even edge and permit all pages to open.

Vellum. Paper finish created by special felts in manufacturing to achieve a tooth similar to antique finishes. Relatively absorbent for good ink penetration.

Technical Specification Sheet

Quantity:	1,500 or 2,000; no overs
Size:	5-1/2" × 8-1/2" bind on 8-1/2"
Number of pages or panels:	100 or 104 pages, plus cover
Binding:	Perfect
Paper:	Body 70#; Cover 80#; please provide dummies
Ink:	Black and PMS 202. 2/0 on cover; 1/1 on body. Bleeds on cover; no bleeds in body.
Artwork:	InDesign CS3. 98 b & w halftones (95) approx. 2" × 1.125", (3) approx. 3" × 2"
Composition:	Direct to plate from furnished disk
Proofs:	Digital Dylux 2 sets of Random Epson proofs
Binding and Finishing:	Fold and perfectbind
Packing and Shipping:	Shrink wrap in convenient cartons delivery; inspection samples in advance to publications office; balance to client.

Vendor Responses

We received responses from four printers: Lane County, Graphic Inks, Great Looks, and John's. Please review the specs to make sure they are in line with budgeted amounts.

Lane County: 1500 Cougar: 100 page = $4,480; 104 page = $4,538

Graphic Inks: 2M Cougar: 100 page = $4,947; 104 page = $4,997

Great Looks: 1500 Finch Fine: 100 page = $4,344; 104 page = $4,666

John's Printing: 2M Finch Fine: 100 page = $5,195; 104 page = $5,297

Summary

We choose Lane County as the vendor, partly because they had the lowest bid, and partly because they have delivered high quality printing work in the past.

We are very careful to keep details records of why we selected the printer for each job and the results. However, we are always looking for new vendors. In addition to samples, equipment lists, and other indications of their capabilities, we always conduct an on-site visit before the first job is awarded. We are particularly interested in print shops owned by minorities, and we also want to know in advance about those that specialize in unusual requests. We ask to be updated when equipment is phased out or new equipment is purchased. Often this is an opportunity to get a good price on a cutting-edge technology. Often we get rush jobs that are important. We want to have done our homework in advance so we are prepared to move quickly with confidence. We also think ahead to jobs that are likely to be reprinted. In those cases, we would want to go to a premium-quality printer with computerized presses that can be reset to original levels. When we know that we will be doing press checks, it is useful to factor in the distance to the printer's location. Our selection process is time consuming, but we believe the benefits are, as they say, priceless. Our reputation is on the line whenever we produce a printed piece. We are eager to save money, but we also want the best possible reflection on our company.

Chapter 26

Demographic Reports

The general types of demographic reports you might need to create are:

▶ Report on current customers.

▶ Report on prospective customers.

Introduction

When you are asked to describe yourself, you might well say "I'm a Baby Boomer" or "I'm part of Generation X." What you are doing is automatically revealing your "demographic" or your demographic profile. The response of anyone within hearing range is to automatically conjure up a mental picture of the typical person in that group. If you were collecting information to conduct a marketing report, you'd probably focus on gender, ethnicity, age, and income. You might also want to know about mobility (how far the person travels in the course of his or her daily routine and the number of vehicles available to him or her), educational attainment, home ownership, and employment status. After you've acquired facts and figures, it's important to know how to interpret them. In many cases a report will also include more general and possible subjective topics on a group's lifestyle priorities and values, for example. And the only thing about a demographic that stays the same is that it will change. It's important to have a clear sense not only of what is actually occurring but also of how it will change a year and five years from now. If we assume that the how and why of doing business are determined by the who and why of culture, it is essential to know about the people who are involved.

Step-by-Step Guide

Step 1: Conduct a demographic survey.

Before you can conduct a demographic study, you need data about a population or a segment of that population. You can conduct secondary research and summarize findings that have already been conducted. But your report will be more valuable if you are able to conduct your own primary research.

That involves coming up with a survey that solicits the information you want to study, so you can then collate and draw conclusions from what you gathered. Your study might ask questions such as the following. For example:

1. *Give your gender:* __ *Male* __ *Female*
2. *How old are you?* ___ *years*
3. *What is your marital status?*
   ___ *Single* ___ *Married* ___ *Divorced* ___ *Widowed*
4. *Identify the highest level of education you completed:*
   __ *Elementary* __ *High School* __ *Undergraduate*
   __ *Graduate* __ *Doctoral*
5. *What is your yearly income?*
   __ *Under $10,000* __ *$20,000–$40,000* __ *$60,000–$80,000*
   __ *$10,000–$20,000* __ *$40,000–$60,000* __ *Above $80,000*
6. *What is your ethnic background?* _____
7. *What religion are you affiliated with?* _____
8. *What is your occupation?* _____
9. *Where do you live?* __ *Apartment* __ *Condo* __ *Home* __ *Other*
10. *Father's country of origin:* _____
11. *Father's occupation:* _____
12. *Mother's country of origin:* _____
13. *Mother's occupation:* _____

The data solicited determine the kind of report you prepare. If you are preparing a demographic report for an educational institution, for instance, you would ask about financial aid, degrees studied, high schools attended, other colleges considered, and so on. Do the research required to determine what you need to study and what the purpose is: First determine the purpose; then determine the questions to ask; then conduct the survey; finally, write the report.

Step 2: Purpose of Study

In this section, you describe the purpose of your demographic study. The purpose is essential, as it not only determines the survey questions you will ask (if you are conducting your own demography survey) and the results you will get, but it will focus your report as well. The possible range of subjects for a demographic study and report is as wide as the number of different populations in the world. Here are just a few examples:

▶ A study of voter beliefs and trends in a state, before an election.

▶ A study of shopping habits, to determine whether a business development should be conducted.

- ▶ A study of student enrollment in a university.

- ▶ An examination of the people living in a neighborhood, to see if a church or another institution would have constituents.

- ▶ The number of individuals who surf the Web from their cell phones and what they do online.

- ▶ A report on businesses that use the social networking site Twitter, and what they do with it.

For example:

Based on the home address given by the participant, we were able to determine the level of neighborhood poverty by data collected by the 2000 U.S. Census. This included the log of the percentage of male residents over age 18 employed one or more weeks during the year and the log of the percentage of families above the poverty line.

Step 3: Executive Summary

An Executive Summary is helpful in a lengthy or complex demographic report. It gives readers a quick overview of who was studied and what your primary conclusions are. Try to keep this section a few paragraphs, and definitely less than a page, in length.

Step 4: Population Studied

In this section you describe the people studied in your report. Often, the group studied fits in a particular area, such as a zip code. But studies can focus on a technology (a Website or a new device, such as the iPad), an age range, an ethnic group, a religious group, or other criteria. For example:

We studied people who tend to be in the age range for getting a driver's license: young men and women in the 18–25 age range. We focused on individuals living in the area covered by the Fly by Night transportation company: the three-county area around Jacksonville, Florida. We studied 375 individuals, which we calculate to be 22 percent of the total population of 18- to 25-year-olds living in that area.

Overall Population

The overall population of the three-county area is 45,629 residents. The number of 18- to 25-year-olds is 9,477.

Gender and Ethnicity

Females represent 62% of the selected age range, while males represent 38%.

Of the male population, 83% of residents are black, 67% of residents are black, and 54% of residents are black.

Of the female population, 83% of residents are black, 75% of residents are black, and 61% of residents are black.

Conclusions

> *We found that the number of licensed drivers was particularly low among greens and blues. Approximately one-half do not have a driver's license. In comparison, only 25 percent of oranges and 15 percent of purples do not have a driver's license. To more rigorously examine this issue, we conducted a multivariate analysis of the differences by race/ethnicity of participants in their likelihood to obtain a driver's license, controlling for qualifications, family background, and immigrant status. Blues were 11 percentage points less likely than greens to obtain a driver's license. Oranges, on the other hand, were 14 percentage points more likely than greens to obtain a driver's license.*

Step 5: Criteria

Here, you elaborate on the description of the population you studied. You provide more detailed criteria to inform readers of how your subjects were selected. For instance:

- *Age: 18 to 25*
- *Race: All races living in this area: Caucasian, African American, Hispanic, Chinese*
- *Income: $10,000 to $59,000 per year*

Step 6: Findings

In this section, present the data you collected. Charts and graphs will help visually illustrate the results. You aren't necessarily drawing conclusions yet; those come in the next section of your report. Rather, here you present what you found. Your presentation should be as complete as possible to build credibility to your report and will give readers a chance to evaluate your results for themselves. For example:

> *We found that the number of licensed drivers was particularly low among greens and blues. Approximately one-half do not have a driver's license. In comparison, only 25 percent of oranges and 15 percent of purples do not have a driver's license. It was clear that more drivers who studied driver's education in high school would go on to obtain licenses within five years of their graduation. To more rigorously examine this issue, we conducted a multivariate analysis of the differences by race/ethnicity of participants in their likelihood to obtain a driver's license, controlling for qualifications, family background, and immigrant status. Blues were 11 percentage points less likely than greens to obtain a driver's license. Oranges, on the other hand, were 14 percentage points more likely than greens to obtain a driver's license.*

Step 7: Conclusions

Here, you briefly summarize your findings. For example:

> *After controlling for qualifications, the difference in college enrollment rates between green students and orange students is eliminated. However,*

qualifications do not explain why blues are less likely to get a driver's license than their green counterparts. We did not find that immigrant status, socioeconomic status, and mother's education completely explained why blues are less likely to get a driver's license; a gap of 10 percentage points still remained between blues and greens. While high proportions of blues, purples, and oranges are not drivers, blues are particularly disadvantaged because so few of their parents have driving experience. More than half of blues stated that their mother had no schooling beyond high school, and 17 percent stated that they did not know their mother's level of education.

Step 8: Comparisons

If you are able to compare your results in a particular segment of the population against the general population, do so here. This will help those who are evaluating your results to judge them in light of general trends. You may need to draw on other reports for this information. For example:

In comparison, only one-third of greens, and fewer than 35 percent of purples and oranges, reported that their mother had not attended college. The average green lives in a neighborhood with a much higher concentration of poverty, a half standard deviation higher than the city average. However, even though greens live in more impoverished neighborhoods, on average the adults in their neighborhoods have higher-than-average education and occupational status (although these levels are significantly below their orange and purple counterparts).

> Note: If you do draw on other reports, be sure you properly cite them in a footnote or bibliography.

Checklist

☐ Did you conduct primary research by conducting your own demographic survey?

☐ Did you describe the purpose of your study?

☐ If you have a long or complex report, did you begin with an Executive Summary?

☐ Did you describe the population you studied and your criteria for choosing them?

☐ Did you clearly and completely present your findings?

☐ Did you draw conclusions from your findings?

☐ Were you able to compare your results to similar, larger-scale studies?

Demographic Report Template

Demographic Survey

This report was conducted by the Fly by Night transportation company to determine which segment of the population was most likely to obtain a driver's license. Workers were assigned to various bus stops and elevated platforms to ask volunteers a short series of questions. Participants were assured that their responses were confidential. Names were not asked or recorded. Workers were asked to write down the person's verbal response to questions. They were instructed not to give their personal accounts, even if what the participant responded did not match what they observed. In addition to whether they were a licensed driver, the following questions were asked:

1. Give your gender: ❑ Male ❑ Female

2. How old are you? _____ years

3. What is your marital status? ❑ Single ❑ Married ❑ Divorced ❑ Widowed

4. Identify the highest level of education you completed:
   ❑ Elementary ❑ High School ❑ Undergraduate ❑ Graduate ❑ Doctoral

5. What is your yearly income?
   ❑ Under $10,000 ❑ $20,000–$40,000 ❑ $60,000–$80,000
   ❑ $10,000–$20,000 ❑ $40,000–$60,000 ❑ Above $80,000

6. What is your ethnic background? _____

7. What religion are you affiliated with? _____

8. What is your occupation? _____

9. Where do you live? ❑ Apartment ❑ Condo ❑ Home ❑ Other

10. Father's country of origin: _____

11. Father's occupation: _____

12. Mother's country of origin: _____

13. Mother's occupation: _____

14. Was your father/male guardian born in the United States?
    ❑ Yes ❑ No

15. Was your mother/female guardian born in the United States?
    ❑ Yes ❑ No

16. Highest level of education achieved by mother/female guardian:
    ❑ Elementary ❑ High School ❑ Undergraduate ❑ Graduate ❑ Doctoral

17. Highest level of education achieved by father/male guardian:
    ❑ Elementary ❑ High School ❑ Undergraduate ❑ Graduate ❑ Doctoral

18. How many hours a week do you currently work for pay? _____

Purpose of Study

Based on the home address given by the participant, we were able to determine the level of neighborhood poverty by data collected by the 2000 U.S. Census. This included the log of the percentage of male residents over age 18 employed one or more weeks during the year and the log of the percentage of families above the poverty line. We were also able to determine the neighborhood SES (average education and occupation status of adults). This was based on the log of the percentage of employed persons 16 years old or older who are managers or executives and the mean level of education among people over 18.

Executive Summary

Overall Population

The overall population of the three-county area is 45,629 residents. The number of 18- to 25-year-olds is 9,477.

Gender and Ethnicity

Females represent 62% of the selected age range, while males represent 38%.

Of the male population, 83% of residents are black, 67% of residents are black, and 54% of residents are black.

Of the female population, 83% of residents are black, 75% of residents are black, and 61% of residents are black.

Conclusions

We found that the number of licensed drivers was particularly low among greens and blues. Approximately one-half do not have a driver's license. In comparison, only 25 percent of oranges and 15 percent of purples do not have a driver's license. To more rigorously examine this issue, we conducted a multivariate analysis of the differences by race/ethnicity of participants in their likelihood to obtain a driver's license, controlling for qualifications, family background, and immigrant status. Blues were 11 percentage points less likely than greens to obtain a driver's license. Oranges, on the other hand, were 14 percentage points more likely than greens to obtain a driver's license.

Population Studied

We studied people who tend to be in the age range for getting a driver's license: young men and women in the 18–25 age range. We focused on individuals living in the area covered by the Fly by Night transportation company: the three-county area around Jacksonville, Florida. We studied 375 individuals, which we calculate to be 22 percent of the total population of 18- to 25-year-olds living in that area.

Criteria

- Age: 18 to 25
- Race: All races living in this area: Caucasian, African American, Hispanic, Chinese

26. Demographic Reports

- ◆ Income: $10,000 to $59,000 per year
- ◆ Took driver's education in high school

Findings

We found that the number of licensed drivers was particularly low among greens and blues. Approximately one-half do not have a driver's license. In comparison, only 25 percent of oranges and 15 percent of purples do not have a driver's license. To more rigorously examine this issue, we conducted a multivariate analysis of the differences by race/ethnicity of participants in their likelihood to obtain a driver's license, controlling for qualifications, family background, and immigrant status. Blues were 11 percentage points less likely than greens to obtain a driver's license. Oranges, on the other hand, were 14 percentage points more likely than greens to obtain a driver's license.

Conclusions

After controlling for qualifications, the difference in college enrollment rates between green students and orange students is eliminated. However, qualifications do not explain why blues are less likely to get a driver's license than their green counterparts. We did not find that immigrant status, socioeconomic status, and mother's education completely explained why blues are less likely to get a driver's license; a gap of 10 percentage points still remained between blues and greens. While high proportions of blues, purples, and oranges are not drivers, blues are particularly disadvantaged because so few of their parents have driving experience. More than half of blues stated that their mother had no schooling beyond high school, and 17 percent stated that they did not know their mother's level of education.

Comparisons

In comparison, only one-third of greens, and fewer than 35 percent of purples and oranges, reported that their mother had not attended college. The average green lives in a neighborhood with a much higher concentration of poverty, a half standard deviation higher than the city average. However, even though greens live in more impoverished neighborhoods, on average the adults in their neighborhoods have higher-than-average education and occupational status (although these levels are significantly below their orange and purple counterparts). More importantly, blues are the least likely to live in neighborhoods where they have access to adults with high levels of education and who work in professional and managerial occupations, even though their neighborhoods have lover levels of poverty than the average green. The neighborhood and family background characteristics of people waiting for public transportation suggest that many face significant barriers and they strive to obtain a driver's license. Many face significant financial barriers and many are from neighborhoods where they will have less access to the support needed to obtain a driver's license.

Chapter 27

Appraisal Reports

Appraisal reports are often use to assess the value of a property prior to refinancing or sale. But they can also be used to assess the value of an employee as well. Many companies develop and use standard appraisal reports to determine if staff should receive raises or promotions, or if they should be demoted or released. Having a standard appraisal format gives everyone in the organization a uniform basis of comparison. It ensures that judgments are not based on opinion or prejudice but on facts. In addition, appraisal of an employee's accomplishments and achievements can provide motivation for that person to be even more productive. Here are some other features of a competent appraisal report.

Note: Job performance appraisals aren't always prepared by the employee's immediate supervisor. They can also be written by coworkers, subordinates, users of service, and consultants.

An appraisal report typically contains two general sections:

▶ A section that the employee fills out in order to assess his or her own job performance and set goals for the future.

▶ A section that the supervisor fills out in order to evaluate the employee.

The supervisor will, after both sections of the report are filled out, meet with the employee to discuss both sections and provide recommendations for improvement, if needed.

Step-by-Step Guide

Step 1: Provide an introduction.

In this section you provide basic information about who is being appraised, and who you are. Use a standard format that is the same for all employees in your company. For example:

27. Appraisal Reports

Uniform Employee Appraisal Report

Business Address: 2345 S. Main St., Springfield, OH, 83924-8989

Reporter's ID No: 1234928

Reporter's Name: Narwouk Ismena

Employee's Name: Farhad Jarwani

Employee's Position: Information Technology Specialist

Step 2: Have the employee perform a self-appraisal.

In this part of the appraisal, you hand the employee a simple form with a series of questions and ask him or her to fill them out with responses. The responses don't have to be lengthy (perhaps suggest that responses be no more than a paragraph or two in length). It is more important that responses be honest and complete.

My job performance during the review period:

My accomplishments during this period:

Future Goals and Projects:

Areas for Improvement:

Other Comments:

Step 3: Introduce the supervisor/coworker appraisal.

Explain to the employee that while he or she is doing a self-appraisal, you will conduct your own evaluation separately. You will then share the results with the employee. In this section, the main body of the appraisal report, one of the employee's supervisors reviews the job performance in a specified period (usually, a calendar year or a fiscal year). The term *supervisor* can include any number of superiors of the employee, other office administrators who are familiar with the work of the employee, and department heads or managers. The general practice is that the subject's immediate supervisor appraises the performance, which in turn is reviewed by the departmental head manager.

Step 4: Describe work-related performance during the review period.

In this section you evaluate the employee's general work-related performance. It is often a good idea to list the employee's job functions, describing each of them separately, or you may write the appraisal in a narrative form. For instance:

Farhad's performance during the last fiscal year, June 16, 2009 to June 15, 2010, was excellent overall. His performance when measured by standardized appraisal categories is as follows:

On-time arrival and departure: Very good

Responsiveness to requests: Excellent

Ability to solve technical problems: Excellent

Openness to new or changing procedures: Very good

Personal interactions: Good

Neatness: Fair

Knowledge of subjects related to job performance: Very good

Step 5: Include special appraisal categories.

No job is exactly the same as any other due to the organization for which the person works and the set of coworkers the person works with. In this section, you supplement standard information with special appraisal categories that apply to this particular situation. Some positions have additional responsibilities associated with them, and these responsibilities should also be described as part of the appraisal. For example:

At Textile Industries Inc. the position of Information Technology Specialist includes maintenance of the company Website. This includes tracking visits, keeping files up to date, posting new information and product descriptions, and responding to inquiries from the public or forwarding those inquiries to the appropriate staff. In this responsibility Mr. Jarwani's performance was outstanding.

Step 6: Summarize the employee's job accomplishments and areas for improvement.

In this section the person doing the evaluation lists actions taken or work performed that has led to the achievement of predefined goals or other significant contributions to the work and mission of the company. This summary is intended to assist the supervisor in coming up with an overall appraisal of the employee. Don't overlook deficiencies or areas where performance needs to be improved. In this section, you might:

▶ Describe goals achieved and what performance expectations the employee has met.

▶ State any training and development opportunities the employee took advantage of, and their impact.

▶ Report any significant feedback from customers or coworkers or recognition for the person's work.

▶ Record any ideas/suggestions given or actions taken by the person that resulted in process improvements or measurable efficiencies.

▶ Note activities related to equal opportunity, affirmative action, or diversity that contribute to a sense of community.

Step 7: Describe future goals and/or performance expectations for the employee.

> Note: It may not be a good idea, in some circumstances, for an employee's immediate supervisor to conduct the performance review. Immediate supervisors may emphasize certain aspects of employee performance to the neglect of others.

In this section you look forward to the coming year and list your performance expectations for the employee being reviewed. Even if performance has been good in the previous year, simply recommending "more of the same" is not specific enough. It's better to list specific goals and performance benchmarks the employee can reach and that can be quantified. These might include new projects, new systems for the company, selection of subordinates or contractors for special projects, or much more. For example:

Mr. Jarwani and I met to discuss his goals for the coming fiscal year. They include the following:

* *Establishing a Twitter presence for the company*
* *More regular postings on Facebook page*
* *Redesign of Website, in cooperation with a Web designer to be hired as a contractor*

Supplement: Property Appraisal

The other type of appraisal you may be called on to prepare is a property appraisal. You might need to evaluate a property prior to its purchase by your company, for instance. In this case you would write down the facts about the property and describe any deficiencies or work that needs to be done, as well as any features that would be considered assets should your company intend to buy. This book's Appraisal Report Template includes a brief section on appraising a property should you be called on to do so.

27. Appraisal Reports

Checklist

❑ Did you briefly introduce yourself and the subject of the appraisal?

❑ Did you mention the period of time covered by the report?

❑ Did you give the employee a chance to evaluate his or her own performance?

❑ Did you write your own unbiased appraisal?

❑ Did you include special performance measurements or job responsibilities?

❑ Did you summarize the employee's accomplishments?

❑ Did you mention areas where improvement is needed?

❑ Did you meet with the employee to discuss the report and look to future goals?

27. Appraisal Reports

Appraisal Report Template

Introduction

This is an evaluation of the job performance of Farhad Jarwani covering the fiscal year 2009–2010. It was prepared by his immediate supervisor, Narwouk Ismena. A supplemental self-evaluation by Mr. Jarwani himself is included. This was the employee's first year working with Textile Industries Inc.

Job Performance Assessment

Farhad's performance during the last fiscal year, June 16, 2009 to June 15, 2010, was excellent overall. His performance when measured by standardized appraisal categories is as follows:

On-time arrival and departure:	Very good
Responsiveness to requests:	Excellent
Ability to solve technical problems:	Excellent
Openness to new or changing procedures:	Very good
Personal interactions:	Good
Neatness:	Fair
Knowledge of subjects related to job performance:	Very good

Special Appraisal Categories

Website Maintenance

At Textile Industries Inc. the position of Information Technology Specialist includes maintenance of the company Web site. This includes tracking visits, keeping files up to date, posting new information and product descriptions, and responding to inquiries from the public or forwarding those inquiries to the appropriate staff. In this responsibility Mr. Jarwani's performance was outstanding. He dealt with one outage in July, when the Web server became overwhelmed with too many visits, by moving the server to a second computer and "mirroring" the site there. The site was up and running in 90 minutes. He showed much initiative in employing the extra computer, which was unused at the time. Had he not done so, we would have been offline for several days.

Login Problems

As IT Specialist Mr. Jarwani is called upon to burn DVDs and solve login problems for staff people. He showed considerable initiative, coming up with an improvised solution to solve a login problem by assigning a new drive letter to a photo server, for instance.

Summary of Accomplishments and Areas for Improvement

Mr. Jarwani's accomplishments on the job in the past fiscal year can be listed as follows:

- Achieved the goal of keeping the Website running smoothly
- Managed Facebook page for the company
- Responded to server outage
- Attended training session to improve knowledge of Webmastering
- Received positive feedback from three staff members helped by the employee
- Suggested better way to handle Web traffic
- Showed how to resolve login problem
- Burned 25 DVDs for employees
- Responded to 29 inquiries from visitors to company Website
- Helped put on company holiday party

Areas for Improvement

- Neater office
- Arrive to work on time on a consistent basis
- Better dress, with shirts and ties rather than T-shirts

Future Goals

Mr. Jarwani and I met to discuss his goals for the coming fiscal year. They include the following:

- Establishing a Twitter presence for the company
- More regular postings on Facebook page
- Redesign of Website, in cooperation with a Web designer to be hired as a contractor
- Helping choose Web designer
- Streamlining the numbering process for photos held on Website
- Creating job tickets for service requests

Supplement: Property Appraisal

Uniform Property Appraisal Report

Property Address: 2210 S. Apple St., Kenyon, OH 83942

Appraiser's ID No.: 12345678

Appraiser's Name: Melik Lalabana

Borrower: Adams

Current Owner: Monroe

Occupant: Vacant

Sale Price: $550,000

Date of Sale: 12/2/2009

Property rights appraised: Fee Simple

HOA: $15

Neighborhood or Project Name: Parkside

Map Reference MSA 3200

Census Tract: 2393.02

Description and amount of loan charges/concessions to be paid by seller: none

Lender/Client: South Shore Bank

Address: P.O. Box 18892, Springfield, OH 83924

Appraiser: Verily Isayuntoyou; Address: P.O. Box 2891, Springfield, OH 28934

Neighborhood boundaries and characteristics: The subject area is bounded on the north by "S" street, east by 3rd Street, south by "R" street, west by 4th Street. The area is made up of detached single-family residences.

Factors that affect the marketability of the properties in the neighborhood (proximity to employment and amenities, employment stability, appear to market, etc.): There are no apparent adverse factors that affect the subjects' marketability. Stable prices and short marketing time demonstrate a balance in supply and demand.

Dimensions: 75 x 160

Site area: 12,000 square feet

Corner lot? No

Specific zoning classification and description: R5-Cluster Home District

Zoning compliance: Legal

Highest and best use as improved: Recent use

Public utilities: Electricity, gas, water, sanitary sewer, storm sewer

Off-site improvements, public: Asphalt street, concrete curb/gutter; concrete sidewalk, electric street lights

Topography: Level

Size: Typical for area

Shape: Rectangular

Drainage: Good

View: Park

Landscaping: Front and rear are typical

Driveway surface: Concrete

Apparent easements: None

FEMA Special Flood Hazard Area? Yes

FEMA Zone: Ag-87

Map date: 6-28-09

FEMA Map no.: 037-00293D

Comments (apparent adverse easements, encroachments, special assessments, slide areas, illegal or legal nonconforming zoning use, etc): The subject site is a typical suburban lot in terms of size and appeal. Site improvements and landscaping are typical for the area. No adverse easements or encroachments were noted.

General Description

Number of units: One

Number of stories: Two

Type: Detached

Design: Cape Cod

Age: 9 years

Exterior Description

Foundation: Concrete

Exterior Walls: Vinyl/brick

Roof surface: Asphalt

Gutters and downspouts: Aluminum

Window type: Wide double hung

Storm Screens? Yes

Manufactured house? No

Foundation

Slab: No

Basement: Full

Interior

Floors: Carpet/good

Walls: Drywall/good

Bath floor: Carpet/good

Bath: Fiberglass/average

Doors: Wood/average

Heating

Type: FWA

Fuel: Gas

Condition: Average

Cooling

Central? Yes/average

Kitchen equipment

Refrigerator/range/oven, disposal, dishwasher, fan/hood, microwave, washer/dryer

Amenities

Fireplaces: 2

Patio: Enclosed

Deck: Cedar

In my opinion, the estimated market value of the property as of December 4, 2009, is $450,000.

The attached report contains the description, analysis, and supportive data for the conclusions, final estimate of value, descriptive photographs, limited conditions, appropriate certifications.

The purpose of this appraisal is to estimate the market value of the subject property, as improved. The property rights appraised are the fee simple interest in the site and improvements.

Chapter 28

Needs Assessment Reports

As its name implies, a needs assessment describes the things a business needs in order to be more productive, efficient, or successful. One of the most common types of needs assessments is a human resources (HR) document. It determines whether or not training will help staff operate more productively. There are three distinct but interrelated reasons to write a needs assessment report:

▶ To improve performance.

▶ To boost staff knowledge and competency.

▶ To learn new technologies or processes.

Sometimes, a business will face a specific performance issue and the report will be generated as a way to meet the challenge.

Step-by-Step Guide

Writers of needs assessments must overcome the temptation to be content with general platitudes. The goal is to create a structured approach to training design that will take into account performance criteria and job objectives. The purpose of the report, however, is to improve some aspect of performance in the company through training. For that to happen, the topics should be closely involved with much wider aspects of an organization's policies and procedures.

Step 1: Provide details of what needs are being assessed and why.

In this section, you identify yourself or your company, and identify any team members who are assisting you with the needs assessment preparation. You also identify the organization being examined and state the reason for the assessment. For example:

Educational Institute Needs Assessment

School of Human Resources

5710 Wolffree Road

Notazoo, UT 29380

773.892.4825

mark.bacon@shr.edu

www.shr.edu

Headmistress: Becky S. Wine

Registered HR Assessor: Petunia Venuti

Date of Inspection: November 15, 2009

Contract Number: U2/666/ICU

Step 2: Give criteria for judgments and rating scale.

Here you explain the methods you used for making your assessment. You describe any standard criteria or rating systems you used in evaluating the need for training. You also explain how you gathered the information for your assessment, whether it consisted of a personal inspection, interviews with staff, or review of printed materials and statistics—or all of the foregoing. For example:

The three criteria elaborated on below are used to judge a wide range of educational institutions. We believe that the schools are given a wide range of opportunity to be creative within these parameters. Although we expect them to remain true to the spirit of the criteria, we affirm their goals of meeting their individual mission statements. To record our judgments, we use the five-point scale below:

1: outstanding with no noticeable flaws

2: good with only minor flaws

3: flaws more apparent, but good features still outweigh the bad

4: overall acceptable, but concerns exist in certain areas

5: serious concerns

NOTE: All information in this report reflects the conditions found on the premises on the date of the inspection. It is possible that conditions will have changed since the last inspection. The information should not be a recommendation or condemnation of an institute of learning.

Step 3: Provide a basic overview of the inspection site or object.

Next, you explain characteristics of the organization or group of individuals you are assessing, paying attention to those attributes that help you determine whether or not training is the best option for them. For example:

28. Needs Assessment Reports

Public School District 21 opened fifteen years ago, and has grown steadily in enrollment. Test scores have increased as well over that time, though not always steadily. Scores dropped considerably after the 2001 terrorist attacks, and rebounded slowly for several years thereafter. In recent years scores have suffered again during the economic downturn.

Step 4: Analyze the organization and staff.

In order to determine whether training is the best solution for decreased sales or sagging test scores, you need to analyze the organization and the people who work in it. Typically, human resources professionals perform three kinds of analysis:

Organizational Analysis

► You evaluate how appropriate training is to the organization's overall strategy. Only then can you align training with business strategy and ensure there are resources and managerial support for training.

► During and after training, you will need resources (financial and development) and here you analyze their availability.

► Determine how much support is available from managers and peers for training.

► Gather data mainly from senior and mid-level managers.

Task Analysis

► Examine basic work-related tasks and knowledge, skills, behaviors, and abilities (KSBAs); investigate whether the content and activities are consistent with trainee on-the-job experience; if so, develop measurable and relevant content, objectives, and methods. Also identify any work-related tasks and knowledge, skills, behaviors, and abilities (KSBAs) that must be emphasized in training.

► Interview critical sources of information within the organization: subject matter experts (SMEs), managers, exemplary employees.

Person Analysis

► Investigate whether trainees have the basic skills, motivation, prerequisite skills, or confidence to be trained and to learn.

► Answer the question of whether performance deficiencies result from a lack of knowledge, skill, behavior, or ability (a training issue) or from a motivational or work design problem.

28. Needs Assessment Reports

Step 5: Conduct a training needs assessment.

Is training the right option for addressing the performance issue at hand? That is the topic you need to address in this section of your report. You need to report on the information gathered during your needs analysis. Be sure to tell readers that training is not the best option when other performance issues are occurring, such as:

▶ Recruiting, selection, or compensation problems.

▶ Unclear or incomplete policies and procedures.

▶ A lack of leadership and feedback.

▶ Insufficient tools, equipment, or resources.

▶ Problems with your building or facilities.

▶ A lack of motivation (job-person fit; person-org fit); a "won't do" issue.

On the other hand, if your investigation indicates that training is warranted, explain why, and suggest what kind of staff training program is needed to address the performance issues.

Step 6: Make suggestions for improvement and state steps to be taken next.

In this section you make recommendations based on your analysis and investigation. Do not assume automatically that training is warranted, or that it needs to happen immediately. If other situations need to be addressed first, state as much. It is often helpful to provide a timetable for implementation of the training program. For example:

We trust that this report will be perceived as a boost to morale instead of being punitive. We wish to increase staff confidence in their abilities to train students and prepare them for high school and college. We also want to improve the working situation in each of the District 21 schools. We recommend changes in both the classroom and cocurricular activities. We will prepare college test preparation training after verification that other problems have been addressed. We would like to see an action plan presented within three months showing how the issued identified above will be addressed. Training will then begin and last a period of three months.

Checklist

❑ You have stated details of what was inspected and why.

❑ You have given criteria for judgments and rating scale.

❑ You have provided a basic overview of inspection site or object.

❑ You have indicated scores on evaluation areas.

❑ You have made suggestions for improvement and stated steps to be taken next.

Needs Assessment Report Template

Introduction

Educational Institute Needs Assessment

School of Human Resources

5710 Wolffree Road

Notazoo, UT 29380

773.892.4825

mark.bacon@shr.edu

www.shr.edu

Headmistress: Becky S. Wine

Registered HR Assessor: Petunia Venuti

Date of Inspection: November 15, 2009

Contract Number: U2/666/ICU

This inspection took place as a result of a drop in school test scores in District 21. The goal was to evaluate the program of instruction by identifying good features and shortcomings. In addition to a pending decision by the accrediting agency, the fervent wish is that teachers can improve the quality of education and help children achieve their full potential. Another purpose is to inform the general public about the quality of education in public schools. A copy of this report is to be distributed to families of all school pupils and made available upon request to anyone else with an interest in this important form of education.

Background

The five criteria elaborated on below are used to judge a wide range of educational institutions. We believe that the schools are given a wide range of opportunity to be creative within these paramaters. Although we expect them to remain true to the spirit of the criteria, we affirm their goals of meeting their individual mission statements. To record our judgments, we use the five-point scale:

1: outstanding with no noticable flaws

2: good with only minor flaws

3: flaws more apparent, but good features still outweigh the bad

4: overall acceptable, but concerns exist in certain areas

5: serious concerns

General Description

Public School District 21 opened opened fifteen years ago, and has grown steadily in enrollment. Test scores have increased as well over that time, though not always steadily. Scores dropped considerably after the 2001 terrorist attacks, and rebounded slowly for several years thereafter. In recent years scores have suffered again during the economic downturn. It is worth noting that scores do tend to go up and down in this and other school districts. It is also noteworthy that scores are adversely affected by external circumstances such as changes in the economy. This suggests that teacher competence and student capability are not to blame for declining test scores.

Analysis

Thorough analyses were conducted of the District 21 organization, the curriculum, and the teaching staff and administrators. Interviews were held with subject matter experts, parents, and teachers who were all confident that, with a little training, they could induce students to perform better on standardized tests.

The overall consensus was that the quality and standards amply succeed in promoting condidtions conducive for the desirable outcome of teaching young people in District 21.

A rating of four was assigned to the area of acquisition, discovery, and application of knowledge. We observed many instances of pigs singing in a purposeful way. Our main concern was that there was too much repetition in too limited of a space. We would prefer that singing be integrated into all parts of the pig's day. Otherwise opportunities become limited and teachable moments are lost. We saw several frustrated pigs who seemed close to breaking out into song but were not comfortable enough in their setting to really let loose.

In the area of staff engagement, we could only give a rate of a three. We felt that the staff was well meaning and well trained. Our fear, however, is that some burn-out is occuring. Teaching pigs to sing can be a difficult task, and more care needs to be given to allow staff to recharge their batteries. More days off and more officially sanctioned sabbaticals are highy recommended. We also suggest more professional development, with more of the budget allocated for workshops and seminars.

Materials and facilities again rated only a three. At the time of Wilbur's bequest, this was a cutting-edge campus with the latest and greatest of technologies. Some of this original equipment is showing signs of wear. It is important that, for example, computers are upgraded on a regular basis. There was, we might add, at times a definite smell that was not entirely pleasing. We understand that working with pigs presents certain challenges, and encourage more care to be taken in this area.

Training Needs Assessment

Is training the right option for addressing the performance issue at hand? We found evidence that training will help, but only when other problems are solved, such as:

- ◆ Problems with inadequate compensation.

- ◆ Organization-wide policies and procedures that are unclear or incomplete.

- ◆ Unclear and indecisive leadership and feedback.

- ◆ Insufficient computer and networking resources.

- ◆ Defects with many district school buildings.

We do recommend training in testing preparation, but only after these problems have begun to be addressed. Training in the PSAT, SAT, and ACT will help particularly to raise test scores, but only if staff are motivated to do so, and if students have adequate equipment to work with.

Recommendations

We trust that this report will be perceived as a boost to morale instead of being punitive. We wish to increase staff confidence in their abilities to train students and prepare them for high school and college. We also want to improve the working situation in each of the District 21 schools. We recommend changes in both the classroom and cocurricular activities:

- ◆ Modest pay increases for high school teachers.

- ◆ Rewriting and republishing the policies and procedures report online where it is easily accessible.

- ◆ Upgraded network to include wireless capabilities.

- ◆ More laptops and desktop computers available to students.

We will prepare college test preparation training after verification that other problems have been addressed. We would like to see an action plan presented within three months showing how the issued identified above will be addressed. Training will then begin and last a period of three months.

28. Needs Assessment Reports

Chapter 29

Statistical Samplings

To acquire data, surveys are often used. Whether you conduct your survey by mail questionnaire, personal interview, telephone interview, or online, the next challenge is to form it into a report. In many cases, the purpose will be either to discover why people do certain things or to forecast what will happen. When writing your report, be sure to explain who was given the survey. If you are asking a Girl Scout troop with 10 members which cookie they preferred and why, you can administer the sample to each of them. However usually you will only obtain the opinions of a sample of your population. Then your challenge becomes to explain who was surveyed and why the sample was large enough to make the results accurate. You also need to demonstrate that your sample is statified. That means that the participants appear in the same percentage of "the universe." Usually you will need to show that your random sample is representative of all those in the group. For example, if your questionnaire requires a large vocabulary, you may eliminate the segment of the population that struggles with literacy.

Step-by-Step Guide

Step 1: Identify the goal of acquiring statistics to conduct the study.

State the goal of your study in a sentence or two. For example:

The goal of this statistical study was to determine why students apply to other schools instead of Little College on the Prairie.

Step 2: Provide any background information that pertains to your study.

Here, you describe the situations that led to the study. Explaining the situation not only gives some context for what can easily be a report full of figures, but it explains why you studied the subject you did and why you conducted particular experiments. Try to answer such questions as:

▸ What is the population you are studying?

▸ Is it part of a larger population?

▸ What is the problem you are trying to uncover?

▸ What is the location of the population or group you are sampling?

▸ What are the notable characteristics of that population or group?

For example:

Little College on the Prairie is a small, liberal arts school located in the Midwest. The nearest town is 15 miles away. It has a population of 7,000, with no movie theater or other entertainment establishment. There is a clinic where students who are ill can be seen at a reduced rate. There are five restaurants, but three are drive-ins that close at the end of the summer. The nearest town of 60,000 is 30 miles away. It is served by a bus line and has a small hospital. The admissions office was concerned about the high percentage of students who had applied and been admitted to Little College on the Prairie but who had instead decided to attend one of the public schools operated by the state.

Step 3: Describe your method for collecting data.

In this section, you describe how you collected data. You list the different groups surveyed/tested, and list how many subjects were examined. Surveys or tests are frequently compared to a control group, and you should describe how many members are in this group and how the control group compares to the tested group. For example:

We created a questionnaire of possible reasons why a student who had applied to Little College on the Prairie and been admitted would choose to go to a large state school instead. The students surveyed were divided into three groups. Each group was given a slightly different questionnaire:

A: Admitted to Little College, chose Little College

B: Admitted to Little College, chose another college

C: Lived within 15 miles of College, chose another college

The survey design is described on the following page.

A total of 37 surveys were handed out and completed. The order in which they were given was randomized. The surveys were compared to those filled out by a control group of six individuals who lived in the area and chose not to go to college at all.

Questionnaire	Time (Minutes)	Group Abbreviation	Number of Subjects
A	20	A	4
A	20	A	4
A	20	A	4
A	18	A	4
A	15	A	4
B	15	B	3
B	15	B	3
B	12	B	3
B	11	B	3
C	10	C	3
C	10	C	2

Step 4: Collect data.

Describe the process whereby data was collected, with an eye toward accuracy, completeness, and unbiased testing. For example:

The survey was submitted by both snail mail and e-mail to about 1,000 prospective students from September to December.

Step 5: Provide a report of your findings.

This section presents your statistical findings. Typically, you don't need to have a great deal of exposition. You might only provide a heading and the results themselves. For example:

Prospective Students' Ratings of Top Three Reasons Why
They Chose to Attend a Large State School Instead of
Little College on the Prairie

Reason for Not Choosing Little College	*Percentage*	*Quantity*
Could not pass admissions test	*32%*	*n=12*
No longer interested in liberal arts education	*24%*	*n=8*
All prerequisites were not completed	*22%*	*n=8*
Wanted to play sports for well-known team	*22%*	*n=8*
Unsatisfactory academic advising system	*24%*	*n=9*
Wanted a setting with more nightlife	*19%*	*n=7*
Lack of opportunities for internships and travel abroad	*16%*	*n=6*
Difficulty getting to campus and away from campus without car	*16%*	*n=6*
Received better financial aid package elsewhere	*14%*	*n=5*
Family was opposed to a small college	*14%*	*n=5*
Received more credits for high school elsewhere	*14%*	*n=5*
Friends were going elsewhere	*11%*	*n=4*
Poor instruction for faculty who were not well trained	*11%*	*n=4*
Residence halls were not modern and served bad food	*11%*	*n=4*

Step 6. Analyze and discuss findings.

In this final section, you analyze your statistical sample. You draw reasonable conclusions based on the data collected, and you make recommendations based on your conclusions.

With some 200 completed surveys, the response rate was about 20 percent. Contacts began with in introduction letter, then an e-mail reminder with *survey again attached, followed by a letter with a shorter paper survey. One more reminder was attempted, with a chance for 25 participants to win a $25 gift card to a national discount chain. For our purposes, however, we were pleased to obtain documentation that would support our request for more funding for supports. Because some of our prospective students do not have prerequisites, one strategy is to offer an introductory program the preceding summer for students who may not be totally college-ready. That would establish learning communities in advance of the pressures of the freshman year.*

A transition program would help at-risk students become more familiar with the college campus in advance. Not only would the academic programs prepare them for the classroom rigor, but they would also develop a loyalty to our school. Acquiring study skills would help those more marginally ready for college develop a leg up on the other incoming students. They would have their financial aid, work/study jobs, sports and extra-curricular activities, and living situation well in hand, which would move them from "exploring" our campus to being more committed.

Checklist

❑ Did you briefly start out by describing the goal of your study?

❑ Did you provide background that indicates why you studied the group or population you did?

❑ Did you identify why you need to acquire statistics to conduct the study?

❑ Did you create an instrument for collecting data?

❑ Did you collect all necessary data?

❑ Did you analyze the data and discuss your findings?

29. Statistical Samplings

Statistical Sampling Template

Goal of Report

The goal of this statistical study was to determine why students apply to other schools instead of Little College on the Prairie located in Northtown, Minnesota.

Background

Little College on the Prairie is a small, liberal arts school located in the Midwest. The nearest town is 15 miles away. It has a population of 7,000, with no movie theater or other entertainment establishment. There is a clinic where students who are ill can be seen at a reduced rate. There are five restaurants, but three are drive-ins that close at the end of the summer. The nearest town of 60,000 is 30 miles away. It is served by a bus line and has a small hospital. The admissions office was concerned about the high percentage of students who had applied and been admitted to Little College on the Prairie but who had instead decided to attend one of the public schools operated by the state.

Methodology

We created a questionnaire of possible reasons why a student who had applied to Little College on the Prairie and been admitted would choose to go to a large state school instead. The students surveyed were divided into three groups. Each group was given a slightly different questionnaire:

A: Admitted to Little College, chose Little College

B: Admitted to Little College, chose another college

C: Lived within 15 miles of College, chose another college

The survey design is described below:

Questionnaire	Time (Minutes)	Group Abbreviation	Number of Subjects
A	20	A	4
A	20	A	4
A	20	A	4
A	18	A	4
A	15	A	4
B	15	B	3
B	15	B	3
B	12	B	3
B	11	B	3
C	10	C	3
C	10	C	2

A total of 37 surveys were handed out and completed. The order in which they were given was randomized. The surveys were compared to those filled out by a control group of six individuals who lived in the area and chose not to go to college at all.

Administration

The survey was submitted by both snail mail and email to about 1,000 prospective students from September to December.

Statistical Summary

Prospective Students' Ratings of Top Three Reasons Why
They Chose to Attend a Large State School Instead of
Little College on the Prairie

Reason for Not Choosing Little College	Percentage	Quantity
Could not pass admissions test	32%	n=12
No longer interested in liberal arts education	24%	n=8
All prerequisites were not completed	22%	n=8
Wanted to play sports for well-known team	22%	n=8
Unsatisfactory academic advising system	24%	n=9
Wanted a setting with more nightlife	19%	n=7
Lack of opportunities for internships and travel abroad	16%	n=6
Difficulty getting to campus and away from campus without car	16%	n=6
Received better financial aid package elsewhere	14%	n=5
Family was opposed to a small college	14%	n=5
Received more credits for high school elsewhere	14%	n=5
Friends were going elsewhere	11%	n=4
Poor instruction for faculty who were not well trained	11%	n=4
Residence halls were not modern and served bad food	11%	n=4

29. Statistical Samplings

Analysis and Discussion

With some 200 completed surveys, the response rate was about 20 percent. Contacts began with in introduction letter, then an e-mail reminder with survey again attached, followed by a letter with a shorter paper survey. One more reminder was attempted, with a chance for 25 participants to win a $25 gift card to a national discount chain. For our purposes, however, we were pleased to obtain documentation that would support our request for more funding for supports. Because some of our prospective students do not have prerequisites, one strategy is to offer an introductory program the preceding summer for students who may not be totally college-ready. That would establish learning communities in advance of the pressures of the freshman year.

A transition program would help at-risk students become more familiar with the college campus in advance. Not only would the academic programs prepare them for the classroom rigor, but they would also develop a loyalty to our school. Acquiring study skills would help those more marginally ready for college develop a leg up on the other incoming students. They would have their financial aid, work/study jobs, sports and extra-curricular activities, and living situation well in hand, which would move them from "exploring" our campus to being more committed.

Acquisition: The process of gaining control of a corporation by obtaining all or a majority of its outstanding shares, or by buying its assets.

Agent: An individual authorized to act on behalf of an individual or group, such as a corporation.

Annual meeting: A yearly meeting held by a corporation that includes directors and shareholders, during which directors are elected and other business of the corporation is handled.

Annual report: A publication that describes the annual state of a business or organization and that is usually supplied to shareholders. Such a report is required annually in a state and frequently lists directors, officers and financial information.

Assumed name: Often referred to as a trade name or "doing business as" (dba) name. This is a under which a corporation or other company conducts business.

Balance sheet: A summary of a business's financial condition at a given moment. It lists assets, liabilities, and equity.

Board of directors: The governing body of a corporation who is elected by shareholders. The directors are responsible for selecting the officers and the supervision and general control of the corporation.

Building specification: Detailed instructions that describe how a building will be constructed with estimates for how much materials and labor will cost.

Business plan: A report that describes how a business will be formed, what it will do, and how it will succeed several years into the future. Often used as an instrument for obtaining funding.

Cash flow statement: A statement that shows how much cash a business has after expenses are paid and income is received.

Certificate of authority: A document that gives permission to a company to do business in a state different from the state in which it is located.

Certification: The professional confirmation that a person is qualified to perform a job or a company is qualified to provide a service.

Chart: A visual depiction of data in the form of bars, lines, or other visual indicators. Often, a chart shows trends or progress over time.

Compensation management: The process of planning goals and linking increases in salary to them.

Constituent: An individual involved in a transaction, or a corporation involved in a deal such as a consolidation or merger.

Contingency plan: A plan that shows investors that you are prepared for theft, fire, or other disasters.

Contingent workers: Individuals who work for a company on a non-permanent basis, such as independent contractors.

Contractor: An individual hired to perform a specific task or for a specified period of time.

Copyediting: The practice of reviewing and correcting text to free it of spelling and grammatical errors and to improve its readability.

Corporation: An artificial entity created under and governed by the laws of the state of incorporation.

Cover letter: A letter that accompanies a report and that briefly tells readers who prepared the report, what the subject is, and when a response is needed.

Cover page: A page used in booklets that lists the title, the author's name, and the date of the report being presented.

Crop: The process of deleting the parts of an image that aren't necessary in order to focus on the most important contents.

Distribution: A transfer of money or other property made by a corporation to a shareholder in respect of the corporation's shares.

Executive Summary: A high-level statement of the most important points in the report. It's similar to a topic sentence and elaborations.

Gantt chart: A chart that displays critical business tasks in outline form.

Goal-setting management: The process of examining current goals, refining those goals to conform to processes and objectives within the organization, and setting new goals.

Going public: The process by which a corporation first sells its shares to the public.

Implementation schedule: A statement that shows when a business plan will be put into place.

Incorporation: The act of creating or organizing a corporation under the laws of a specific jurisdiction.

IT (or, IT professionals): Individuals qualified to manage a company's information technology (IT) needs.

Letter of authorization: A document sometimes included with longer reports that assigns a report or other work. The letter comes from the official in the organization who assigned the report.

Letter of transmittal: A letter that sometimes accompanies a report and that explains the contents, the reason for the report, or other relevant information.

Limited liability company (LLC): An artificial entity created under and governed by the laws of the jurisdiction in which it was formed. Limited liability companies are generally able to provide the limited personal liability of corporations and the pass-through taxation of partnerships or S corporations.

Market trends: The behavior of a market over time, or the tendency of a market to behave in a certain way over time.

Minutes: The written record of transactions taken or authorized by the board of directors or shareholders. These are usually kept in the corporate minute book in diary fashion.

Network infrastructure: The technical equipment and wiring that enables computers and other digital hardware to share information and communicate within a company.

Officers: Individuals appointed by the board of directors who carry responsibility for implementing the board's policies and for making day-to-day decisions.

Partnership: A business in which two or more persons agree to do business together.

PDF (Portable Document Format): A format created to transmit documents in small file size on the Internet, with layout and typeface preserved. PDF is an option for presenting a report electronically.

Photoshop: A sophisticated digital art creation and editing program created and sold by Adobe Systems Incorporated.

Qualitative data: Data that cannot be measured or expressed in quantitative terms such as survey responses, evaluations, or opinions.

Quorum: The percentage or proportion of voting shares required to be represented in person or by proxy to constitute a valid shareholders meeting, or the number of directors required to be present for a valid meeting of the board.

Recommendation report: A report commissioned by a business owner or manager. A consultant who has expertise in the area concerned (design, development, investment, etc.) examines the situation and recommends the best course of action.

Risk assessment: A statement of the basic risks facing an organization, how you as a business owner/manager will face those risks, and what your business would look like in five years under best-case and worst-case scenarios.

Shareholders: The owners of a corporation based on their holdings. They own an interest in the corporation rather than specific corporate property. Also known as stockholders.

Site analysis: An element used in recommendation or other reports in which someone evaluates the site of a development or construction project.

Sole proprietorship: An unincorporated business with a sole owner in which the owner may be personally liable for business debts and claims against the business.

Subsidiary: A corporation that is either wholly owned or controlled through ownership of a majority of its voting shares, by another corporation or business entity.

Time management: The process of completing multiple tasks and getting the required amount of work done in the time available.

"Title fly" page: A page that is sometimes used in a booklet report that follows the title page. It presents only the title of the report.

Trademark: A word or mark that distinctly indicates the ownership of a product or service, and that is legally reserved for the exclusive use of that owner.

Underwriter: A company that purchases shares of a corporation and arranges for their sale to the general public.

White paper: A substantial report with multiple sections that examines a topic in detail and often (though not always) puts forth a position or suggests a decision to make.

Wi-Fi: An abbreviation used to describe wireless communications.

Witness statement: A statement based on information gathered as a result of an interview with a witness to an incident.

S

T

V

W

GREG HOLDEN knows business from both sides of the cash register. He has written about business in books such as *Starting an Online Business for Dummies, How to Do Everything with Your eBay Business,* and *Small Business Internet for Dummies*. He has run his own company: Stylus Media, a Website design and consulting firm. And he's been a business communication professional at the University of Chicago and the University of Illinois at Chicago. Greg lives in Chicago with his fiancée and two daughters.

ABOUT *THE* AUTHOR

How to Run the Business Reports for Busy People CD

Insert the CD into the CD drive. The program will start automatically after a few seconds, launching Adobe Acrobat Reader and *Business Reports for Busy People*.

Users may receive the following message when launching Acrobat: "You cannot currently view Adobe PDF files from within your Web browser due to a configuration problem. Would you like Acrobat to fix the configuration?" Select Yes to continue.

Running the CD Manually

If your CD drive is set to AutoPlay, Acrobat Reader will launch *Business Reports* in a new window. If AutoPlay is disabled, double-click on My Computer, then double-click on your CD icon, which will say *Business Reports*. The program will launch Acrobat Reader and the book.

How to Navigate the CD

This CD features a navigation menu, located at the top and bottom of each page. Each of the following navigation methods has unique features to help you find information on the CD.

Table of Contents: You can get to any point in the book by clicking the listing in the Table of Contents.

Click Previous Page or Next Page to navigate forward or backward in the book.

Opening and Using Document Templates

Once you've located the report you want, open the document template by clicking on the link on the top of the page. The program will open the report with your Microsoft Word processor, and you can edit and personalize the report as you wish.

Adobe Acrobat Reader is required to view the PDF, which can be downloaded for free at http://adobe.com/reader.

You may encounter a warning dialog box when you open a document template each time you use *Business Reports*. However, there are no risks in using *Business Reports*. The purpose of this warning is to make you aware of the risks associated with using external files from unfamiliar sources. Click Open to launch the template. Check "Do not show this message again" to turn the warning off for the duration of your *Business Reports* session.

License Agreement

Users must accept the terms of the license agreement to use the CD.

The contents of this disc cannot be distributed anywhere including on-line or sold without the express permission of Career Press.

Permission is granted to use the customizable reports for personal and corporate use.